TRUE BLUE

[handwritten signature/inscription]

True Blue

THE CARM COZZA STORY

Carm Cozza with Rick Odermatt

Yale University Press   New Haven and London

Designed by Sonia Scanlon
Set in Joanna type by The Composing Room of Michigan, Inc.,
Grand Rapids, Michigan.
Printed in the United States of America by Vail-Ballou Press,
Binghamton, New York.

Library of Congress Cataloging-in-Publication Data
Cozza, Carm, 1930–
True blue : the Carm Cozza story / Carm Cozza with
Rick Odermatt.
p.   cm.
Includes index.
ISBN 0-300-08099-9 (cloth : alk. paper)
1. Cozza, Carm, 1930–   2. Football coaches—United
States Biography.   3. Yale University—Football—History.
I. Odermatt, Rick, 1940–   II. Title.
GV939.C68A3   1999
796.332'092—dc21
[B]   99-24185

A catalogue record for this book is available from the
British Library.

The paper in this book meets the guidelines for permanence
and durability of the Committee on Production Guidelines for
Book Longevity of the Council on Library Resources.

10 9 8 7 6 5 4 3 2 1

To my family—
my wife, Jean, for all the years of love and support she gave me,
and my daughters,
Kristen, Kathryn, and Karen, for their love and loyalty

Contents

Preface

For thirty-two years, Coach Carm Cozza avoided the spotlight. He did all he could to deflect attention from himself so that Yale's football players, not its coach, would be the heroes of autumn Saturdays in Yale Bowl. His efforts were entirely proper, but over time they had a reverse effect. The more he deflected attention onto his players, the more prominent he himself became. When he retired at the end of the 1996 season, he was one of the best-known and most respected college football coaches in the nation.

The Cozza story is laced with these paradoxes. In his three-plus decades as coach, the average crowds in Yale Bowl dwindled from forty thousand to half that, yet he will be remembered as both successful and popular. He was reared in the Midwest during the Depression, one of five children in a poor immigrant family, yet he became an icon of poise and class in a world of elitist academicians. He had four sisters and no brothers, three daughters and no sons, yet he thrived in a man's world of collegiate football. Even as most admired him for never bending the rules, some criticized him for not following the pack. He was celebrated for embracing traditional values in a world fascinated with those who ignore them.

Perhaps the ultimate paradox is his decision to write this book. Here is an intensely private man going public for the first time. For all his fame, the flesh-and-blood Carm Cozza remains a mystery to all but his players and family. We know of his loyalty, compassion, and wisdom from the testimony of others. We have heard Don Kagan, then dean of Yale College, say in 1989, "Carm is quite possibly the best teacher at Yale." And we have heard player after player talk of how the coach changed their lives. But we have not—until now—heard Carm tell his own story.

It is a bittersweet story. For all the championships, all the players who went on to the National Football League or to positions of responsibility, even fame, Carm feels the sting that somewhere on his watch Yale football lost a little of its national luster. But the most triumphant part of the story is Cozza's response to the changing landscape of Yale and Ivy League football. If Yale football failed to keep pace with the times, Cozza was not diminished in the process. To the contrary, he was recognized over time as the ultimate teacher-coach of student-athletes. In spite of competitive temptations to do otherwise, he coached by the rules. His adherence to the basic values of hard work, fair play, loyalty, and compassion defines his legacy. The poignant, overarching theme of Cozza's story is the lasting personal relationships he forged with his players, more than a thousand of them. Already, he says, he misses that intimacy with "my young men."

Carm came to Yale about the time I joined the sports department at the *New Haven Register* in 1964. At first, I knew him only by reputation. My sports editor, Charley Kellogg, and the "beat writer," Bill Ahern, left no doubt that he was someone to be respected and admired. In time, I made his acquaintance and began to write stories about him and the Yale football team. Still later, I grew to know him personally, though not well, and the more I saw of him, the more I admired him as a beacon of all that is right in the world of collegiate sports.

I was honored when he telephoned me in the first year of his retirement and asked me to help him write his story. I am grateful to have had the opportunity to help turn his thoughts, his memories, and his emotions into the words on these pages. We spent many hours together as we prepared this book, and even more than before I am convinced that in his own quiet way Carm Cozza is a genuine American hero.

Rick Odermatt

TRUE BLUE

CHAPTER ONE

The 29–29 "Loss"

It seems odd that after all the wins and losses, the most memorable game I coached at Yale was a tie. But that's a fact, and nothing I can do now or could have done then will ever change it.

Some people insist that it wasn't a tie at all. The headline the next day in the *Crimson*, Harvard's student newspaper, read: Harvard wins 29–29. When you are as heavily favored as we were that afternoon in 1968, anything less than outright victory has the sting of a loss. And believe me, I felt the sting as severely as anyone. I still feel it.

What happened that afternoon in the bedlam of Harvard Stadium, especially in the last two minutes and forty seconds of the game, simply shouldn't have happened. I still hurt for the wonderful young men on that team, especially the seniors who took off their pads that day for the last time in their lives. They deserved a better ending to their football careers. They should have had a chance to belt out one last chorus of "Bulldog, Bulldog." That was always a big part of winning. The players would gather in the locker room and sing the Yale song. They'd wait for me to start—God knows why, with my voice—then it was like an explosion. They'd all join in and sing just as loud as they could. At times, it was all I could do not to choke up. That team, especially the seniors, deserved one last victory song as much as any team ever did. Instead, they dressed in stunned silence. Hardly anyone said a word. It was heartbreaking.

The very fact that we were lopsided favorites tells you how good we were. We weren't the only undefeated team going into the game, after all. Harvard was unbeaten, too. Imagine that. They came into the game with an 8–0 record, they were playing in their own stadium, and no one gave them a chance. But the odds were understandable if you had followed the Yale team over that season and the one before it. We had won sixteen games in a row, the longest streak in the nation, and were ranked in the Top 20. We had scored in twenty-two straight quarters and had averaged 456 yards of total offense and thirty-six points per game.

Most of all, of course, we had two superstars in Brian Dowling and Calvin Hill. They had support from a lot of fine players—the two senior ends, Bruce Weinstein and Del Marting, and the big tackle Kyle Gee are just three who come to mind—but Brian and Calvin were in a class by themselves. They were really special.

Brian had a magic about him, an aura. The students hung signs from their windows that said things like "God wears No. 10." Well, you almost believed it. He was a quarterback with superhuman mystique. When he entered a room with teammates or alumni or anyone else, everyone just gathered around him. He had that special something, like Frank Merriwell, the larger-than-life Yale athlete in Burton L. Standish's turn-of-the-century novels.

And Calvin did, too. The two of them couldn't go anywhere without somebody knowing who they were. That's why I was so thankful that they were level-headed young men. If they had had a little bit of ego, it really could have been a problem. Everybody wanted them out every night. Every organization wanted them to speak. Every fan wanted to be with them. The glory could easily have gone to their heads. But they were great kids.

Garry Trudeau was a student then, and he added to the excitement by portraying Brian as BD in his Yale Daily News cartoon strip Bull Tales—the forerunner of Doonesbury. He drew a caricature of a quarterback with his helmet on and No. 10 on his jersey. He never mentioned Brian by name, but everybody knew who BD was. He portrayed Brian as an intellectual college football superhero, and that just stoked the football emotion around campus. The students—Brian included—couldn't wait to see the strip.

Harvard week '68 was a wonderful time in many ways, but it was really hectic. Fortunately, we were playing up there in Cambridge. I always liked playing the Harvard game away because you didn't have quite as much media attention or personal distractions—people asking for tickets and things like that. But for this game it didn't make any difference. We could have played in Alaska and the distractions would have been there. There was so much fanfare I had trouble concentrating on anything. I doubt that the players did much studying. I don't know how they could have.

The excitement didn't happen overnight, you understand. It had been building for two years. In fact, I should go back to 1967, just to set the scene. I remember the Dartmouth game that year in particular. Our winning streak was just getting started. It was only four games, but we had beaten our last three opponents, all Ivy League teams, by a combined score of 97–14. It was a rainy Saturday morning and Dartmouth was coming in undefeated. After our pregame breakfast, the players gathered as they always did in the room we had set up for them downstairs in the Ray Tompkins House. It was a comfortable room hidden in the basement of the Gothic stone building on the edge of the campus where the university houses its athletic offices. It had an atmosphere something like a common room in a fraternity, where the players could study, talk, or play a game. It was important that they had a place to spend some quiet time together, particularly in the last hours before a game.

On that Saturday morning, I was especially concerned about Dartmouth, and I figured the players were, too. I invited Brian to play a game of pool, thinking I would calm him down. I waited for the right moment and I said, "Now Brian, I don't want you to worry, we're going to be all right. The ball is going to be a little wet, but you've got big hands and—" Well, he knew right away where I was going, and he didn't even let me finish. He looked at me and said, "Coach, don't worry, we're going to kill 'em." That's when I really got nervous.

But Brian had it right. The first five times we touched the ball, we were in their end zone. It was 35–0 before I shifted my feet on the sideline. We were just scoring at will. It was still early in the game when we got to forty-nine points, and I figured I'd give one of the young kids a chance to kick an extra point. He was just a little kid, and when I looked for him on the sidelines, I couldn't find him. So Brian went for the two-point conversion. Now we had more than fifty points and Bob Blackman, the Dartmouth coach, was really upset. And he had a right to be. He thought we were trying to rub it in. The only thing I could do was pull all the starters out of the game, and that's what I did right away. But I felt bad. I couldn't even enjoy the win.

That game just added to the excitement around campus. The student body was going wild over the team. There were impromptu pep rallies all the time. Once I had to come out of Mory's, the storied campus restaurant, during one of our Tuesday lunches with the news media because the kids were chanting outside. I had to leave staff meetings to talk to the students. All around campus there were signs hanging on the walls of the college dormitories—Brain Dowling wearing a cape, things like that. The week before the Princeton game, the dining halls stopped serving oranges because they looked too much like Princeton's orange headgear, and students were throwing them all over the place. One student was actually injured by a flying orange. You couldn't believe the atmosphere that whole week. I just thought, "Please, bring on the game!"

Then came time to leave for Princeton, and the fanfare almost caused a disaster. We boarded the buses at the curb outside Ray Tompkins House, and the students came out to give us a sendoff. They were all around us, chanting, which was fine until they started rocking the bus. You get two hundred students pushing on the side of a bus, you don't know what's going to happen. I told the driver to get us out of there before the students could tip over the bus. We made it out of town without any damage, but that illustrates the kind of passion there was on campus.

It's funny how little things stick in your mind after so many years. What I remember about that Princeton trip is something I told Brian before the game. We hadn't beaten Princeton in six years. I coached two of those losses, and Yale had lost for four years before that. We were ahead near the end of one game when a fellow named Stupski blocked a punt and they ran it in for the winning touchdown. The next year, incidentally, Stupski came to Yale Law School, but that's another story.

Anyway, a couple of years earlier, when I was an assistant coach sitting up in the press box, I watched the Princeton running back

Cosmo Iacovazzi throw the football up into the stands behind the end zone every time they scored a touchdown. That really graveled me. And there was something else that got under my skin. It's traditional at Yale, Harvard, and Princeton games for the fans of the winning team to wave white hankies in the stands during the final minutes. But no one had told me about this tradition, so when it first happened to us against Princeton, it really bothered me.

So I said to Brian, "When we're safely ahead at the end, I want you to take that ball and throw it as high up in the stadium as you can." I was only joking, of course, but what does he do? In the first quarter, Calvin rolls out and throws back to Brian, who runs it in for our first touchdown, and he takes that damn ball and fires it halfway to the top of the stadium. I didn't see him do it because it was down in the corner on the left side and it was a full house. So I didn't realize what he'd done until I saw the film the next day. Then I just about died, thinking, hey, we hadn't won the game at that point, it was only one touchdown. Fortunately, we did end up winning, 29–7, which gave us the Ivy League championship, regardless of what happened the next week against Harvard. It was my first championship, my coaching staff's first championship, and Yale's first championship in seven years. For good measure, we beat Harvard the next week, 24–20, to finish the Ivy League season undefeated.

The next year, we picked up where we left off, and so did the enthusiasm on campus. With Brian Dowling and Calvin Hill back to lead a solid, senior-oriented team, we kept right on winning, and winning big. Probably the worst coaching I ever did was when Brian and Calvin were here. The only thing you had to do was get them to practice and keep them from catching a cold. As far as Xs and Os were concerned, you hardly needed a playbook.

Calvin was the one player I had in thirty-two years who probably could have been a star at any position on the team. He was the No. 1 draft pick in the National Football League and became Rookie of the Year with the Dallas Cowboys. People forget that he was a quarterback in high school. That's why Jim Root, our offensive coordinator, devised a halfback pass: Brian would pitch out to Calvin, who would pass the ball downfield to Brian. I'm sure Calvin knew that he was good enough to be the quarterback here, but he came in and made the adjustment with no questions asked. He knew he could contribute in so many ways from the tailback position. And he probably threw the ball as much as some quarterbacks.

For all his physical ability, the best thing you could say about Brian was that he was a winner. He never lost a game that he started from the sixth grade until he graduated from college, unless he was injured. That tells you something right there about his ability to win. Whenever he stepped on the field, you just knew he was going to find a way to make things happen. The one game Brian started that we didn't win was against Rutgers in his sophomore year. We lost 17–14, but Brian tore up his knee and had to be taken out. As it turned out, that wasn't the worst thing that happened to him that day. Later that night, his father died of leukemia. I had to break the news to him the next morning over breakfast in his college dining room. I felt terrible. I had to put him on the plane to Cleveland on crutches. I flew out for the funeral the next day.

Calvin wasn't shy, but he wasn't an extrovert either. Brian was the same way. They weren't the type of kids who couldn't wait to talk. They had an air of confidence, yet they weren't obnoxious in any way. They were gentlemen, both of them, and a dream to coach. Every coach should have people like that, especially starting in a new situation like I was. I could trust them. They were great leaders without trying to be. And they were close friends. That helped a lot.

One of the exciting things about watching those two was the way they were always improvising. It was like they were drawing plays in the sand. At first, it made me nervous, but when I saw what they could do, I learned to just sit back and watch them do their magic. Brian was never in trouble. You were in trouble if you started chasing him around, because he would scramble and use everybody on the field, including the referee. I don't know how many referees got knocked down trying to get out of the way. We had set plays, obviously, but when Brian was in trouble, Calvin had a knack of getting loose somehow, somewhere, and Brian would find him. He would just put the ball in the air, knowing that Calvin could out-jump anything and anyone. And he did. He was 6-foot-4 and a 26-foot long jumper, an Olympic-caliber athlete.

Brian had great peripheral vision, the best I ever saw. He saw more on the field in an instant than you could see on the film if you looked at it three times. He was just gifted. He also had a great running sense. He wasn't a speedster, but he made something happen with every step. He just electrified a crowd. If you were a coach or a player on that team, you had more fun than you could ever have imagined.

By the time Harvard week came around in 1968, things were really crazy. We had the nation's longest winning streak and were ranked in the Top 20—and that was in the days before the split of Division I-A and I-AA. We were playing The Game—Yale-Harvard had long since earned those capital letters—against another undefeated team, with the Ivy League championship at stake. The news media were all over us. The Dartmouth game had been in ABC's national telecast, and with all the great things happening to us, and all the publicity Brian and Calvin were getting, there was no way to hide. The news media were determined to be a part of this game. Not just the big papers, either—there were reporters from papers I never heard of.

Our big concern early in the week was Calvin Hill. He had bitten his tongue in the Princeton game, and it had become infected. He was in the infirmary until Thursday. That was the only time I ever saw Brian concerned, wondering whether Calvin would be ready to play. Nothing ever bothered Brian, at least not outwardly. I don't know what made him tick inside. I visited Calvin in the infirmary every day, and finally I was able to reassure Brian that he was going to play. Brian became his usual confident self after that.

But I was concerned. I was worried that our players weren't giving Harvard the proper respect. I had seen their films, and I knew that they were a solid football team. They weren't undefeated by accident. I told Brian that Harvard was better than most teams we'd played and asked him how the team felt. "Coach," he said, "that's not a problem. The Harvard game is the Harvard game. It doesn't matter if they've won every game or lost every game, we're going to go after them." What he couldn't answer, nor could I, was how many people were going to try to pull him apart during that week. How did I know who would be calling him? There could be gamblers. Anybody. Who knew?

I was probably more concerned than I needed to be, but everyone seemed to feel we couldn't lose, and that really bothered me. Our coaches never, ever would say, "Hey, we're going to win." But you could see in the meetings the air of confidence in everybody. With all the fanfare and Calvin's questionable health, I was really nervous. I remember our final home practice, Thursday afternoon. That's always an emotional time, and that year the emotions were at a peak. We were leaving for Cambridge the next day, so it was the last time we suited up in our own field house and walked through the tunnel under Derby Avenue to the practice field. For the seniors, it was the end of an intense four-year experience. I like to think that the discipline and effort and camaraderie of those practices had lasting meaning in the lives of all my players.

I didn't often get an opportunity to step back and reflect on the big picture during practices. You can't always take time to enjoy the moments, however special they might be. But the scene at the end of the final home practice every year is different. It's our tradition for the players to form two lines and have the seniors run between them. The underclassmen are just supposed to give them a whack on the shoulder pads as they go by, but with all the emotion and everyone whooping it up, it's a good thing the seniors are in full pads, because they take some real shots. It's all in good fun, of course, but I was always glad to see them come out the other end in one piece.

It's one of those moments that reflects the best of what college football is supposed to be about. It might seem like an odd ritual to an outsider, but it was a way for these wonderful, intelligent, dedicated young men to express how much they meant to each other. They had worked hard and sacrificed for a common goal, and this was a private moment of togetherness before the final battle. I stood aside in the cold November twilight and watched that great senior class, especially those two superstars, Brian Dowling and Calvin Hill, run the gauntlet. To be honest, my first thought was, "What am I going to do next year without them?" They hadn't played their last game, and already I missed them.

Kickoff on Saturday afternoon was a relief. It was good to have the week of interviews and phone calls and planning and fitful nights behind us so that we could finally get down to business. Once we started playing and I saw that we were manhandling Harvard, I felt better.

The scene in Harvard Stadium was incredible. Its capacity is supposed to be about thirty-eight thousand, but there must have been even more there that day. They put extra seats right down at ground level. The crowd was so close to the field that I couldn't always find the down marker. Once I yelled into the headphones to the coaches upstairs, asking them what yard line we were on only to have four or five alums on the sideline answer me. That's how close they were. It was actually dangerous, almost like the old basketball courts where people were right up to the sideline. There wasn't a vacant spot, let alone a seat, in that stadium. And the noise was the loudest I ever heard, just unbelievable. If I took off my headphones, it was just constant screaming. I had to put them back on because I couldn't hear myself think.

Well, we had things pretty much our way for most of the game, except that we made more turnovers than we typically did. Calvin fumbled, and his teammates followed suit. Remember, Calvin hadn't practiced all week. He was fit to play, but I don't think he would have been able to stand up and give a lecture. Still, he was such a good athlete that I knew if he just showed up, he would be outstanding. And he was.

The game went pretty much the way you would draw it up on paper—until the final two minutes and forty seconds. At that point, we were safely ahead 29–13, and a lot of people actually started to leave the stadium to beat the crowd. But from then on, everything that could go wrong in a football game went wrong.

Actually, fortunes began to turn against us with just more than three minutes left. We were driving toward a fifth touchdown, which would have doomed Harvard for sure. But we lost the ball on a fumble at their 14-yard line when Bob Levin tried to lateral to Calvin. The turnover didn't seem terribly significant at the time, and when we threw the Harvard quarterback, Frank Champi, for a 12-yard loss with 2:40 to play, it seemed inconceivable that they could mount a comeback. But we were called for defensive holding downfield on the play. Instead of having them backed up with third down and twenty-two yards to go at their own 17, they had a first down at our 47.

Even then, we might have stopped them but for an apparent inadvertent whistle after a Harvard fumble. I don't know to this day whether a whistle was blown, but when a pitch from Champi was mishandled and hit the ground, our players pulled up short, assuming that the pitch had been ruled an incomplete pass. Harvard tackle Fritz Reed scooped up the ball, and before we realized what was happening, he had scrambled to our 15-yard line. Later, when I asked our players why they hadn't reacted, they said, "Coach, we heard a whistle."

That play led to a Harvard touchdown and two-point conversion with forty-two seconds left. Harvard was given two chances for the conversion. On the first try, Champi threw incomplete to Pete Varney, but we were called for interference. On the second try, Gus Crim ran it in to cut our lead to 29–21. Naturally, they tried an onside kick. When they recovered it at our 49, the stadium went absolutely crazy. The clock never started on the kickoff. There were still forty-two seconds remaining when they lined up for the first play from scrimmage.

Again we were hurt by an infraction. Mike Bouscaren was called for grabbing the face mask, a 15-yard penalty that set them up with a first down at our 20. With three seconds left, Champi hit Vic Gatto on an eight-yard touchdown pass, then connected with Varney for the two-point conversion that tied the score and ruined our season. Incidentally, if they had failed on that two-point try, they would have had another chance. We were called for holding on the play.

After Harvard scored the first of its two late touchdowns, there was an incident on our sidelines that stirred a lot of interest when it finally came to light. It's a true story, though I didn't say anything about it at the time. I have a feeling that Calvin, or maybe Brian, said something after a few years had passed.

Before Harvard lined up for the game's last drive, they came to me and wanted to go in on defense. I think it was Brian who did the talking. He was the captain. He just said, "Coach, put us in." Well, I was tempted. I really wanted to do it. We were in a 3-deep mode, and I would have put one of them in at safety and the other at defensive halfback. They didn't know all our defensive keys, of course, but with their talent, they just might have found a way to stop Harvard from scoring. But I told them I wouldn't do it. It would have meant taking two players out of the game. I told them, "We would destroy two young men if we took them out now."

I don't regret that decision at all. I would have let down a wonderful team by sending in Brian and Calvin. We had gotten that far because of the talents of all the players, their dedication, their commitment. You don't win sixteen in a row with one or two individuals, even two superstars. It was a team effort. I got a lot of credit for that decision, but hey, it was a spur-of-the-moment thing. I just didn't think it was the thing to do.

Well, Harvard did score the two-point conversion, on its second try, and that was the beginning of the end. With the inadvertent whistle and the unnecessary penalties, the game got completely out of control. I felt totally helpless. I think the assistant coaches felt helpless, too. I remember them on the sidelines screaming about the officiating. There's no doubt in my mind that the officials got caught up in the emotion of the game. Not that they purposely gave us the shaft, but they did get swept away in the excitement. I don't fault them totally for that because I don't know how they could have avoided it. But when I looked at the film, I saw some calls that didn't have to go Harvard's way.

Incidentally, I watched the game film that Monday only to critique the officials, and I have never seen it since. I've seen parts of it in our highlight film, but I never wanted to see the whole game again. One thing did perturb me. The next week, I drove up to Boston with Brian when he got an award at the Boston Gridiron Club and discovered that one of the officials was the president of the club.

Once things started to go wrong at the end, the roof just fell in on us. Of course, we made our share of mistakes, especially when we didn't handle the onside kick that gave Harvard that last possession. The kickoff went to Brad Lee, who was a pitcher on the Yale baseball team and had really good hands for an offensive lineman. But he failed to recover it. He got labeled for it, too, which really bothered me, because you're either lucky on those onside kicks or you're not. Besides, one play didn't tie the game. Harvard still had to do something after it recovered the ball.

I hated to see those penalties called, not only because they affected the game but because I didn't want those players who were penalized to shoulder all the blame. I tried to take the pressure off them after the game by saying positive things about Harvard, pointing out that they never gave up, even when we had them on the ropes. The news media asked me about the officials, but all I ever said was that I thought they got caught up in the emotions of the game. Later on, when the subject came up, I'd tell a story about our trainer, Al Battipaglia, who had a great sense of humor. Al sees the ref running off the field after the game and says, "Hey, Ref, where you going? You look like you're in a hurry."

The ref says, "Yeah, I'm in a hurry, these Yale people are going to kill me."

"Well, you're not afraid of death are you?"

"Sure, I'm afraid of death," the ref says.

"Haven't you heard of reincarnation?"

"No, what's that?"

And Al tells him, "Well, after you die, you come back as something else. Looking at you, you're sort of tall and skinny, you'll probably come back as a blade of grass. Some horse will come along and munch on you and in due course, you'll be digested and deposited and I'll come by and say, 'Hi, Ref, you haven't changed a bit.' "

After the game, it was pandemonium. Everybody from the Harvard side poured onto the field, and as I recall, they took the goalpost down. I did manage to get to John Yovicsin, the Harvard coach, to shake his hand, but we were like sardines on the field. You couldn't see a piece of grass. There were a lot of tears in Yale players' eyes as we walked off that field. And in Yale fans' eyes, too.

Even after we got back to the locker room, it was hard to talk to the players because the press was grabbing them and people were just wandering in and out. I don't think I even made it to the formal press conference. But I do remember telling the players that although their disappointment was deep, they had been one of the great teams in Yale history. I didn't want them to leave thinking that the world was over—even though I did. I felt as though tomorrow might never come. It was the worst I ever felt until my last season, after the loss in my last home game and the loss the next week up at Harvard.

Anyone who saw the game knew we outplayed Harvard, statistically and every other way. Without all those bad breaks at the end, there was no way we would have tied. But one thing I remember clearly about the aftermath of that game is the way both Brian and Calvin handled the press. The reporters were all over them, of course, but instead of making excuses or blaming the officiating, they complimented Harvard. They handled it with class.

I was never right after a loss until I saw the kids the next day. The hardest thing is when you lose that last ball game because you don't see them the following week until the team dinner. That's one reason I never gave them Sundays off during the season. It was selfish: I needed to see them. Until I could see the players and talk with them and go over the film, I wasn't okay. So I hurt that entire week after The Tie.

I was really downhearted on Sunday and Monday. I felt as if we had been robbed, like everything had been taken away from us. I felt terrible for my staff, for myself, and even more so for the players, especially the seniors. But the more the years go on, and the more I think about it, the more I think that maybe this was the best thing that could have happened to those seniors, because they had had life their way so much. Maybe they learned some lessons that helped them—that everything isn't automatic, that life isn't always fair. In fact, we talked about that at the banquet, about how strong people overcome things like this. I remember telling them, "This may help you deal with some adversity you will experience later in life that you have absolutely no control over. And you had absolutely no control over the last two minutes and forty seconds of this game. Nor did I." I told my staff the same thing. And to this day I feel that way, that this game was sort of played in heaven and dropped on us. The game made me realize, like Yogi Berra says, "The game isn't over until it's over." I never again had a sigh of relief until the gun went off, because I knew what could happen.

A lot of people thought it was the greatest game they had ever seen. The sportscaster Curt Gowdy invited us to appear on his Sunday morning television show, The Way It Was. Calvin, Brian, and I flew out to Hollywood to be on the show with Coach Yovicsin, Vic Gatto, Frank Champi, and Pete Varney of Harvard. Coincidentally, my old coach Ara Parseghian was on the show, too. He was coaching at Notre Dame then and had just lost the national championship to Southern Cal.

I think I received more publicity, more letters, and more questions about that damn 29–29 tie than about all the other games I coached combined. In the days after the game, the news media wouldn't let up. I got to the point where I just didn't want to hear the phone ring. One day I answered it with an abrupt "Hello!" Kingman Brewster, the Yale president, was on the line. I felt terrible because here was a guy who died with every down we played. I remember Ted Blair, who played for Yale in 1921, '22, and '23, calling with tears in his voice. Blair's support through the years was so strong he became known as "Mr. Yale Football." A lot of wonderful people called and just about cried on the phone. It's odd when you think about it because we didn't even lose the game.

Without a doubt, that was one of the greatest teams and most exciting seasons in the history of Yale football, yet the players will be remembered as much for that infamous tie as for all their great accomplishments. But the funny thing is, Brian Dowling and Calvin Hill and all the others were a part of a game that probably never would have been mentioned again if we had won it the way we could have . . . and maybe should have.

CHAPTER TWO

Proud Italian Stock

I t took a long time for me to decide to write this book. I can't tell you how many times over the past ten or fifteen years some former player or alumnus said to me, "Coach, you should write a book." That's understandable because the story of Yale football is compelling. A lot of wonderful young men put on that blue-and-white uniform and took the field in Yale Bowl to become a part of one of America's oldest and most storied sports traditions. Some of them were great athletes. Others—most of them, I suppose—were less than great, but they made up for their lack of talent with dedication. Each one of them brought something special to the program, something even more important than their football skills. They were fine young men who bettered my life and the lives of everyone around them.

Clearly, the story of these gifted scholar-athletes and the assistant coaches who helped me shape their lives is a tale worth telling. I have never doubted that. And, ultimately, that's why I finally took pen in hand. Still, I was reluctant because I knew I could not write this memoir without revealing something of myself and my family, and frankly, that makes me uncomfortable. Not that I'm not proud of my life and career. On the contrary, I'm very proud of my roots, my family, and my accomplishments. But my wife, Jean, and I have always found comfort as far from the spotlight as a high-profile job allowed.

A few kind folks have described me as humble, and I thank them for that, but that's not the point. The fact is that I owe everything to a succession of absolutely wonderful people. I was helped from cradle to retirement by one strong, caring person after another, and they are the ones who deserve to be the focus of this book. Among them were my mother and father (both Italian immigrants), my sisters, my wife, our three daughters, my teammates, my coaches, all the players I coached (and learned from), and the men and women of Yale who wouldn't let me fail.

My God, when I think about it now in the context of this book, I realize how blessed I was.

Our home in Parma, Ohio, was only about ten miles from downtown Cleveland, but when I was growing up in the 1930s, it was really out in the sticks. We lived in a two-story house that my dad built with his own hands. It was the kind of house nobody builds anymore. He didn't use two-by-fours, he used six-by-sixes—huge, solid lumber. My mother told me he built it with a horse and wagon. I guess that's how he dragged the timbers in and raised them. I don't really know how he did it. He must have had some help, but it's an incredible house that still stands today, though it looks kind of out of place now on a street with mostly ranch houses. One of my sisters still lives in it.

We had chickens and a garden—we sort of lived off the earth, just like a lot of people did then. We owned only about half an acre, but it was out in the country, and there was land all around us that we could use. Growing up, I thought all that land was ours. No one else used it, and apparently no one cared if we did. There were orchards in the backyard and grape arbors out front. Coming from an Italian family, I was responsible for helping my dad make wine.

My mother, who was born Carbita DeLuca, and my father, James, both came to this country from Italy when they were young. My dad came over by himself, as far as I know. He never talked much about his family history. He was from the northern part of the country, and had blue-green eyes and a light complexion. My mother had brown eyes and darker skin. She came over with her whole family from Calabria in the south. They settled in the same neighborhood in Cleveland. They met and were married when they were still in their teens. It was a rough area of downtown Cleveland, and my dad didn't want to raise his family there. So when my sisters came along, he bought a piece of land up on a hill in Parma, way out in the boonies, and that's where he built our house.

I was born in 1930, the youngest of five kids and the only boy. My youngest sister, Ange, was ten years older than I, and the others—Pat, Theresa, and Josephine—were older than Ange in about two-year increments. For as long as I can remember, we were the only ones living in the house, but for a time, when I was just a baby, there were something like eighteen or twenty people from our extended family living there. My grandfather on my mother's side had taken ill and couldn't work, so my parents took in the whole family. I had aunts and uncles who were about the same age as my sisters, and my folks treated them like their own. After my grandmother and grandfather died, my father provided for all those kids.

Pop worked with his hands his whole life. I wouldn't call it polished carpentry. It was more like rough construction, but he could build you anything you wanted. He built a platform in our yard so my sisters could be married at home. It was a tough life in many ways, but he never made excuses. When I was in college I went to a union meeting with him, and I remember seeing how the mostly Italian laborers on a construction job were treated. He had to pay to get a job or to get the best shovel. I think that made me work harder in college. I never wanted to be in a position like that.

He was a wonderful dad who believed so much in his family. He was very loving in the little things he did, like teaching my sisters to dance. But he could be strict, too. One time my oldest sister, who was married and living upstairs at the time, was leaving the house with her husband to go out for the evening. My father said to them, "I want you home by 11 o'clock." He was the provider and the disciplinarian, no doubt about that. All he had to do was look at you to get his point across. He wasn't a big man, but he had a way about him. And he was really strong from all that manual work.

My mother, meanwhile, ran the household. She planned the meals, handled the money, and in many ways she was the strength of the family. She was there for me more than anyone as I was growing up. Not that my father didn't want to be with me more than he was, but he worked from morning to night. I'm sure there were times when I said to my mother, "Why can't Pop come with me?" But I understood that he had to work.

It was great to grow up seeing the respect my mother and dad had for each other. Mom saw how hard Pop worked all his life, and she appreciated that he never blinked an eye when her side of the family had to move in temporarily. My parents had a common bond: they both lived for their family. Their whole lives were wrapped up in my sisters and me. My dad insisted that we eat our evening meal together. He was adamant about that. Sometimes I'd come in a little late and I'd get that look, but I don't remember a single night when we weren't all there for the evening meal. I realize now how important that time together every day was to our family.

My parents spoke mostly Italian in the home, though they both tried hard to learn and speak English. My mother got to the point where she spoke it very well. Dad spoke mostly broken English, except when he was upset—then it was pure Italian. My sisters and I spoke only English, which was a big mistake. I could have learned two languages, two beautiful languages. I can still understand a little Italian, but I can't really speak it. In those days, of course, you didn't want to be the foreign kid on the block. Italians were apt to be looked down on. I didn't experience too much of that, but I think my parents did, and maybe my sisters, too.

My mother would tell us, "You're Americans." And I think my dad felt the same way. He was very proud of his adopted country, even though he loved Italy. He was proud of what he accomplished here—raising a family, earning a living. One of his great achievements was getting his U.S. citizenship. He had to learn to read and write in English because he had to take a written test. He had learned the language phonetically, by hearing it and speaking it, but he hadn't learned to read or write it. I tried to help, but it was hard for him. I remember him saying to my mother, "Why can't the test be in Italian? I could do it in Italian." But he stuck to it and accomplished what he wanted. He was probably close to fifty when he became a citizen, and the achievement really made him stand tall.

Those years in Parma were tough times in America. Just about everyone was feeling the effects of the Depression in one way or another, and our family was no different. Three of my sisters had to leave school to get jobs. Only my youngest sister had an opportunity to graduate from high school. But as I look back, I don't think of us as poor. We didn't have a lot of material things, but we had a lovely home, the best of food right there on the land, and an abundance of love in the family. I wish everybody had what we had growing up.

As far back as I can remember, I knew I wanted to be involved in sports. I never walked anywhere, my sisters told me—I ran, for the sheer joy of it. I always had a glove or a bat or some kind of ball in my hands. I pitched apples by the hour at the trees behind our house, pretending I was Bob Feller on the mound in Cleveland. After dinner, I did my chores as fast as I could so I could get back outside and play. I was totally wrapped up in sports. Now that I think about it, I'm not sure where my enthusiasm came from. No one else in my family had the slightest interest in athletics. There was no television then, so I didn't learn about sports that way, and there were only a couple of kids my age in the neighborhood. The best we could do was play three-man softball or make up some other game. So I don't know how my love for sports started, but I was consumed with it right from the beginning.

I certainly didn't get it from my father. He had no feel for American sports. When he came home at night, he had his dinner, then worked in the garden or just sat outside. He loved doing that. He loved music, too, and wanted me to be a musician. Well, I couldn't carry a tune from me to you, but I made one attempt to play an instrument just to please him. When I was in elementary school, someone came to our house looking for kids to join a musical group. My mom said, "Your dad thinks you should try it." So I did. I played the Hawaiian guitar. I couldn't play a lick, but I worked at it for maybe two years until my parents realized that I wasn't going to be a great musician. They made me practice half an hour a day, which I hated. I couldn't wait to finish so I could get my bat and ball and go back outside. But I learned something about discipline from that experience.

All I wanted to do was play sports, partly because I realized early on that I had natural ability. There were some older boys up the road, and sometimes we'd round up maybe a dozen kids and make a diamond in a vacant field for a game of softball. I was the youngest of the bunch, but I ran faster, threw harder, and hit better than any of them. I hope that doesn't sound boastful, but that's the way it was. I had natural talent. Some kids are good at music or art or whatever. I was good at athletics. Maybe I got my athleticism from my mother, who always won the races at Parma's summer festival. This was before I was born, or shortly after. Wherever it came from, I was blessed with speed and a very strong arm, which I think I developed by throwing apples at the trees behind our house. My sisters would tell you I threw the apples at them, but I'm sticking with my own version of the story.

When I was about ten, I got my first baseball glove. It was very small, almost like a toy glove, but it meant everything to me. I took it to bed with me, along with my ball and bat. I remember getting my first spikes, too. Every Saturday morning, I went grocery shopping with my mother in Cleveland to help her carry the bags. We walked about a mile, then took the streetcar into the city. One morning, she took me to Newman's, a big sporting goods store that was owned by Paul Newman's father. I'm pretty sure he was the one who sold me the spikes.

My dream was to play major league baseball for the Cleveland Indians, and years later the dream almost came true when I played in their minor league system. They were my favorite team, and just about everybody else's in that area, too. I was a big-time fan, I mean big-time! In my mind, Bob Feller was the greatest pitcher of all time. And Lou Boudreau, the shortstop and manager, was special. I admired Jim Hegan, their catcher, and Al Trosky, the first baseman, and Joe Gordon at second base. I can still recite most of the names on that team.

In the summer, I played baseball in the Sand Lot League, which was like Little League today. I was the pitcher most of the time, but when I wasn't on the mound, I'd play another position, because I could hit, too. One year our coach took us to old League Park in Cleveland to see the Indians play. This was before Municipal Stadium was built. He had a friend with the Indians—I don't remember who it was, but I think he might have been one of the coaches. Anyway, my coach said to him, "I want you to see this kid throw." I was in awe of the big stadium and the major league atmosphere. I stepped onto the field—this was an hour or so before the game— and pitched to a guy wearing an Indians uniform. That was one of the thrills of my life. After the game—I think Cleveland played Detroit—we went to a dairy called Sodas, where my sister worked. She gave us chocolate milk. Funny what sticks in your mind.

Of course, I was a big Cleveland Browns fan, too. That was when they were just starting their run of championships under Paul Brown. I idolized Otto Graham, their quarterback. Once he made an appearance at our high school with Lou Groza, the great kicker and tackle. Thirty years later, Otto Graham was the coach at the Coast Guard Academy at the same time I was at Yale, fifty miles away. It's a small world.

I met my wife in the second grade. It sounds funny to say that, but it's true. Jean lived about a half-mile from me, right next to my friend David Bruening, whose dad was our doctor. David and I listened to Cleveland games on the radio, then put on our store-bought baseball uniforms and played in the little road between his house and Jean's. Sometimes she would play, too, and that's how I got to know her. She was a good athlete who could hit as well as David.

So I've known Jean for almost my whole life. I didn't think of her in a romantic way when we were young, of course. We were just buddies. Later on, probably about freshman year in high school, we were at a party, dancing with different people, and when I danced with her, I saw that this little tomboy had grown into a young woman. That's when we started dating. It was a natural thing because we had always liked each other. It's rare, I know, but I have to say that neither of us ever dated anyone else. That probably wasn't right for her, or maybe me either, but that's the way it was. Her family was structured like mine: she had a brother ten years younger and two older sisters. But they had a more affluent lifestyle. Her father, Robert E. Annable, was vice president of the Society for Savings bank in Cleveland.

The world was very different then. We didn't have a lot of the things kids have today, like computers, Nintendo games, or a house full of toys. Drugs were unheard of. An exciting date in high school was to see a movie, then go to a little hamburger place called the Whip for a milkshake or a Coke. We had parties, of course, and on Friday nights, we'd go to the Teen Canteen, where they had records and dancing. The world wasn't as small as it is now. People weren't always traveling to Europe or the Coast or wherever. I don't remember my father being away from home a single night. And I don't think I ever traveled out of the Cleveland area as a kid, except for a car trip to Soldier Field in Chicago when I was playing the Hawaiian guitar with that musical group in elementary school.

Our high school, Parma-Schaff, was a rural school. I had to walk quite a distance to get the bus because we lived beyond public transportation and didn't have an automobile. It was a wonderful school with great kids. I could not have enjoyed my high school experience more than I did. I remember going two or three years without missing a day. It wasn't because I enjoyed sitting in English class all that much, but I didn't want to miss the interaction with the students, and I certainly didn't want to miss any practices.

One sports season ran right into the next. We would go from football to basketball to baseball, and I even found time to run a little track. In all, I was awarded eleven varsity letters and elected captain of the basketball and baseball teams. I was also class president for three years, not that I campaigned for the office or even submitted my name. They just threw names in the hat and the students voted. I certainly wasn't the brightest kid in the class, but I got my name in the paper a lot as an athlete and got along well with the other kids. That's all it was.

I got a lucky break in the first football game of my sophomore year. Parma-Schaff was a senior-dominated team, but for some reason the coach unexpectedly sent me in at tailback in the middle of the opening game. I was so taken aback, I forgot my plays. Our captain, Andy Wolf, said something to me that woke me up, and I guess I had a pretty good game. The next day the Parma paper had a story about the sophomore who was the hero of the game.

We had good seasons in all the sports, particularly in my senior year. We were undefeated in football and played for the city championship of Cleveland in baseball. In fact, we played the title game in the new Municipal Stadium. There were some personal honors, too; I was named the team's most valuable player in football and baseball. I remember going with my coach and my father to an awards dinner at a hotel in Cleveland as a member of Cleveland's All-Scholastic football team. It was sponsored by Ohio State, and my dad was in awe of that.

My one setback was a football injury in my junior year. Oddly enough, I didn't feel the full effect of it until almost two years later, when I was operated on after graduation. I was carrying the ball against Glenville High when these two huge kids jumped on me. I kept running until my knee just popped. It was only a small tear of the cartilage, and because they didn't have the sophisticated medical procedures they do now, the doctors decided to let it heal by itself. It did heal, to a certain extent, and I played most of that year and all of my senior year before having surgery. The knee bothered me the most in basketball, probably because of the hardwood floor, but I was the captain in my senior year, and there was no way I was going to quit. Running straight ahead didn't give me a problem, but sometimes when I planted my foot to cut, the knee would go out. It didn't give me a lot of pain. It would just slip out, then pop back in place. But just knowing that it could go out at any moment affected the way I played. That whole experience increased my mental toughness.

It's easy to get nostalgic for my high school years. Much has changed in America since those days, when we respected our elders and our teachers and never locked our doors. As a coach, I was aware that I had a different upbringing than many of the young men who played for me. Their families were different. The pressures and distractions on them bore little resemblance to the concerns Jean and I experienced in Parma in the 1930s and 1940s. It was a safer world then, and a simpler time. Still, the students who came to New Haven to study and play football and spend a few precious years of their youth were so bright, so well-adjusted, and so focused that they never ceased to amaze me. I was twice-blessed, once by the solid family roots of my Italian heritage and again by the opportunity to spend parts of four decades in the company of the young men of Yale.

Because I was the youngest in the family, and the only boy, my four older sisters treated me almost like their son, especially when I was little. In some ways that was special. But it seems that I was spoiled and mischievous. I was always throwing things at them and generally giving them a bad time. They were patient, but once in a while, one of them would have to sit on me. They would yell my dad's name, and that would stop me immediately. My mother treated me like her pride and joy. In fact, she probably coddled me a little as her late-in-life baby. She let me enjoy life and feel my way, but when I crossed the line, I was in trouble. When I think of her now, I realize that I became like her in the way I treated my family and my players. I would tolerate just so much, then draw a line.

My mother and my sisters were proud of everything I did. They encouraged me throughout my high school career. I was very close to my youngest sister, Ange. She bought me my first automobile when I was a senior in high school in 1948. It was a 1932 Model B Ford that she got from a friend for $275. She bought it with the understanding that I would pick her up from work when I could and take my mother to market or wherever she needed to go. I was only too willing to do that.

When I had the chance to go to college, my mother and sisters couldn't have been more supportive. In fact, it was probably because of them that I went to college at all. I wanted to sign a baseball contract with Cleveland right out of high school. The scouts had watched me in the Sand Lot League, which was the best summer league for young players in Cleveland. I threw something like six no-hitters, and one in high school, too. I figured I probably could make it in baseball, and I didn't want to wait. But my parents and sisters told me I should seriously consider my opportunity to go to college.

My father took more interest in my athletics when he realized I was going to be able to go to college at no cost. I'm sure he would have found some way to pay my tuition, no matter what sacrifices had to be made, but to be able to send me for free, that really impressed him. I'm sure he was proud of my athletic success in high school, even if he couldn't fully understand it. He couldn't help but notice the publicity I was getting, but he really had no feel for sports. He couldn't understand what football was all about. Once when he was working on a construction crew building a high school stadium, he watched the players bumping into each other during practice and had no idea of what they were doing. That night, he told my mother, "I hope our son never plays a dumb game like that." He wasn't joking. He didn't want me to play. When I was a freshman, I needed a signed permission slip from one of my parents before I could go out for the team. I was afraid to ask my dad, and I knew my mother would be in trouble with him if she signed it, so I went to Ange. She said she would sign it, but only if she could tell my mom. I said okay, but don't tell dad. Of course, he found out in due time. He didn't stop me from playing, but he said to me—in Italian—"If you break a leg, I'll break the other one."

It became evident in my senior year that I was going to be offered a football scholarship. I was recruited by several colleges, including Ohio State. Unfortunately, the weekend I went there for my visit, I was still on crutches from the knee operation I had after graduation. I don't think that went over too well, and I wasn't offered a scholarship. I was also recruited by two other Ohio schools, Miami University in Oxford and John Carroll University, just outside Cleveland. Herb Eisley, the coach at John Carroll, came to the house to recruit me, and George Blackburn, who was then the assistant and later the head coach at Miami, also came to the house. I think that's when my dad realized that maybe there was something real about this.

Coach Blackburn was nervous the day he came to our house because his wife was expecting a baby at any moment. He asked to use our phone so he could check on her. I was embarrassed to tell him we didn't have one. Ultimately, I chose Miami University because a lot of my former teammates were there and because I could play both football and baseball. My father was proud that his son was going to college. He might not have understood football, but he understood what a college education could mean, and he knew that an athletic scholarship could help make it a reality.

My first semester at Miami University was almost a disaster. I shudder to think of how close I came to throwing away everything I had achieved. Going away to college was a difficult transition for me for a variety of reasons. For starters, it was my first time away from home. I knew that sooner or later I was going to have to break the ties, but I didn't want to go too far. Oxford was only about four and a half hours away, on Ohio's border with Indiana, but it might as well have been in another country. I missed my family, and I missed Jean, who was 150 miles to the east, at Ohio University in Athens. I was struggling in the classroom, too. As a science major, I was in with guys who were pre-med students and really burning the midnight oil. I wasn't doing that. I was just trying to get by.

And to top it off, I wasn't allowed to play football because I was still recuperating from the knee surgery. Now I realize that the injury was probably a godsend, because I needed the time to study and adjust to college life. That's why I was always against freshmen eligibility for varsity football at Yale. College, especially in the Ivy League, is a big enough adjustment without making a huge commitment of time and energy to football. At the time, though, I missed being able to play. I really could have used that release, out on the field competing. And I was worried when I saw 140 freshmen trying to make the team. A lot of them were older guys, too, who were there on the GI Bill. They had a red team, a blue team, a green team. You name it. I said to myself, there's just no way I'm ever going to get a chance to play.

Suddenly, I had gone from a high school star to a college nobody, and a struggling nobody at that. I was so discouraged and homesick that after a few weeks I jumped on a train and went home. If I hadn't felt I was letting my family down, I might not have gone back to Oxford. But being home for a few days and having some home-cooked food made me feel better. After I went back, I settled down, my grades began to improve, and I was okay after that. I'm sure that living through that uncertainty was good for me. It helped me become a stronger person inside. But it was no fun at the time.

CHAPTER THREE

First Time East of Pittsburgh

Once I got settled, my years at Miami University were wonderful. I played both football and baseball, got a fine education, and was coached by two of the all-time greats of college football, Woody Hayes and Ara Parseghian. Not only that, but I had two future coaching greats, John Pont and Bo Schembechler, among my teammates. John was also my roommate and later the best man at my wedding.

Imagine that. Where could I have gotten a better foundation for a career in coaching than at Miami University from 1948 to 1952? I wasn't certain at the time that I wanted to be a coach, because I still had aspirations of playing major league baseball, but being exposed to those remarkable men and a lot of other wonderful teammates was invaluable no matter what course my life might have taken. Twelve of the coaches or players on that team became head coaches in college or the pros. Besides Ara, Woody, Bo, John, and me, there were Bill Arnsparger with the New York Giants, Clive Rush with the New England Patriots, John McVay with the New York Giants, Doc Urich at the University of Buffalo, Jim Root at New Hampshire, Jay Fry at Kitchner College in Ontario, and Norbert Wirkowski with the Toronto Argonauts. That's how Miami became known as the Cradle of Coaches.

The only bad thing about my college years was being separated from Jean, though in retrospect it might have been a good thing to have her in Athens and not with me in Oxford. A little distance was probably good for both of us at that time, although neither of us was happy about it. We had to satisfy ourselves with a weekend visit to one another's campus whenever we could.

Actually, Sid Gilman, who later coached the San Diego Chargers, was the coach at Miami when I was recruited, but he left before I got there, and George Blackburn took over. Blackburn was the assistant coach who had come to our house to recruit me. He coached for only one year, however, and I never got to play for him because of my knee injury. Woody Hayes replaced him in my sophomore year and was my coach for two seasons before leaving for Ohio State. Then Ara Parseghian replaced Woody for my senior year.

Woody and Ara were as different as two coaches could be, which was a bonus, because I got to observe two opposing styles. I learned that there is no right or wrong approach to coaching as long as you are true to yourself. Later on, I observed John Pont as a head coach, and he had yet another way of dealing with his players and assistants. I expect I borrowed a little something from all three of them as I developed my own style.

Woody was a yeller. Oh boy, was he a yeller. Unfortunately, a lot of people remember the ugly scene on the sidelines many years later, when he got a little too physical with one of the opposing players. I can't say that he was right or justified at that moment, but I can tell you that there was a caring, loving heart inside that fearsome exterior. I tell people that he hit me a lot harder and a lot more often in practice than he hit that kid on national television. He treated his own players like that. We feared him, but we respected him, too, and grew to admire him.

Woody loved to tell the story about the first time I handled the ball as a sophomore at Miami. He sent me in to receive a punt, but I bobbled the catch. I shudder when I think of that moment. Here I was, a raw sophomore trying to make a team with literally dozens of big, strong running backs, and the first opportunity I got, I dropped the ball. Fortunately, I scooped it up before the onrushing tacklers got to me and ran it back for a touchdown. It wasn't talent or determination or even good luck that enabled me to score that touchdown. It was stark fear of what Woody would do to me if I hadn't. It might have been a long time before I got a second chance.

Despite his bluster, I enjoyed playing for Woody Hayes. His last game as the Miami coach was a bowl game victory over Arizona State in Phoenix. It was called the Salad Bowl when we played in it in 1950. Today it's the Fiesta Bowl, played in Tempe, Arizona. That was an important win for us, and I think it was the game that got Woody the job at Ohio State.

We had good teams at Miami. The Mid-American Conference was just starting then, and I don't think we ever lost a league game. I remember playing at Wichita in 1951, when Ara was coach. We had a black running back named Boxcar Bailey, who was about 6-foot-2, 215 pounds, and could run like a deer. We had at least one other black player on the team, and when we showed up at the hotel, we were told they couldn't stay there. Ara said, "Don't unpack, we're leaving." And we did. We moved to another hotel.

I started the summer after my junior year working in construction with my father, but the job didn't last long. I got a call from Tom Pequignot, my baseball teammate at Miami. He said he was in Sleepy Eye, Minnesota. I asked him if he had been drinking, because I had never heard of a town called Sleepy Eye. But he assured me it was a real place and told me he was playing for a semipro baseball team that could use my services. Well, that sounded a lot better than running a jackhammer in the hot sun, so I packed my glove and headed north. Semipro ball was allowed under NCAA rules at the time. The manager put me in the outfield, which concerned me at first, because I had played mostly in the infield when I wasn't pitching. But I was fortunate to hit a home run in my first game and was accepted right away.

We didn't make much money in Sleepy Eye, but we didn't need much, either, because the townspeople helped us out with housing and food. In fact, I saved enough by the end of the summer to buy Jean an engagement ring. Fortunately, she accepted my proposal, and on June 28, 1952, just days after my graduation from Miami and hers from Ohio University, we were married. We spent the first months of our marriage—our honeymoon I suppose—in Cedar Rapids, Iowa, where I played the outfield for the Cleveland Indians' farm team in the Three-I League. I was signed by Hall-of-Famer Hank Greenberg, who actually pitched batting practice to me before he signed me. Fourteen years later, I coached his son, Glenn, at Yale. I also was offered a professional football contract after graduation with the Green Bay Packers. It was for $5,000, but you got the money only if you made the team. I never reported, and I doubt that I would have made it. I gave myself a B as a football player and an A as a baseball player.

At the end of that season in Cedar Rapids, I went back to Miami as a graduate assistant coach under Ara Parseghian. I was paid only a small stipend for coaching, but I had an opportunity to take courses toward my master's degree and to participate in the ROTC program. The United States was still fighting the Korean war, so the officer's training was really important. Jean got a job teaching elementary school in Oxford, and we managed the best we could. Fortunately, the war ended that year, which allowed me to drop out of ROTC and take a high school teaching and coaching job at Gilmour Academy, a small private school outside Cleveland. My year assisting Ara had given me the coaching bug, and I thoroughly enjoyed the year at Gilmour, where I was assistant coach in football, basketball, and track and taught tenth grade biology. A man named Ray Janasek was the head coach in all three sports and the athletic director.

I was certain that I was going to be drafted after that year, and I told the headmaster at Gilmour that I wouldn't be returning for a second year. That proved to be a miscalculation. I never got a call from the military, and I had to scramble for a job the next fall as a permanent substitute teacher at Collinwood High School in Cleveland. I taught biology and mechanical drawing and coached junior high basketball and track.

We moved again after that year, when Ray Janasek asked me to come back to Gilmour as head football coach and his assistant in basketball and track. I was lucky to have a solid team of seniors, and we ended up winning the league championship in my first year as a head coach. It was an enjoyable time, but it lasted just one year because of an offer from John Pont that I simply couldn't refuse. John, who had served in the military before college and was a little older than I, had taken over as head coach at Miami University when Ara Parseghian moved on to Northwestern. He asked me to join his staff as freshman coach for football, and I also coached the freshmen in basketball and baseball. Jean and I and our first two daughters were only too happy to move back to Oxford, where I earned the handsome salary of $4,500. I was still playing semipro baseball in the summer and the only downside to teaching and coaching during the school year was that I had to miss spring training. It was always late June before I reported to my team, and by then the other players had been playing for several months. That really put me behind. In all, I played pro or semipro baseball for eleven years, from my junior year in college until 1963, when I left for Yale. I was in the Indians' organization in 1952, and the White Sox organization in 1953.

The money from baseball helped subsidize the down payment on our home in Oxford. I did a lot of the work on that house myself, using the skills I had picked up from my father. It was a prefab house, and I hired a lot of helpers, but I acted as the general contractor and did all the landscape work. I would come home from practice and climb onto the backhoe. After a couple of seasons as freshman coach at Miami, I moved up to the varsity. We spent seven happy years in Oxford until John accepted the head coaching job at Yale in 1963. We had good teams in those years. In fact, Miami beat Purdue, Indiana, and Northwestern and never lost to a Big Ten team. I think the win over Purdue was a big factor in John's getting the job at Yale.

I was still a young coach at thirty-two, but I applied to be John Pont's replacement and was among the final candidates. But the job went—rightly so—to Bo Schembechler, who was then an assistant to Woody at Ohio State. Bo did a terrific job in Oxford before moving to the University of Michigan, where he became a legend. He asked me to stay on at Miami as his assistant, but I decided to follow John to Yale instead. Bo and I remained close friends and colleagues throughout our careers.

My initial visit to the Yale campus was the first time I had ever been east of Pittsburgh. I had played a football game at the University of Pittsburgh, but that was the farthest east I had ever been.

I remember the day I arrived in New Haven. It was dreary and rainy, and frankly the city and the campus seemed rather unappealing. The urban scene was very different from the beautiful rural campus in Oxford. I had driven east with a couple of the other coaches, and for the first few months I shared a room with John Pont in the Ray Tompkins House, just downstairs from the football offices. My family didn't join me until our three girls got out of school in June. It took some time to get used to New Haven. It was a culture shock for the son of an Italian laborer from the Midwest to be transported suddenly into the elite, old-money atmosphere that marked Yale and the Ivy League at that time. But the people at Yale and in the community were wonderful, and before long my family and I felt right at home. It was a big help that the city had a large Italian-American community. I told my mother back in Parma that all the Italians weren't in Italy. There was a good number of them right here in New Haven.

I credit Charlie O'Hearn, the Yale vice president; Sam Chauncey, the secretary; Delaney Kiphuth, the athletic director; and Kingman Brewster, the president, with making us feel welcome. Delaney was the one who helped us understand how Yale sports worked and what the Ivy League stood for. Still, as helpful as those four men were, it was the players themselves who ultimately convinced me that I was right to cast my lot with the likes of Walter Camp, Pudge Heffelfinger, Albie Booth, Larry Kelley, Clint Frank, Levi Jackson, T. A. D. Jones, and so many other Sons of Eli. The Yale kids were just remarkable. I was immediately impressed with how bright they were, and how coachable. You never had to push them. I was amazed at how they could excel in the classroom in such a tough academic environment and still work so hard on the football field. More than three decades later, I was still impressed.

The Yale kids wanted to be thought of as any other college football players, not as bookworms just playing for the exercise. They loved to win, and they hurt inside when they lost just like the players at big-time football schools. What made them different was their thirst for knowledge and their desire to be the best they could be at everything they did. And their ability to accept a victory and a loss with the same grace.

Yale had a very different way of doing things than I was used to in the Midwest. At Miami, if we wanted a kid and he qualified academically, we simply offered him a scholarship. That was the end of that. At Yale, a kid could qualify ten times over and maybe not get in. That was quite an awakening. But when I saw crowds of forty thousand and fifty thousand for Ivy League games in the Bowl—and I don't mean just for the Harvard game—I figured that they must know what they're doing.

I had heard the name Walter Camp, but I never paid much attention to it and never put him together with the university until I got here and read his book about the founding of football right here at Yale. The whole campus just reeked with tradition, and I got caught up in it right away. I should point out, incidentally, that John Pont's staff in 1963 was the first group of full-time coaches at Yale. The previous coach, Jordan Olivar, and all his predecessors had been part-time coaches who shut down operations after the season and resumed their regular professions until the next fall. I think that's why Jordan left. Yale wanted him to take the job full-time, but he couldn't afford to give up his lucrative insurance business. It was mind-boggling to see the quality of athletes Yale was getting when the only recruiting being done was by alumni and two full-time assistants, Harry Jacunski and Gib Holgate.

That, briefly, is how I ended up at Yale, at a salary of $9,000, I might add. I can say without hesitation that I never once regretted coming here. In fact, I feel blessed that I was given the opportunity. I had a few offers over the years to move to other schools, including the head coaching job at an Atlantic Coast Conference school, but I always decided to stay put, and I'm glad I did. I had my share of frustrations, but no regrets.

Coaching college football is often a vagabond existence, especially for young coaches. My tenure at Yale—thirty-four years, including my time as an assistant—was an exception to the rule. So it was no surprise when John Pont announced after just two seasons that he was leaving to take the head coaching job at Indiana University in the Big Ten. I hated to see my old friend leave, and I think he hated to leave, too. He really loved it here, but the lure of the Big Ten and the chance to return to the Midwest was too much to refuse. Although he never said it, I often thought that if he had it to do over again, he would have stayed at Yale.

Chuck Mercein was the key running back during John's two seasons. He was 6-foot-2 and weighed about 220 pounds, which was really big for a back at that time. He played several years for the New York Giants as one of their "Baby Bulls" and was with the Green Bay Packers in the famous "Snow Bowl" NFL championship game in 1967. With people like that, John had seasons of 6–3 and 6–2–1 at Yale, though he didn't beat Princeton either year and split with Harvard.

John's first Harvard game in 1963 was postponed a week because of the assassination of President John F. Kennedy. Not many people know this, but the president, who was a Harvard grad, was planning to attend The Game in the Bowl that Saturday. We heard the news of the shooting on Friday afternoon during the junior varsity game, and I told John that we were probably going to have to postpone our game. I think most of the schools around the country were watching to see what we would do, and when we made our announcement, almost everyone else did the same thing. We played the game the following Saturday and won 20–6.

John invited all of his assistant coaches to go with him to Indiana, but I viewed his departure as an opportunity to apply for a head coaching position. After seven years as an assistant at Miami and two more at Yale, I felt I was ready. I didn't apply for the Yale position, however, because I didn't think I had a chance. There were some big names in the running, including Bud Wilkinson and Joe Paterno. But I interviewed at several other schools, and in January, the same week John left, I was offered the head coaching job at the University of New Hampshire. Needless to say, I was excited as I drove back from Durham, New Hampshire. I was thinking about breaking the news to Jean and the girls. They had become quite comfortable in our home in nearby Orange, and I wasn't sure how they would feel about being uprooted again. I planned to tell them that New Hampshire had a rural campus much like the one at Miami of Ohio.

You never know what destiny awaits you, however, and when I got home that evening, I received a phone call that changed my life. It was Delaney Kiphuth, the Yale athletic director, asking me to wait twenty-four hours before I said yes to the people in New Hampshire. I was shocked at the call because it was obvious he was considering me for the Yale job, even though I hadn't applied. I found out later that some of the players had spoken to him on my behalf, and sure enough, the next day, January 29, 1965, Delaney officially asked me to be John Pont's successor. The salary was $16,000. I thought for about sixty seconds and said yes.

It was a banner day for me. My mom and dad were proud, and Jean and our daughters were, too, though the girls were still a little young to understand. Unfortunately, my dad died that year, at seventy-seven. I was thirty-four at the time and had no way of knowing that I was beginning a job I would keep until I was nearly twice that age. If somehow I could have known then what I know now about the path that lay ahead, I would have begun the journey without a second thought.

My first game as head coach at Yale was against the University of Connecticut. In later years UConn became a strong opponent, one of the toughest on our schedule every year, but at that time, the Huskies were considered a patsy. We had beaten them all sixteen times we played them, including ten shutouts. The perception of them as a sacrificial lamb was a little out of date, though. UConn was upgrading its program as a member of the Yankee Conference, and several of our recent games had been close. Still, there wasn't a single fan or alumnus of either school who expected the small upstate college to beat Yale that September day in 1965, when the Elis' rookie coach marched his first team into Yale Bowl.

What I didn't know at the time was that we were facing a team that was about as emotionally charged as a college team could be. Connecticut had an extraordinary coaching staff. Rick Forzano, who went on to coach at Navy and the Detroit Lions, was the head coach. Lou Holtz, who later coached at Arkansas, Notre Dame, and the New York Jets, was an assistant. So were Sam Rutigliano, a future Cleveland Browns coach, and Dan Sekanovich and Dave Adolph, both future NFL assistants.

Forzano understood the psychology of the game between the underdog state college and the storied Ivy League power, and he used it brilliantly to UConn's advantage. During the summer, he and Holtz had driven to New Haven to take pictures of the Bowl and to dig up some of its sod. They showed the pictures and the sod to their players to demonstrate that the Bowl was just another stadium. Meanwhile, I had hired a staff of five assistant coaches, all former players at Miami University. They were Jim Root, Bill Mallory, Bill Narduzzi, Neil Putnam, and Seb LaSpina. We all exchanged the red-and-white of Miami for the blue-and-white of Yale. Jack Blake, the ticket manager, who had a great sense of humor, said the football office was beginning to look like an old-age home for Miami coaches. That was true to some extent, except that Jim Root and I were the only two over thirty, and we were only thirty-four. Harry Jacunski, the freshman coach who had been one of the Seven Blocks of Granite at Fordham in the 1930s and played for the Green Bay Packers in the '40s, was a father figure to the coaching staff as well as the players. We also had Bill Irons, Tris Carta, and Buddy Amendola as part-time assistants on that first staff. Amendola, who later became our defensive coordinator, had been the football captain at Connecticut.

I made more coaching mistakes that first year than in all the other years combined, but I also learned more than in any other year. A lot of what I learned was from my players. If you weren't smart enough to know who to play, the players would find a way to let you know. They would give you hints, or they would say things like, "Coach, maybe you ought to consider this or that." They never tried to tell me what I should do. They were too smart for that. But they found a way to get the message across. And sometimes they were dead right.

I'll give you an example of a player giving the coach a lesson. I acted as the offensive coordinator that first year and let Bill Mallory pretty much run the defense. I guess I let myself get a little too attached to the offense. At one practice, we were having a tough time moving the ball, and I voiced my frustration that we—the offense—couldn't move the ball. Afterward, our captain, Dave Laidley, who was a middle guard, came to me and said, "Coach, aren't you our coach, too?"

The day finally arrived for my first game as coach at Yale, and I was a lot more worried than I was excited. I thought we were pretty well prepared, but when it's your first time out as the head man, you never know. We had lost our big running back, Jim Groninger, to injury, and I was still not sure who to play at quarterback, Tone Grant, Pete Doherty, or Watts Humphrey. I wish I could say my first game ended successfully, but it didn't. I will never erase the image of UConn's defensive back, Gene Campbell, running right in front of our bench with an interception that cost us the game. It was a pass into the deep flat from Pete Doherty with just a couple of minutes left to play, but Campbell picked it off and ran it back for a touchdown and a 13–6 UConn win. Naturally, I second-guessed myself for calling the pass, but we were behind 7–6 and had to make something happen.

You can imagine the reaction in the Yale community. Delaney Kiphuth got a bunch of letters that he was too much of a gentleman to show me, but I'm sure most of them called for my head. We managed to beat Connecticut eleven of the next thirteen years, but that didn't help the situation after that first game. At the team meeting on Sunday afternoon, you could hear a pin drop. Everybody was really down, and I knew that somehow we were going to have to regroup. Later I came to find out that the kids overcame it better than I did. That's the quality of the individuals we worked with at Yale. We had a solid captain in Dave Laidley and a strong bunch of kids who didn't let the embarrassing loss get them down.

Fortunately, we won our second game over Brown, though we needed a late field goal by Dan Begel for a 3–0 victory. But hey, a win is a win, especially when it's your first one. Who knows what a second loss might have done to our confidence? We won just three games that first season, but we recruited a freshman class that was probably the best in all my years. Brian Dowling, Calvin Hill, Bruce Weinstein, and the others had a great freshman season in 1965, gained experience during a 4–5 sophomore season, then launched the sixteen-game winning streak that ended in the celebrated 29–29 tie at Harvard in 1968.

CHAPTER FOUR

The War Years

Alot of things changed from the time Brian Dowling and Calvin Hill cleaned out their lockers in November of 1968 to the following August, when a new Yale team reported for two-a-day practices. Not only had those two superstars graduated, leaving us with a squad of what I would call normal-type players, but the whole campus had under gone a dramatic change in student attitude and behavior. It's hard to imagine how different the university environment was from one season to the next. Somehow, in the span of barely nine months, the giddy excitement of the big game in Harvard Stadium had been replaced by the restless cynicism and smoldering anger of a fundamentally changed Yale community.

One season, perhaps Yale's greatest season, came to a delirious climax, albeit a disappointing one, in a game that embodied the lofty ideals of college football, and the next one began with a football team caught in the middle of pervasive student anxiety over the war in Vietnam, racial injustice, and authority of any kind. I doubt whether there was ever a time when the job of coaching college football changed more significantly than in those few turbulent years of our country's involvement in Southeast Asia. With little warning, many of the long-held bedrock assumptions of the player-coach relationship crumbled.

This rebellion—and that's really what it was, rebellion—was not unique to Yale, of course. Campuses across the country were suddenly caught up in the passion of student unrest. The most obvious cause was discontent over an unpopular war, but the anger, fear, and confusion spilled over into opposition against other symbols of authority as well. For the first time, young people were challenging their professors, their parents, the president of the university, the police—and, of course, their football coaches, too. Our players began to ask why they had to get up early on game days for a team breakfast. They wanted to know why one player was starting and not another, especially if one was white and the other was black, or why there weren't more passing plays in the playbook. Until then, I don't remember a player ever questioning that sort of thing. But they did then. Big-time.

They were troubling times, but they were good times, too. They were important times, with new challenges and new opportunities for coaches to really make a difference in young men's lives. More than ever before, those of us whose job it was to use football as a tool to educate the future leaders of our country recognized the importance of our calling and the influence we held over our charges. I felt then, and I still feel, that strong parents and strong educators were more important to our nation's youth during those several tumultuous years than at any previous time in history. Maybe not more important than they are now, with the dangers and distractions kids face today, but during the Vietnam war era, more than ever before, a college football player's life was complicated by passions and pressures outside of schoolwork, girlfriends, family, and football.

There had been other troubling times—two World Wars, the Depression—but people's reactions then were entirely different. Those events brought the country together, made families closer, and, if anything, seemed to validate the need for unquestioned, military-style discipline on and off the football field. But the late 1960s and the 1970s tore the nation apart. It was a fractious time, when players at Yale faced not only the rigors of their studies and football but the thinly veiled scorn of classmates who questioned the regimen and discipline of a warlike team sport. It was a time when players turned more than ever to their coaches to help make sense of the things going on around them. It was a time when some coaches fought against the rebelliousness while others welcomed the opportunity to play more meaningful roles in the lives of the young men entrusted to their care.

I don't mean to overdramatize the roles we played as coaches. Surely there were many others who helped harness and direct this youthful energy, but I mention these difficult times to explain how broadly and abruptly the role of college coaching changed. Not every coach accepted the challenge. I think more coaches left the profession at that time than at any other. Many of them couldn't adapt. Many of them simply wouldn't change. I talked with other coaches around the country, and we were all faced with the same things. Those who tried to hold onto the blind discipline that had marked college football for generations either quit or were asked to leave. It was the General Patton types who had the greatest problems.

The changes in young people's attitudes were obvious. Until then, if your parent, your teacher, or your coach told you to do something, you did it, no questions asked. I can just imagine what Woody Hayes, my old coach at Miami of Ohio, would have said if I had been so bold as to suggest a new play or, God forbid, to question a decision he'd made. In the long run, though, I think this new environment was a good thing. It kept teachers and coaches on their toes. It made us really think through what we were doing before we did it, because we knew that we could be challenged on every decision. We had to be prepared to defend every minute of our practice schedules, because someone was sure to ask why we were spending twenty minutes on the kicking game, or why we were working on an off-tackle play that hadn't worked the previous Saturday. Everything was why, why, why, and you had better have answers.

Some of my assistant coaches may have questioned what we were doing, but I think they followed my leadership. I made sure that they understood that we would be better coaches and a better team if we listened to our players, respected their right to an explanation, and tried to learn from their questions. I have always said that you can learn more from your players than from any book or coaching clinic. My message to the staff was to remember that the reason the school buildings were there, the reason we were there, the reason every professor was there was to benefit the students. That's why we were being paid, to educate those young men—and that meant more than teaching them the Xs and Os of a football play. It meant molding them as leaders of our community. I always felt that our players would have a head start on being leaders because of the great education they received at Yale, and because of the way they handled the outside pressure of being a part of a football team. I still believe that.

It didn't take a genius to see that things were changing in the fall of 1969. The first clue was the way the students looked. They started to appear shabby, letting their hair grow and wearing long beards. It was all part of the antiestablishment attitude. I knew what was happening on campus. I understood the peer pressure the players were feeling. The student body was asking them why they were playing football, why they were submitting themselves to the arbitrary authority of the coach instead of joining in campus protests. And I knew that many of the players were sincere in their opposition to the war. So I can't say I was surprised when our captain, Andy Coe, came to me early in the season and asked that the team be allowed to wear black armbands as a symbol of antiwar protest.

Andy was a fine leader. He was the son of a minister and an earnest young man. He walked into my office in the Ray Tompkins House to speak on behalf of the team, but I could tell that he was speaking his own mind as well. He said that the players wanted to wear the armbands on their uniforms during our games. Furthermore, he said, they wanted to march on Washington as a team to make a visible statement against the war.

I told him no, that we weren't going to do those things as a team, that the Yale uniform was not something we could use to make political statements. I let Andy know that I sympathized with the players' feelings, but that there was a right way and a wrong way to make those feelings known. Fortunately, Andy understood. I don't know whether he agreed with me entirely, but he accepted my position, and in his role of captain, he persuaded the players to drop their request.

I was torn in my feelings about the war. It was an unpopular war that half the people in the country were opposed to. But I was disturbed by the methods of protests that many students were choosing. And I was upset that blatant disobedience to all established authority was not only accepted but applauded in many quarters. The players were caught in the middle of all this passion, and I'm sure that they had mixed feelings, too. Many of them were genuinely angry about the war and wanted to show solidarity with the protests of their peers. On the other hand, they understood and respected the need for discipline and structure on a football team. They knew that the breakdown of authority could not extend to the football field without negative consequences. My job, as I saw it, was to help them understand the dilemma they were caught up in. They needed to know that questioning authority on campus and respecting the rules within our football family were not mutually exclusive. I encouraged them to be members of the university as well as members of the football team, and I reminded them that football was an integral part of their lives, but only a part of it. Stone Phillips, who was our quarterback in 1975 and '76 and is now the co-anchor of NBC's *Dateline*, spoke about that principle when he came back for a golf tournament the summer after I retired. During his public remarks after the tournament, he reminded people how I always preached that family came first, academics second, and then football.

During those difficult years I made a point of talking with the players as often and for as long as I could. I made sure they knew my door was always open. I met almost daily with the captains and the other seniors who were the leaders of the team. I also had conversations with the team as a whole. I let them know that I understood and respected their feelings. I told them that I was upset, too, because I didn't think the war had a real meaning, but that for us to act as renegades wasn't going to help the situation. At times it was hard to find the right words to say to them, because I felt very much like they did. On the other hand, I didn't like the disloyalty that was so much a part of the protests on campus. We always preached loyalty to one another, as well as to parents and elders. I was angry when I saw students—and especially football players—showing disloyalty to our leaders in Washington.

That's not the way I was raised. My mother and father would have been extremely disappointed in what was happening on college campuses then. They believed in this country and the opportunities it gave them. They never said negative things about the president, not even in a kidding fashion. Sometimes they'd say, "I wish he had done this" or "He shouldn't have done that," but they never, ever criticized him in a disrespectful way. And they would never allow me to be disrespectful in any way to anyone older or in authority. That just wasn't done.

Whether they wanted to be or not, our players were campus leaders. Football teams build leadership, and even in those rebellious times the young men who played the game were expected to set certain standards. So it was important to remind them that everything they did must be in a positive vein. They probably got tired of hearing me tell them that we didn't need to add fuel to the fire. The campus and the country didn't need more dissension, more heartache. I think every one of them believed in our country and loved our country. It was just that they didn't agree with everything that was going on in Washington.

The one thing I could never understand was why so many students held it against the soldiers who were being shot at and killed. Why didn't the protesters treat the soldiers with respect when they came home? Why did they burn the flag? I still can't understand that. If they had this great concern for other people—and after all, that's why they were in such turmoil, because they thought people were being treated unfairly—then why did they turn on the young men and women who fought for this country and tried to make it better? They heard about that from me, I'll tell you! I told the players I didn't want to hear them talking about a professor in a disrespectful way, or the president of the university or the athletic director or anyone else, unless they understood their job and knew what they were up against. "I don't think you have that right," I told them. I stayed strong on that, and I'm glad I did.

Even that was touch-and-go, because they questioned authority big-time. That's why my door was always open, so we could talk about it. More than ever, that was the time to be a good listener. Coaching was needed then more than it had ever been. The players needed supervision. They needed a sense of discipline. They needed guidance and they needed someone to talk to. It was important to let them express themselves, let them get their feelings on the table and see what you could do to help them get through their troubles. I think some kids felt guilty, to be honest with you, about not being in the service. Some of them had close friends who were killed, and that made them bitter. Protesting the war was their way of expressing their anger and frustration.

I feel fortunate that we had strong character on that 1969 team, especially in the senior class. I tried to tell them that they certainly could voice their opinions and let people know they were not comfortable with the way some things were in the country. They were free to discuss their concerns with their peers, their professors, or anyone else. I let them know that they were right to do whatever they could to make their point, as long as it was constructive. Being full of youthful exuberance, they thought they could make a difference, and I'm not sure they couldn't, but marching on Washington and throwing stones at the White House, so to speak, wasn't going to help.

There were people who wouldn't stand for the national anthem. That bothered me, and I think it bothered our players. I was concerned because I thought the fiber of the country was beginning to come apart. I felt it was a time when we needed really strong parents, strong educators, and strong coaches. But at the same time, we needed to let our young people grow at their own pace. Years later, I got a letter from Brian Clarke, who people know today for his acting roles on General Hospital and Eight is Enough. He had been the first player to challenge team rules by wearing a beard. I don't think I ever told him he had to shave it off, but we talked about it and eventually he trimmed it so he looked more presentable. The letter he sent me was really beautiful. He thanked me for letting him grow and express himself. Later in life, he realized that not all kids had been given that opportunity in college.

That's what the players needed most. They needed people in positions of authority to listen to them, respect their views, and allow them to express themselves. I don't think they understood it then, but many of them realize now that many of their extreme positions were just expressions of youthful passion and a necessary part of growing up. The trick was to strike a balance between letting them express themselves and maintaining discipline. I continued to make players wear a shirt and tie when we traveled. It wasn't fashionable then, but I told them that they were a class outfit representing a class university, and I wanted them to look the part. A few of them challenged me, but I think ultimately they respected me and themselves because of it. If you don't have discipline, you lose your team. You can't let 150 guys go their own way. Most of all, I didn't want the players to lose the warm feeling they had for one another and their coaches. I wanted them to realize that family is the strongest thing you can have in life, and that a football family is an extension of your real family. I wanted them to hold on to that feeling. If they did, I thought, we would survive.

We lost one of our players, Woody Knapp ('65), who was a defensive back when I was an assistant to John Pont. He was a fighter pilot who was shot down and killed. I remember thinking, here's one of the nicest, most wonderful people you ever want to meet and he gives his life for something the people in his own country don't respect. It bothered me that we weren't giving these soldiers the same respect we did during World War II and the Korean conflict. I was young during those wars, but I remember how the nation respected the military. The attitudes were very different during the Vietnam era, and that was unfair to our soldiers and sailors. They hated the protesters for not giving them the respect they deserved, and because they knew that some of those kids wouldn't have fought even if they were drafted. They would have fled to Canada to avoid their duty.

I was concerned about the direction of football, not only on our campus but on other campuses, too. But I found that the players still wanted the discipline of football. They still wanted to be at practice, still wanted to work hard and enjoy the camaraderie. And they still enjoyed the competition.

That's me, circa 1940.

The Cozza family, circa 1940;
back row, from left: Theresa, Dad, Mom, Josephine; front: Pat, me, and Ange.

The house my father built in Parma, Ohio. (Photo taken in 1990s).

My Parma-Schaff High School letterman sweater.

Pitching for the Miami University baseball team.

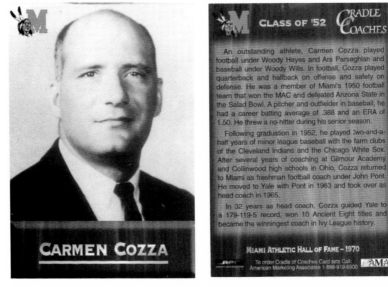

Trading card from the Miami University of Ohio "Cradle of Coaches" series.

Coach John Pont's 1963 Yale coaching staff meets in the football conference room of the
Ray Tompkins House; from left: Harry Jacunski, John Pont, me,
Ernie Plank, Herb Fairfield, Jay Fry, Jake VanSchoyk.

My wife, Jean, and my daughters, Kathryn, Karen, and Kristin,
at our home in Orange, Connecticut, 1964.

Head coach at 34, I stand on a snowy Yale campus, 1965.

With Athletic Director Delaney Kiphuth, 1965.

My first coaching staff, 1965; from left, me, Bill Narduzzi, Bill Mallory, Neil Putnam, Seb LaSpina, Jim Root. (Yale University Sports Archives)

Karen, me, Kris, Jean, and Kathy, 1965. (Yale University Sports Archives)

Brian Dowling stiff-arms a would-be tackler from Harvard in Yale's 24–20 victory, 1967.
(Yale University Sports Archives)

Nick Davidson, me, Bob Levin, and Brian Dowling on the way to
the Cornell game, 1968.

Calvin Hill, left, and captain Brian Dowling, leaders of the undefeated,
once-tied 1968 team. (Yale University Sports Archives)

The 29–29 "loss" to Harvard, 1968. (Yale University Sports Archives)

Brian Dowling (10) threads a crowded sideline at Harvard Stadium in 1968.
(Yale University Sports Archives)

Garry Trudeau's *Bull Tales* strip in the *Yale Daily News* in 1967 and 1968 helped inflame student passions. Any similarity between the lead character, B.D., and Brian Dowling was entirely intentional. (Yale Daily News)

Brian Dowling, Bruce Weinstein, and Calvin Hill, Class of 1969.
(Yale University Sports Archives)

Spring practice, 1969. (S. Frinzi, Yale University Sports Archives)

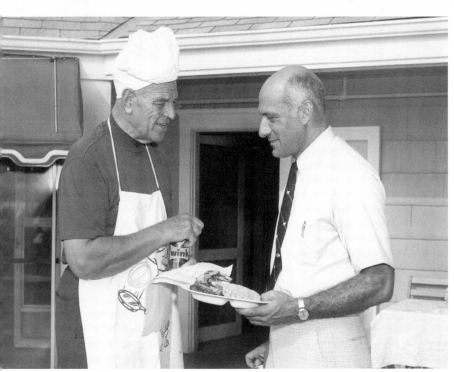

With Ted Blair—"Mr. Yale"—who hosted a barbecue for the football team every year. (S. Frinzi)

Jean and me with Yale president Kingman Brewster at Ted Blair's barbecue, 1969.

President Kingman Brewster, with me and team captain Andy Coe on his right and Athletic Director Delaney Kiphuth on his left, speaks at the annual team dinner attended by Fred the Dog. (Milton M. Smith)

A kiss from daughter Kris at a team practice.

Doing stretching exercises with the team. (Yale University Sports Archives)

Don Martin (45) and Dick Jauron (25), both future NFL stars, follow the blocking of Earle Matory (73). (S. Frinzi, Yale University Sports Archives)

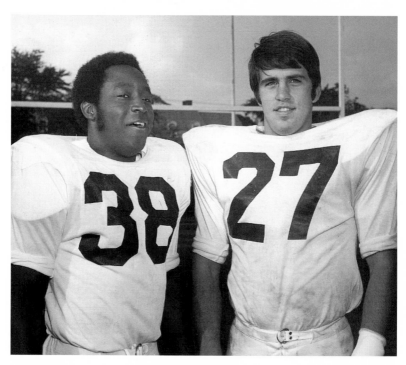

Ron Lindsey (38) and Jack Ford (27), 1972. (Yale University Sports Archives)

Two other elements added to the student angst. One was the growing popularity of drugs. The other was the issue of black-white confrontation on campus and in the nation at large. Racial pressure was the strongest in the early 1970s that I can ever recall. Black students were angry. They felt that maybe they weren't getting a fair shake, and for the most part, the white athletes supported them. It was a tough subject to deal with. Probably more coaches lost their jobs because of black-white issues than over any antiestablishment issues. Coaches had to be colorblind just to survive. We faced a strange paradox: we had to treat every player the same, and at the same time we had to make certain allowances for some minorities because of their backgrounds and upbringing. Dealing with the raw-edged racial sensitivities of that time required an extra measure of patience and especially communication. It's always hard to explain to a player that although he thinks he's the best at his position, that might not be the case in the eyes of the coaches. That is tough to get across, especially to parents who always think their sons are the best. If you add race to the equation, the result can be explosive.

One black player who really challenged me was Tyrell Hennings, an outstanding running back in the early 1970s. He insisted that he be allowed to wear different colored tape on his shoes. He told me that it was the only way his mother could recognize him. This young man came from a difficult background, and I tried to take that into account, but I knew that as a member of a team, he couldn't be allowed to act as an isolated individual. I couldn't let him dictate what he was going to wear on Saturday afternoons. I reminded him that he had a number on his uniform, and his mother could pick him out that way. I said I didn't want to hear any more about it. In time, we became close. In fact, the longer we were together, the friendlier we became, and the more each appreciated where the other was coming from.

Fortunately, Rudy Green, another fine running back, was also on that team, and he was Tyrell's opposite. The kids elected him captain in 1974, the first black captain at Yale since Levi Jackson in 1949. He was a good, steady player, but beyond that, he could laugh at himself and roll with the punches. I'm sure he heard a lot of nasty things in those days about black athletes, but he always had a smile on his face. He was a wise and wonderful choice for our captain. We've been friends ever since.

I think sometimes that my own upbringing helped me understand some of the minority kids who were from poor families. In some ways I had been a little deprived, too. So when players told me about the problems they had, I could relate to them. I could say, hey, my family didn't have an automobile or a telephone when I was growing up, so don't give too much weight to your problems. You can do anything you want to do in this world. You are at this wonderful university, which means you have been given a great opportunity to be the best you can be in your chosen profession. And excuses will get you nowhere.

For the most part, the white athletes supported the black athletes, but I was always concerned about cliquishness. I didn't like it when all the black players would eat at one table. If I saw that, I would sit down and eat with them myself. I made a speech at the beginning of every year and told the players that their fraternity or residential college or the group of friends they hung out with on campus had no bearing on the team. And that included their social standing or their race. I made sure that they understood that we were a team, and that everyone was a part of it. That meant we were all here to help one another be better athletes and that we would be a better team because of it.

The Yale football players were not my only concern in those years. Jean and I had three young girls growing up, too. We talked a lot about drugs and dissent and the peer pressure they were feeling. Jean did a wonderful job of being there for our daughters. She gave up her teaching career so she could spend time with them. I appreciated and respected that. I tried to be there for the girls as much as I could, but so often I wouldn't get home until after they had gone to bed. That's why I made it a point to drive each one of them to school in the morning, so we would at least have that private time. Jean was wonderful with the players, too. Many times we would have a player out to our house for dinner, and we did it more than ever during the war years. I would tell Jean about some young man who was having a problem, and we would have him over. She would talk to him like a mother. We established some lasting relationships that way. I remember Bob Kenney, an end and punter on my first three teams, as one example. He and his girlfriend, now his wife, were contemplating marriage, but he wasn't sure if the time was right, and he needed someone to talk to. Jean helped him through it, and eventually things worked out well. Bob still remarks about it. He thought that was very special.

The early 1970s were tough times. But in many ways they made the young men who lived through them better people later in life. I think they learned a great deal from the experience. They learned a great deal about themselves, and what was right and wrong. In many ways, I think they were fortunate to get an education beyond the classroom.

In the first weeks of that 1969 season, it was easy to get caught up in the campus upheaval, but I had a team to coach and a football season to play. And while the peer pressure and the antiwar protests were one concern, I also had the problem of carrying on the success of the 1968 team without Brian Dowling, Calvin Hill, and Company.

We didn't have the makings of another truly great team. What we did have, though, was a team of good players with great character and determination. And they were players who had learned how to win as underclassmen. In some regards, I think those troubling times made the kids better players, because they had to overcome something else in their lives. They needed something special inside them to stay out for the team. It took a genuine commitment to deal with the external pressure they were feeling on campus and in their residential colleges.

The students were not overtly opposed to football. There were no antifootball rallies or anything as obvious as that. But anything that connoted combat was suspect. The exuberant student mobs that had rocked the team bus and the impromptu pep rallies disappeared.

The Yale football jersey with Brian's No. 10 had been replaced by the closed fist of protest as the icon of choice on banners hanging from dormitory windows. All this made it more difficult for the young men of Yale to submit to the rigors of football. It was a great source of satisfaction that so many of them stayed with the program. Whenever a player told me that he was going to drop off the team, I asked him what was going to take the place of football in his life. Almost all of them had something they wanted to do, like join a musical group or do charity work in the city. I was okay with that. I just didn't want them to quit for the wrong reasons.

But the vast majority of those players kept their commitment to the team. Not only that, they put together winning seasons, including a 7–2 cochampionship year in 1969. We had a strong defense that included defensive end Tom Neville, a future Rhodes scholar, defensive end Jim Gallagher, middle guard Rich Lolitai, and Andy Coe at linebacker.

We lost our opener to Connecticut 19–15 and got beaten by Dartmouth 42–21 in the Bowl, but we won the rest of our games and shared the Ivy League championship with Dartmouth. The dedication and character those "normal-type players" displayed in the midst of the campus turmoil was as great a source of pride to me as the national ranking had been the year before. It took something special for those young men to stay the course through the storm of peer pressure. In the end, they not only honored their commitment, they honored themselves. They were real champions.

CHAPTER FIVE

Hooked on Coaching

The call was waiting for me when I walked off the eighteenth green at the National Cash Register golf course in Dayton, Ohio. It was the summer of 1976, and I was playing in a charity tournament for multiple sclerosis in honor of my old coach Ara Parseghian. As soon as someone told me there was a call for me from New Haven, I had a good idea who it was and what it was about. And I knew my life was about to change.

So I wasn't surprised to hear Kingman Brewster's voice on the phone. He was the president of Yale University and, I'm proud to say, a good friend, too. He didn't tell me what he was calling about, he just said he wanted to talk with me as soon as I got home. Two days later, I flew back to Yale, talked with the president, and accepted the job of athletic director. It was a proud moment for me. I was honored not only because I was being entrusted with the highest position in the athletic department at this great university but because I was succeeding Delaney Kiphuth, a man I respected greatly, and I was being given the job by Kingman Brewster, someone I admired more than I can find words to express.

Accepting the job seemed entirely natural. I was to be the AD and football coach for one more season, then relinquish the coaching position to concentrate on running the department. It is not unusual for a coach to move up to the AD's office after a number of successful years. It's a reward for a job well done and an opportunity to serve your school and its student-athletes at a higher level, though in retrospect I'm not sure there is any more important way to serve youth than as a coach. It was an exciting time for Yale sports, with many important challenges ahead. Women's teams were changing the landscape of Yale athletics, and the number of varsity sports was exploding. In my time at Yale, the number of varsity sports increased from seventeen to thirty-four. I looked forward to working with the coaches in the other sports. They were people I knew and respected, and I was sure I could help them find ways to do their jobs even better.

There was just one thing I didn't count on. I didn't realize how tough it would be to give up coaching. When it came time to step aside, I just couldn't let go. It wasn't until I had to face the prospect of giving up the rewarding personal relationships with all those fine young men that I realized how much coaching meant to me.

To be honest, I thought I could do both jobs. I convinced myself that if I worked hard enough at being AD and football coach, I could show the president I could handle both jobs. But it didn't work out that way. It wouldn't have been fair to Yale to try to keep both positions, working in the football office on the second floor in the morning and running downstairs to the AD's office in the afternoon. I bounced back and forth like that for the first few weeks and months of that 1976 season, but I soon realized that it wasn't a schedule I could maintain. I simply couldn't give my best efforts to both positions.

And that brought me to a real dilemma. It slowly dawned on me that my coaching days were coming to an end. I had promised Kingman Brewster that I would form a committee and bring in a new coach at the end of the season. But as that time grew closer, I was heartsick. If I gave up coaching, I was afraid I would regret it for the rest of my life. But if I backed out of my agreement with the president and gave up the directorship to remain as coach, I would be disappointing a man I respected as much as anyone I ever met. Jean gave me good advice. She didn't suggest what I should do. She just reminded me that life is short and that I should do what makes me happy.

To help you understand the depth of my dilemma, let me tell you about my admiration for the president.

You've heard the expression "He was preceded by his reputation." Well, President Kingman Brewster was preceded by his given name. Accurately so. He was exactly what you would expect from someone named Kingman. His presence was almost regal. It's no wonder that he became the United States ambassador to England when he left Yale.

Whitney Griswold was the president when I arrived at Yale, but he died during my first year, and Kingman was deservedly ushered into the president's office. The courtly way he carried himself could be intimidating if you didn't know him. In fact, I was a little intimidated when I first met him. After all, he epitomized the lofty image of Yale and the Ivy League, and I was a thirty-two-year-old football coach who had never been east of Pittsburgh when I first arrived in New Haven. He was the kind of man you couldn't help but notice, and I was duly impressed.

I met him for the first time when Delaney Kiphuth brought him over to the football offices during John Pont's time as head coach. Kingman made a few remarks, then chatted informally with the coaching staff. He was so distinguished and handsome, and carried himself so well, I admit that I was a little in awe. But after I became the head coach and got to know him a little better, I realized that he had a shyness about him—a little like me, perhaps. He wasn't really the extrovert you might think he was if you judged him by his public persona alone.

One year, he was given an honorary degree during graduation exercises and I remember marveling at how embarrassed he was by all the attention. If anyone deserved an honorary degree, he did, yet as I watched him, I could tell that he couldn't wait to get the ceremonies over with. Another time, when we were traveling together on behalf of the university, whoever booked the reservations had arranged for him and his wife, Mary Louise, to sit in the first-class section, while Jean and I were ushered back to coach. It didn't bother me in the slightest. If he had wanted to be the pilot, it would have been okay with me. But he was thoroughly embarrassed. He came back to where we were sitting and apologized profusely. That's the way he was. There was something about him that was extraordinary to me. He was a gifted scholar, but he could sit and talk with you about anything. He never thought of himself as better than anyone else. He didn't want you to think that he was special in any way. But the less he encouraged you to think of him that way, the more you did.

As the moral leader of the university, he stood for all the right things, even when that meant tough decisions and criticism from people on and off campus. I remember, for example, the trial of Black Panther Bobby Seale in 1970. This town could have blown apart. The courthouse on the green was the focus of the nation, as angry crowds gathered and threatened a violent confrontation with authorities. The National Guard had been called out and was positioned just out of sight in case of trouble. We were worried about bombs going off. In fact, a small one did explode at Ingalls Rink, the Yale hockey arena.

The situation came to a head during a big May Day protest. It was a Saturday night, and thousands of protesters gathered on the New Haven Green, only about three blocks from the athletic offices in Ray Tompkins House. I spent the evening in my office with a loaded rifle. Several other coaches were there, too. I can't say that I would have used the gun, but if a mob had stormed the building, they could have damaged a lot of important equipment and memorabilia. I would have fired into the air to scare them off.

But I think Kingman really calmed the situation, maybe even saved the university and the town from erupting into something ugly. He took a lot of criticism for his public stand that blacks couldn't get a fair trial in this country. But I understood what he meant. He wasn't criticizing the justice system or the country. He was just stating the obvious, that the atmosphere was so charged with racial over-tones that it was sure to affect the way people thought and acted, including jurors. Significantly, the students listened to him, even at a time when they were challenging authority of any kind. I think it was because he was willing to listen to them and physically come out and talk with them. He didn't hide in his home or in his office and they respected him for that. President Brewster taught us all important lessons and left a legacy at Yale that everyone should be able to say what's on his mind without recrimination. He encouraged both faculty and students to think for themselves and not to be afraid to express their feelings, but always to do it the right way.

President Brewster wasn't really a sports fan, certainly not the way Bart Giamatti, his successor as president, was a baseball fan. But he knew a little about football, and he certainly understood the benefits of a winning program for the university. He never wanted to jeopardize academics for athletics, but he believed that football was an integral part of the educational experience. And he knew that it was a sure way to generate school spirit. He came to almost all our games. He sat in the president's row in Portal 16, right above the entrance to the players' tunnel, and he really got into the action. After we beat Harvard one year, I turned around and caught sight of him jumping around like an underclassman, shaking his arms in the air and screaming.

I was so happy for him that day because he wanted to beat Harvard in the worst way. Yet when we lost, I think he felt worse for me than he did for himself. I'm not sure you see that kind of compassion in many presidents, because they have to be so involved in so many things. But there was a real caring about Kingman. There were lots of little human touches about him that I admired, like the time he and Mary Louise found a four-leaf clover in their yard. They set out to find our house in Orange so that they could give it to me for good luck. One fall he had gout so bad that he had trouble getting around without a cane. But it wasn't enough to keep him from driving to the University of Rhode Island for a preseason scrimmage. There he was with Mary Louise and Sam Chauncey, the university secretary, walking up and down the sidelines.

It's an honor to say that Kingman was more than a president to me, he was a friend. In the early 1970s, when the university was involved in a $360 million fund drive, he invited Jean and me to travel around the country with him to speak to alumni groups. We went to the West Coast and Dallas and various other stops. We attended a number of alumni functions and spoke at lunches and dinners, but there was some private time, too, when I really got to know Kingman. We talked about the flavor of the university, and about the facilities. That's why we were raising money, to refurbish the outdoor facilities, the residential colleges, and, of course, the athletic facilities. He understood long before other people did the need to raise funds to keep Yale's physical assets at a peak. You are seeing the benefit of that now.

More than anything, though, Kingman wanted to talk about the kids. He wanted to know how the players were doing in school. He would ask whether they were enjoying their experience at Yale. And he would ask about former players who had graduated. I was honored that he asked me to go with him on those fund-raising trips. Football was big at the time, and he knew that I often traveled around the country meeting with alumni groups. I was trying to spread goodwill for the university and establish a network for recruiting. Whenever the alumni office asked me to go some-where, I went. I even solicited places to go. If I was going to Phila-delphia, for example, to meet with recruits, I wanted to talk to an alumni group while I was there.

You can see why my decision at the end of the 1976 season was so difficult. The president had given me the opportunity to be athletic director at one of the world's greatest institutions of higher learning, and here I was thinking about giving it back. He had entrusted me with the stewardship of a huge intramural program, dozens of varsity sports, and a remarkable complex of truly magnificent athle-tic facilities, most of which, unfortunately, were in need of repair, or soon would be. It was a weighty responsibility, but I felt equal to it. In fact, I looked forward to the challenge. But there was that prospect of giving up my sweats and whistle. As the weeks of that season passed, I realized that what was really important to me was the inter-action with my players.

In the end, there was really only one thing for me to do, and that was to give up the directorship. I thought then that there might be another chance later on to be an athletic director, but if I gave up coaching, I might never get another chance. I have never regretted that decision. Clearly, it was the right thing for me to do. My place was with the players. They were an important part of my life, and I wanted to be an important part of theirs. I really had two families. I had Jean and our three girls, and then I had my football family. As athletic director, I could never have had those close ties with the young men who meant so much in my life, and that was a sacrifice I was unwilling to make.

There was another factor, too. I was in line to be the president of the American Football Coaches Association the next year, and if I gave up coaching, I would have had to pass on that post, too. Still, it was an agonizing decision, and the way some people reacted to it was really unfortunate. It bothered me that President Brewster got the blame for not letting me do both jobs. That was wrong. We had an understanding at the start that I would give up coaching after one season. I had agreed to that, and even though I secretly hoped I could do both jobs, it was unfair to blame him. He took some hits from the alumni, and he shouldn't have. I guess there was a feeling that because we had won the championship that year, there was no reason I couldn't be both coach and AD. We had lost our opener, then won the rest of our games. Even some of my players went to the president to ask him to let me do both.

Kingman knew as well as I did that it was impossible to fill both positions. So did Sam Chauncey, who told me, "Carm, you'll be all right as long as all goes well, but what if something should blow up in one of the other sports and you're in the middle of football? How are you going to handle it?" He was dead right. Kingman said much the same thing. He told me that I would burn myself out because I would never be home between recruiting, traveling, coaching, and being in the AD's office. Still, I felt bad that after one year I handed the job back to him. I don't think he held it against me, because he knew that in my heart I really wanted to be a coach. But I felt bad just the same.

CHAPTER SIX

A Few of the Brightest

ick Jauron was at Harvard Stadium that November day in 1968 when we "lost" 29–29 to John Yovicsin's Crimson. He lived only a few miles northeast of Cambridge in Swampscott, Massachusetts, where he had just finished his senior season as one of the most sought-after running backs in the country. He was named to the high school All-America team by *Parade* magazine and was being wooed by the likes of Notre Dame, Alabama, and Ohio State. He was at the top of our recruiting list, too, of course, as he was at Harvard and who knows how many other schools.

I knew his dad, who had been a coach at St. Joseph's College in Indiana. He was a robust, Woody Hayes type, and I assumed that his son would be the same way, but Dick was just the opposite. He was quiet and unassuming, always shunning the spotlight until it was impossible to avoid it. I really liked that about him. My first contact with him came when I spoke at his high school banquet. I did everything I could during my speech to sell the Yale football program, and Dick knew that I was talking directly to him. After the dinner, I went to the Jauron home, and I was immediately impressed with the young man. He had a way of looking you right in the eye and letting you know that he was taking in every word you said.

It was our good fortune that he made the short trip to the horseshoe-shaped stadium beside the Charles River and witnessed the dizzying excitement of The Tie. It might have been a painful disappointment for our side, but it was an exciting game just the same. The noise and the passion among the fans on both sides convinced the young Massachusetts athlete to narrow his college choice to Yale or Harvard, with two other Ivy League schools, Princeton and Brown, as backup choices. In the end, he chose to wear the blue-and-white of Yale, which proves that even the darkest cloud can have a silver lining.

This young man was not only one of the very best backs I ever coached but one of the humblest team players, too. It was next to impossible for the press to get him to take credit for anything he did in his three record-setting seasons at Yale. When reporters interviewed him about one of his many long-distance touchdowns, he would ask if they had noticed the great block the tight end had thrown to free him. When I tried to give him the game ball after he set the Yale single-game rushing record against UConn, he suggested that it go instead to the family of Herman Wegerich, a Yale player who had died that summer after his freshman season. For three years, Dick consistently and doggedly deflected the attention to his teammates.

I was thrilled when he was named to the Kodak All-America team after his senior season because I knew the honor was based on his exploits on the field and not some promotional campaign orchestrated by the publicity department. He tried so hard to avoid the spotlight that he wouldn't even cooperate when Cappy Jones, the sports information director, wanted to put together a film clip to be sent out to newspapers and TV stations. Cappy asked Dick to sit with me on camera in one of the college courtyards and talk about football, but Dick declined because he felt it was wrong to be singled out as an individual in a team sport.

It was a little surprising that the American Football Coaches Association voted him to the Kodak team, not because he didn't deserve it but because Cornell's running back Ed Marinaro had been an All-American the year before, and I didn't think the voters on any of the various teams would go for two Ivy Leaguers in a row. Dick also was named to the Associated Press All-America second team.

We played Jauron mostly at fullback in his sophomore year because Donny Martin was firmly entrenched at tailback. Imagine two future NFL defensive backs in the same Yale backfield. Still, Jauron led the team in rushing with 962 yards in 182 carries—5.3 yards per carry. In his first game, a 10–0 win over UConn, he ran 116 yards on 22 carries, caught six passes for 81 yards, and scored the game's only touchdown on a 90-degree day in the Bowl. That set the tone for the next three seasons. He ran for 151 yards the next week against

Colgate and found himself in seventh place in the national rushing statistics. Then came games of 117 yards against Brown, 111 against Columbia, and 176 against Cornell, the third-best single-game performance in Yale history. Clint Frank had gained 190 yards in his Heisman Trophy season of 1937 and Levi Jackson had run for 177 in 1948.

After the Cornell game, which we won 38–7, Jauron jumped from seventh to fifth in the national statistics, while the Big Red's Marinaro, whom we held to 67 yards in 19 carries, dropped from No. 1 to No. 2. Dick got his 176 even though we were so far ahead that I pulled him for good with a few minutes left in the third quarter. Had I known how close he was to Frank's record, I might have given him a few more carries.

With Jauron, Martin, quarterback Joe Massey, and end Bob Milligan on offense, 270-pound Hawaiian Rich (the "Pineapple") Lolotai at middle guard, and future Rhodes scholar Tom Neville at defense tackle, we were 5–0 and riding high when an equally undefeated Dartmouth team came to play us at the Bowl. Unfortunately, we got skunked by one of the best Dartmouth teams ever. They held us to 190 yards of total offense, kept Jauron to 67 yards, and beat us 10–0 before a crowd of sixty thousand. The Big Green finished the season 9–0. We got our momentum back with wins over Penn and Princeton but lost 14–12 to Harvard in Coach John Yovicsin's final game.

In spite of our 7–2 season in 1970 and the prospect of Dick Jauron in the backfield for two more years, I began to worry about the direction of Yale football. And uncharacteristically, I didn't keep my concerns to myself. In radio interviews and on my weekly Sunday morning TV show with sportscaster Dick Galiette, I warned Yale officials and alumni of trouble ahead. I sounded the alarm that we would begin to suffer beginning in 1972 if we didn't get the number and quality of recruits we needed. We had fewer than fifty freshmen that year, compared with UConn's 112. I put the blame directly on the admissions office and pointed out that my staff was identifying scores of academically qualified football players who were being denied admission to Yale, then showing up at other schools, including other Ivy League schools. I told sportswriters that under those circumstances there was no way to stop Yale football from fading.

I also expressed my displeasure that the Ivy presidents had limited the league's home squads to sixty players and the traveling squads to forty-five. That was outrageous. Imagine a young man taking time out from the most rigorous academic regimen in the country to practice football, only to find that he wasn't allowed to travel with the team on weekends. Or worse, to be told that he couldn't put on his uniform and stand along the sidelines on Saturday afternoons in the Bowl for fear our sheer numbers would unduly intimidate opponents. Fortunately, the player limits were lifted eventually, but unfortunately, my predictions of a decline of Yale football were proven over time to be true.

We struggled some in 1971. Our 4–5 record was my only losing season in a fifteen-year stretch of 107 wins, 27 losses, and The Tie from 1967 to 1981. We missed Donny Martin, who won sprint championships at the Heptagonal and IC4A track championships before graduating and being drafted by the Oakland Raiders. He was converted to a defensive back and played three seasons in the NFL for the New England Patriots and the Kansas City Chiefs. He returned to Yale as an assistant coach in 1981 and was still on my staff when I retired sixteen seasons later.

Despite the mediocre season, we had some high points, including the opener against UConn, a 23–0 win, when Jauron rushed for 186 yards, passing Jackson into second place on the single-game rushing list, still behind Frank. It was his first game at tailback after playing mostly at fullback during his sophomore season, and it was obvious he was more comfortable in the upback position. Meanwhile, Marinaro ran for 260 yards in Cornell's opening game, and the two Ivy Leaguers found themselves No. 1 and No. 2 in the nation. Later that season, Marinaro, who became a famous TV actor in later years, put on quite a show when Cornell beat us 31–

10 in the Bowl. He gained 230 yards before Coach Jack Musick took him out of the game with 2:30 to go. Marinaro was only a few yards shy of the NCAA career rushing record held by Oklahoma's Steve Owen, and Musick wanted him to break the mark in a home game at Ithaca, which he did.

Jauron had a few explosive games, but we never really jelled as a team. We beat Penn and Princeton but lost to Dartmouth and limped into the Harvard game with a 4–4 record. We drew fifty-one thousand to the Bowl for Coach Joe Restic's first appearance, but we lost 35–16. Jauron rushed for 85 yards but fell just short of the 1,000-yard mark for the second year with 930.

One little sideshow put some flavor into the 1971 season. Bill Guthrie, a local sportswriter, wrote a column headlined "Pizza Power" about the seven Italian-Americans we had on the coaching staff. Guthrie had an acerbic style of writing, designed, I suppose, to get people's goat, or at least their attention. But some people in the local Italian community thought that he went too far with that column. He got so many negative letters and phone calls that he wrote an I-didn't-mean-to-offend-anyone column as a sort of apology. Frankly, I was not particularly upset. I knew that he was just having fun with us. I also knew that he wasn't stupid enough to insult the largest ethnic population in New Haven on purpose. I saw no harm in calling me Carmine Luigi Cozza and placing the athletic offices in the Reymondo Tompkinsino House. He didn't have to make up names when he talked about Bonaventure Dominico Amendola or Sebastian Antonio LaSpina. Those were their names. Most of all, Bill wasn't exaggerating when he talked about our collective love of pizza, which, by the way, many people insist was invented on Wooster Street right here in New Haven. He was dead right about that.

By 1972 the full-house T-formation was pretty much passe in college football, but I resurrected it from the scrap heap to take advantage of a backfield with three explosive running backs—Rudy Green, Tyrell Hennings, and Dick Jauron. We called it the Y-formation, which was roughly the way the quarterback and the three backs lined up behind the line of scrimmage. As good as Jauron had been in his first two years, he was even better as a senior. He had always been an elusive runner. I used to tell people you could spend twenty minutes with him in a phone booth and never touch him. But by his last year, he had gained strength as well and was a full-blown superstar at the Ivy League level. I believe he would have been a premier back on any college team in the country.

Once again we opened the season against Connecticut, and for the third straight year, we beat them, this time 28–7. Jauron, running from the left halfback position, broke Frank's single-game rushing record with 194 yards. I'm sure the UConn folks were glad to be rid of him. He had gained 496 yards in those three wins.

This was the centennial year of Yale football, and after four games, it looked like we were going to observe it with a very good season. After UConn, we beat Colgate, Brown, and Columbia by convincing margins, though we needed an 87-yard touchdown run by Jauron to erase a 14–12 deficit against Columbia in the fourth quarter. There was a terrific picture of that run in the New Haven Register the next day, showing Jauron racing all alone in front of horrified players on the Columbia sideline. He got a good block from Hennings at the line of scrimmage, bounced off at least one tackler, and got another key block at the corner from wide receiver Paul Sortal. After that it was clear sailing. I was so excited I ran onto the field and embraced him. It was the greatest touchdown play I had seen since Brian Dowling hit Del Marting in the end zone to beat Harvard in 1967. On that play, Dowling slipped as he was running to his right and threw the pass back across the field as he was falling down.

On Thursday before the Cornell game, Jauron walked into the locker room before practice, opened his locker, and stared into an empty stall. His helmet, pads, and cleats were missing, and so were all his personal belongings. Above his locker was a hand-lettered sign that read simply: "On waivers." Dick stood there for a moment with a puzzled look on his face until the captain, Bob Perschel, walked over with a serious expression and said, "You better go see the coach. I think Columbia has put in a claim for you." I always got a kick out of that kind of teasing. It helped keep the team loose, but it did us no good that Saturday at Cornell. We gave up seven, count 'em, seven fumbles and lost our first game of the season 24–13.

It wasn't until midway through his senior season that Dick began to get the national recognition he deserved. In the week leading up to the Dartmouth game, he was the fifth-leading rusher in the nation, with 634 yards in 81 carries. That's 127 yards per game and an awesome 7.8 yards per carry. It is worth noting that he was racking up all those yards in a T-formation backfield with two other backs who were carrying the ball a lot. It wasn't like he was getting 90 percent of the calls.

Bill Wallace, writing in the New York Times that week, compared Dick to Duane Thomas, the petulant but talented back for the Dallas Cowboys. Wallace's point was that neither of them said much to the press, but it wasn't really a good comparison, because the two players were very different people. Dick was polite and polished when he talked to reporters. He was honest and always tried to be helpful, but all he ever talked about was his teammates. Dick was quiet by nature, but he was one of the most intense players we ever had. He used to tell me that he was having trouble concentrating on his studies because of football. There wasn't much I could say except to remind him that he had to do both. He took me at my word during Dartmouth week, when he skipped a crucial practice to finish a history paper that was due before the midterm exam that week. Only in the Ivy League!

The missed practice didn't hurt us as a team. We whipped Dartmouth 45–14 in a performance that was as close to flawless as any I can remember a Yale team playing. We got a real bonus from a sophomore quarterback named Tom Doyle, who ran the ball 12 times for 160 yards. We couldn't stand success, though, and lost 48–30 the next week on Pennsylvania's artificial turf. We recovered to beat both Princeton, 31–7, and Harvard, 28–17, for a 7–2 season record.

Jauron's 1,055 yards for the season and 2,947 for his career set Yale standards. The career mark was still in place when I retired, though Rich Diana (twice), John Pagliaro, Keith Price, and Chris Kouri all surpassed his season record. Dick was named one of the nation's eleven Scholar-Athletes by the National Football Foundation and Hall of Fame, along with his Kodak first-team and AP second-team All-America honors. He was also asked to play in the East–West Shrine Game in San Francisco. Pro football fans know well that Dick went on to a nine-year career as an NFL defensive back, most notably with the Detroit Lions, then turned to coaching. After assistant positions with the Green Bay Packers and Jacksonville Jaguars, he was named to the head coaching job with the Chicago Bears.

Nothing that John Pagliaro ever did on the football field—and he did plenty—meant as much to me as a private and very emotional conversation we had in 1976 that helped shape my life. John was the son of a postal worker from Derby, Connecticut, a blue-collar town about ten miles out Derby Avenue from Yale Bowl. He was the product of a loving family and a small high school with one of the proudest football traditions in Connecticut. When he was a young boy, his father brought him to Yale games to watch Chuck Mercein and Calvin Hill carry the ball for the Elis. Later John Pagliaro Sr. watched with pride as his son became a schoolboy legend for Coach Lou DeFilippo at Derby High. And then, when John strapped on the pads of the Yale varsity, the father was a silent fixture along the sidelines at as many practices and games as he could make.

The whole town of Derby took an interest in John's career as he developed into one of the best and most durable backs in Yale history. A cluster of fans in Red Raider jackets was in noisy evidence at all our games, and it grew even larger in John's senior season, when former Derby fullback Mike Sullivan joined him in the starting backfield. Sullivan broke Pagliaro's high school rushing records, then followed him to Yale. We let Big Lou, the coach, roam our sidelines during games. It was the least we could do to repay him for producing half our starting backfield. He would coach his game on Saturday mornings, then rush to the Bowl, arriving sometime after the 1 o'clock kickoff.

Pags, as everyone called him, was a junior in 1976, which was to have been my last year as coach, before my tenure as full-time athletic director was to begin. My hopes were high for a successful final season, even though we had graduated several key defensive players from the 1975 team that had gone 7–2 and finished second to Harvard in the Ivy League. The running backs were Pagliaro, Mike Southworth, and Rick Angelone, another local player who played at Lyman Hall High in Wallingford, just two towns north of New Haven. Stone Phillips was our senior quarterback, with junior Bob Rizzo as the backup.

Our opener at Brown loomed as one of the toughest tests of the season. It was the first time since the 1940s that we had opened with an Ivy League opponent. For the previous eight seasons we played Connecticut and Colgate before launching the conference campaign. Ironically, I had worked to get this changed because I thought it was unfair to open every season against teams that had the benefit of two-week spring practices; all Ivy League schools were allowed was a token one-day, noncontact practice. Then, when the schedule finally was changed, we had to open in a regionally telecast game on ABC against a talented Bears team that was sure to challenge us for the Ivy title. Be careful what you wish for, they say, because you might get it. Sure enough, my worst fears were realized. We lost three fumbles, shanked a punt, failed on two forth-down conversions, couldn't score four times from close to their goal line, and were whistled for two personal fouls. Pagliaro was a bright spot, rushing for 114 yards, but we lost 14–6. It was an inauspicious start to my "final season."

That turned out to be the only low point of the campaign, however. We won our next nine games and tied Brown for the Ivy League championship at 6–1. We had some close calls, though, including an 18–14 win over Dartmouth. That was a bizarre game. We held the Big Green without a first down until there were just three minutes left in the third quarter, but if Bill Crowley, a future captain and Rhodes scholar, hadn't made a crucial interception and Randy Carter hadn't kicked two field goals, we might have lost.

Pagliaro, who works in New York City now for Hearst Magazines, deserved the biggest share of the credit for our 1976 success. Running behind one of the best offensive lines I ever had, he gained 1,023 yards on the season, just 32 fewer than Dick Jauron had gained four years earlier to establish the Yale record. Mike Southworth gave us a solid one-two punch, running for 477 yards out of the fullback position. Both Pags and Southworth had terrific per-carry averages of 5.7 yards.

Pagliaro ran with the highest knee action I ever saw. It was his natural gait and it was perfect for a running back of his size. He was only 5-foot-11 and 190 pounds, but he ran through or bounced off tacklers like a much bigger back because of his determination and his leg strength. The way he ran, with his knees churning up almost to his chest, made it nearly impossible to tackle him below the waist. And if you tried to arm-tackle him, you got a face full of cleats. He had the strongest legs of any back I coached, at least until Rich Diana came along a few years later. He was a swarthy young man of Italian heritage, and with his wild hair, thick black mustache, and the greasepaint under his eyes, he was a fearsome sight to opponents.

The season went so smoothly that I began to think I could handle both the athletic directorship and the head coaching job. The only distraction I had all season was caused by the Yale Precision Marching Band, which was drawing criticism from alumni and fans for its politically charged and risque halftime shows. It sounds petty to mention it after all these years, but it was a real concern at the time. Some of the alumni thought the performances were obscene and were withholding contributions until something was done about it. Although I never saw the band perform, because I was always in with the team at halftime, my gut reaction was to ban them from the Bowl and replace them with high school bands. That would have been a disaster with the liberal wing of the faculty, however, to say nothing of an activist student body that was still pretty stirred up over the Vietnam war. In time, cooler heads prevailed, and the band cleaned up its act enough to mollify its critics.

I figured that if nothing worse than an unruly band diverted my attention during the season, there was no reason I couldn't be coach and athletic director at the same time. To be honest, I hoped to convince President Brewster that I could handle both positions. My conflicting emotions came to a head when my players carried me off the field after my "last game," a 21–7 victory over Harvard. The scene in the locker room was even more touching. I have to admit that I had tears in my eyes. A lot of tears. When I walked in after the regular postgame press conference, they were chanting my name. They hoisted me up on their shoulders again, and we sang a very hoarse rendition of "Bulldog, Bulldog, Bow-Wow-Wow." Then they started chanting "one more year," and I got so caught up in the moment that I said I hoped I could do both jobs for at least one more year, maybe more. That was a mistake. There were sportswriters in the room, and they reported my comments, as they should have.

All of a sudden there was a controversy. Columnist George Wadley wrote an open letter in the *New Haven Register* addressed to the "Powers That Be at Yale," asking them to let me stay on as coach and AD. I appreciated the sentiment and support, but the column was more of an embarrassment than anything else. I wasn't trying to drum up public support, and I knew that's the way it would look. Besides, I had agreed to step down, and it wasn't fair to put President Brewster and the Yale Corporation in the uncomfortable position of reminding me of my commitment and making me choose between the two. Ultimately, the president announced at our captain's banquet that I would have to relinquish one of the two positions. The next morning, I offered my formal resignation as coach and prepared to concentrate solely on the AD's post.

I was devastated, much more than I had expected. I couldn't eat. I couldn't sleep. Jean was very supportive, as she always was, but there wasn't much she could say or do to console me. I was really miserable. Later in the week, I was in my office, gathering a few of my things to move downstairs to the director's office and trying to focus on the immediate task of appointing a search committee for a new coach, when I looked up to see John Pagliaro. "Coach," he said, "can I talk to you for a minute?" He sat down in the chair across from my desk, and I could see there was something very serious on his mind. He seemed almost tearful. "Coach," he said, "do you have to leave now? Can't you stay for one more year and be my coach?"

Well, that did it. That was the conversation, the very moment, when I decided it was a mistake to leave the one thing I had dedicated my life to—working closely and directly with athletes. In that moment I saw clearly that I couldn't stray from this goal. I realized that the self-fulfillment I got as a coach overshadowed anything else I might strive to do, including running Yale's athletic department. That visit to my office will always be my most vivid memory of John Pagliaro. More than any of his touchdown runs or any of the individual honors he won or benefits he brought to the team, I will remember that private moment that meant so much in my life.

Former President Gerald Ford, who had helped coach the Yale defensive line as a graduate assistant coach after his graduation from Michigan, got the 1977 season off to an inspirational start when he visited Timothy Dwight College as a Chubb Fellow. Two of our players, Lou Orlando and Bob Skoronski, handed a letter to the Secret Service men one evening, asking whether Ford could spare some time for an informal chat. To everyone's surprise, Ford agreed and met for more than an hour with five players who lived in Timothy Dwight. Earlier in the week, in a more formal setting, he had spoken to the whole team. I gave him a Yale helmet, and Delaney Kiphuth, who once played for him as a junior varsity player, presented him with a varsity jacket.

I felt great walking back onto the practice field that fall. It seemed like only the day before that I had made the wrenching decision to stay on as coach. I was very aware that if I had made a different choice, I wouldn't be there with a whistle around my neck feeling the adrenaline surge of another season. Frank Ryan, who was the great Jim Brown's quarterback with the Cleveland Browns when they won NFL championships in the years before the Super Bowl, had been installed as the athletic director. I was pleased to have a football man in the job, especially one who had put his academics ahead of his athletics when he played at Rice University in Texas.

Frank stayed in the job for ten years and, frankly, he wasn't always the most popular guy in the department. He certainly didn't have the warm personal approach that Delaney Kiphuth had shown in the twenty-three years before my one-year term. In Frank's defense, it was a tough time to run the department. He was under pressure to cut expenses and level the playing field for the men's and women's teams. That was no easy task. I can't say the department would have been better off under my authority. Some of the things that happened to adversely effect Yale sports, like the advent of the disastrous Academic Index, were not Frank's fault. They were beyond the ability of the Yale AD to control.

With two minutes and thirteen seconds left in the 1977 opener against Brown, we were in deep, deep trouble. Yale was ahead 10–7, but the Bears had the ball on our 2-yard line and were driving behind a huge front line. Brown outweighed us along the line of scrimmage by thirty pounds per man. Brown did what a bigger team should do and ran three running plays right up the gut, the last of which was a keeper by quarterback Mark Whipple, who would return to his alma mater as head coach in 1994. Somehow we managed to keep them out of the end zone, forcing them into a fourth-down play from the 6-inch line.

I had little hope of stopping them a fourth time, however, as I watched their big fullback, Wally Shields, bolt toward the goal line behind a 6-foot-6, 265-pound tackle. With twenty-seven thousand fans in Yale Bowl on their feet, our linebacker George Rapp launched himself over the line of scrimmage and hit Shields shoulder high. Rapp had acted on the advice of Buddy Amendola, our defensive coordinator, who told him to pinch inside and focus on the fullback. Rapp's hit slowed him up enough for tackle Frank Paci, middle guard Dave Humphreville, and monster back Kevin Gardner to finish him off. The other members of that defensive line deserve mention for their part in that goal-line stand, which people were still talking about twenty years later. They were ends Clint Streit and Dan Goodfriend and tackle Bob Skoronski. We gave up a safety in the dying seconds but then sacked Whipple twice to preserve a 10–9 win.

We beat Connecticut 23–12 the next week on a rainy day at the Bowl, then hunkered down for Yale's first intersectional game in nearly thirty years, against my alma mater, Miami University. Obviously, the game held special meaning for me, but it was an important test for Yale, too. Miami wasn't nationally ranked as it had been a few years earlier, but it was a midlevel major college that had beaten Indiana of the Big Ten 21–20 the week before. The whole Ivy League was watching to see how we would fare. I even got a telegram from Brown coach John Anderson wishing us luck.

I was embarrassed on Friday, the day before the game, because Yale employees were on strike, including the cafeteria workers and the grounds crew at the Bowl. I had to ask our sophomores to roll the tarp onto the field after Friday's practice. Predictably, they did it in good humor. That evening, I attended a Miami alumni gathering at a local restaurant. There were about four hundred people there, and they couldn't believe that the opposing coach would show up, but I just felt it was something I wanted to do. Despite my wholehearted allegiance to Yale, I still had a warm spot in my heart for my alma mater.

We gave Miami a good run, leading 14–6 after a nearly flawless first half, but we fumbled three times in the second half and wore down physically at the end, losing 28–14. It might have been our best game of the year, but we couldn't match Miami's depth and speed. The crowd of nineteen thousand was disappointing, but I guess Miami of Ohio didn't resonate with the local fans the way it did with me. We lost again the next week, a 3–0 squeaker to Dartmouth. We missed a good chance to score a winning touchdown at the end after an 81-yard pass play from Bob Rizzo to the future NFL tight end John Spagnola. That gave us fourth and 2 at Dartmouth's 3-yard line, but the Big Green forced a bad pitchout to Pagliaro, and time ran out. After the shaky 2 to 2 start, we reeled off four straight victories, including a 44–0 win over Princeton before a homecoming crowd of twenty-three thousand at Palmer Stadium. I used all eighty-six players in the game, including five quarter-backs.

With a 6–2 record, we drew a near-capacity crowd of sixty-seven thousand for Pagliaro's final game against Harvard. And what a final game it was. Pags rushed 30 times for 172 yards to lead us to a 24–7 win. His season's total of 1,159 broke the record that Dick Jauron had set four years before. The big play of the game was turned in by the other Derby High School running back, Mike Sullivan. We were nursing a tenuous 10–7 lead in the fourth quarter when Mike dropped back to punt. The snap from center was wide to the right and when Mike fielded it, he was off his stride and sensed that if he tried to punt, it might be blocked. He took off around the end and ran 65 yards for a touchdown.

I think the large crowd we attracted that day had to do with the three local backs we used, all of whom had played high school ball in the Housatonic League. Besides Pagliaro and Sullivan from Derby, we had Rick Angelone from Lyman Hall of Wallingford, who converted six third-down-and-short-yardage situations into first downs and ran for 75 yards in 17 carries in the game. Part of Pagliaro's legacy at Yale was to revitalize interest in Yale football among local fans. He was a hard-nosed, lunch-bucket athlete, and that really appealed to the locals.

Pags was selected to the Walter Camp All-America team in a backfield with Grambling's Doug Williams and Texas's Earl Campbell. He was also named a third-team AP All-America and won the Bushnell Award, presented to the Ivy League's most valuable player, for the second year in a row. He signed a free-agent contract with the New York Giants, as did our defensive tackle Paul Denza, but neither one made the team. I was interested in a comment Pagliaro made to sportswriters after his final game. He said that his proudest accomplishment was never missing a single minute of practice or a game for four years. He was, indeed, the iron man of Yale football. Still, I will remember him for the private conversation we had that November day in 1976 more than for any of his gridiron accomplishments.

I'll never forget how his few heartfelt words helped me see just how much coaching meant to me.

The best defensive back we had at Yale never played defensive back. Gary Fencik played wide receiver, though he probably could have played both ways. I know he wanted to, because he never wanted to come off the field. He constantly bugged me to let him play. By his senior year, he was in on every play he possibly could be, kickoffs, punts, and field goals, and he virtually never came out on offense. I figured I'd tire his butt out one way or the other, but he just loved it.

Gary had a defensive player's mentality, and although he never said so, I always thought he would have been happier on the other side of the ball. But we were in dire need of offensive talent from 1973 to 1975, and Fencik had plenty of it. So he had to wait until after graduation to play defense. He was an All-Pro defensive back with the Chicago Bears for a dozen years and earned a Super Bowl ring in 1986, when Coach Mike Ditka's Bears beat the New England Patriots 46–10. He became an investment banker after leaving the NFL.

Gary was on the receiving end of the longest pass play from scrimmage in Yale history. It was at Princeton in 1975, his senior season. We were trapped at our own 3-yard line in the second quarter of a scoreless game. Contrary to my reputation as a conservative play caller, I did like to try a little razzle-dazzle once in a while, and I thought this was as good a time as any. We had a halfback pass in the playbook in which Don Gesicki, who had been a high school quarterback, took a pitchout, faked the run, then pulled up to pass. I suggested to Coach Seb LaSpina, the offensive coordinator, that this would be a good time to use it. He looked at me like I had holes in my head, but I said, "Call it." Well, Gesicki took a pitchout from Stone Phillips, dropped back three yards into our end zone, and hit Fencik on the dead run for a 97-yard score. We ended up winning the game 24–13.

Gary set six receiving records at Yale—most catches and most yards receiving in a game, season, and career. His eleven catches against Harvard in 1974 and the 188 yards he gained against Princeton in 1975 were still on the books when I retired more than twenty years later. And as good as he was as a receiver, Gary might have been even better as a blocker. He just loved to run out in the secondary and take his man out of the play. He was a vicious hitter. I used to say that if he was sent out to block a defensive back and the man ran into the stands, he'd go after him.

The Miami Dolphins drafted him in the tenth round, but his career almost got sidetracked in preseason training camp. He won the team's long-distance run but suffered a collapsed lung in the process. A few days after it happened, he called me from the hospital and said, "Coach, no one's checking on me." I called a couple of my former players who were doctors in the area and they checked in on him right away. Then I called Don Shula, the Dolphins' coach, to find out what was going on. He assured me that he had no idea that Gary was being neglected and promised to follow up. A week or so later, Coach Shula called me back and said that he was going to have to let Gary go. He said he had a feeling it was a mistake, because Gary was a real talent who might well come back to haunt him, but he had to have a veteran player at safety who was ready to play immediately. I understood. Sometimes, you get into a situation where you have to make decisions even when they don't feel quite right. Shula's premonitions were right. The Bears picked him up on waivers, and he developed into one of the premier defensive backs in the NFL for twelve seasons. It was a perfect situation for him, too, because he was from Barrington, Illinois, not far from Chicago.

Fifteen of the players I coached at Yale saw action in the NFL. The first was Chuck Mercein, one of the "Baby Bulls" of the New York Giants, who also saw action with the Packers, Redskins, and Jets. Actually, John Pont was his head coach and I was his position coach. Then came Calvin Hill and Brian Dowling. Brian played in the Canadian Football League before stints with the Patriots and Packers, and Calvin was Rookie of the Year and an All-Pro for the Cowboys before playing with the Redskins and Browns. After them came Rich Diana,

Greg Dubinetz, Joe Dufek, Gary Fencik, Ken Hill, Dick Jauron, Don Martin, John Nitti, Eugene Profit, Jeff Rohrer, John Spagnola, and Chris Hetherington. Details of their careers are in the Appendix.

Chris Hetherington, our quarterback, in 1992, '94, and '95, was the last pro prospect I coached—though you could make a case for Keith Price, who had the third-best season of any running back in Yale history as a sophomore in 1992 but was injured and never regained full strength. Chris, who grew up just a few miles from the campus in North Branford and went to nearby Avon Old Farms prep school, had raw athleticism I hadn't seen since Calvin Hill. He was a standout football, hockey, and baseball player as a schoolboy and came to Yale not as a quarterback but as a split end. He had soft hands and excellent speed. He was also big and strong. He stood about 6-foot-3, weighed 225 pounds, and seemed to get stronger with every hit he took.

This high school pass receiver had the best passing arm on the freshman team at Yale. He had never played quarterback, but he could launch accurate spirals from the pocket or on the dead run. This was not lost on freshman coach Larry Ciotti, who wisely switched Chris's position. He became the best freshman quarterback in the league. Unfortunately, Chris was dogged by injuries throughout his Yale career. First a groin injury, then a hamstring pull either slowed him considerably or kept him out of the lineup entirely. Still, he passed for 1,169 yards as a senior, tenth-best all-time, and was our second-leading rusher, with 540 yards. He was fifth in single-season total yardage, fourth in career passing yardage, and third in career total offense. My God, what would he have done if he had stayed healthy.

I mention Chris's ability and his injuries to make a point. The one time he was entirely healthy was against an undefeated Princeton team at Palmer Stadium in his senior year. We went into the game at 1–4 in the league and 2–5 overall. The Tigers were 5–0 in the conference and 8–0 overall. With Chris healthy, though, running for 59 yards, completing 10 of 17 passes for 170 yards, and drawing the attention of the Tiger defense, we upset them 21–13. Without him, we didn't stand a chance. Chris wasn't drafted, but he signed a free-agent contract as an H-back with the Cincinnati Bengals. He was traded during his rookie season to the Indianapolis Colts, where he became a regular on their special teams. Incidentally, his agent was Joe Linta, a former Yale player and volunteer coach who represented a score of NFL players, including a few multimillion-dollar stars.

CHAPTER SEVEN

As Tough as They Come

I tried never to speak in superlatives. I'm not sure why that was, but if I had a player who was truly outstanding, I'd just say that he was pretty good. If Joe Montana had played for me, I probably would have said something like, "He's as good as any quarterback we have in camp at the moment." My conservative comments drove sportswriters crazy. They called me a lousy quote because I never went out on a limb, never made a controversial statement. With that in mind, let me make a flat-out superlative statement with the benefit of hindsight. Kevin Czinger was the toughest kid to play football at Yale in my thirty-two years as head coach. No question about it. He was also the most unusual personality, probably the outstanding overachiever, maybe the brightest student, and definitely the scariest individual. I loved him because of what he was made of inside. Jean loved him, too. He and Dick Jauron, both No. 40s, may have been her two favorite players to watch.

When I say Kevin was tough, I mean he was competitive to the point of obsession and loyal almost to a fault. If there are two more important personality traits for a football player, I don't know what they are. He was everything you could ask for in a teammate and friend.

The stories of Kevin's exploits on and off the field transformed him into something of a legend even before he graduated. An example of the Bunyanesque tales that were told was an incident after our Ivy League championship banquet in 1979, when a few of his teammates got into a scrap with two young men from the city. I'm not sure what started it, but the two townies got out of a car, and some angry words and jostling ensued on the sidewalk in front of the old Yale Co-Op store. One of our players, Jimmy Dwyer, was in a leg cast up to his hips and in no condition to defend himself.

Kevin was across Broadway, a short commercial street in the middle of the campus, when he saw the commotion. In the blink of an eye, he darted through traffic at full speed, tackled one town kid waist high, and sent him flying over the roof of the car into the street. When the other kid stepped in, Kevin laid him flat with one punch. At least that's the story I was told. I can't vouch for its accuracy. True to his character, Kevin was as angry at his teammates for not defending themselves as he was at the troublemakers from town. But when he turned to his teammates, they just pointed furtively to the side with anguished looks on their faces. What Kevin hadn't seen was there was a policeman only a few yards away who had observed the whole scene. That's why the other players hadn't reacted. Apparently, Kevin finished his work so quickly, the cop didn't have time to react either.

That version of the incident may be exaggerated, but knowing Kevin, it's easy to imagine that it happened exactly that way. I know there was at least some truth to the story because I got a call from the cops at my home just before midnight. They had taken Kevin and the two town kids to the police station in a paddy wagon and were deciding what to charge them with—disorderly conduct, assault and battery, or nothing at all. When I got to the station, the cop took me aside to explain the situation. He seemed stunned at how efficiently Kevin had disposed of the problem, and, quite frankly, I'm not sure even he was entirely honest with me. He told me that he didn't really blame Kevin, that the other kids had started the trouble. The police kept Kevin in jail overnight, but they never filed charges. A few months later, one of the two town kids was murdered with an ice pick. When Kevin heard the news, he was heartsick. I think he even went to visit the mother. That's the kind of kid he was. Inside, he was as kind and decent a person as you ever want to meet.

My affection for Kevin had nothing to do with his being from my hometown of Parma, Ohio—though that didn't hurt. Nor was I impressed that he came from St. Ignatius High School in Cleveland, where Brian Dowling played quarterback in the early 1960s. What I respected most was his intensity. We may have been similar in our fierce competitiveness, but I was never as tough as he was. I don't know anyone who was. You'd better not let him catch you smiling after a loss, because he'd be all over you in an instant. The aftermath of defeat was no time to be lighthearted. I know how he felt, because I was that way myself. It would bother me if I heard someone laughing on the bus ride home after a loss. There wasn't anyone or anything that could make me laugh after we lost. I would hurt so bad inside I didn't even want to smile.

By the way, I always came back on the team bus after road games. There wasn't a single time that I can remember when I rode home with Jean or in a private car. It didn't matter if we had just won an important game or lost a heartbreaker, it was important for me to share as much of the team experience as I could. Maybe I was just being selfish, trying to stay as close as I could to the joys and agonies of the family, which is what a football team is. But if my riding back on the bus said something to the kids about my commitment to them and the team, then it was all to the good.

Fred Leone, the great defensive end who was our captain in 1981, tells the story about his first up-close taste of Kevin Czinger's passion for winning. It was during Fred's sophomore season, when Kevin was a junior. Fred got whistled for a penalty, which Czinger considered an unnecessary lapse of judgment on the sophomore's part. He grabbed Fred by the jersey and damn near lifted him off the ground—and Kevin was a good four inches shorter and maybe thirty-five pounds lighter. Kevin made it clear that sophomores who drew stupid penalties were living dangerously. I guarantee you the experience left an impression on Leone, and he wasn't alone. By the time Kevin graduated, he had earned a reputation throughout the athletic department for his ferocity. You never knew what was going to set him off, but you sure knew when it happened. He had eyes that burned right through you.

His reputation spread to athletes in other sports as well. They tell me that when he climbed onto the bus that shuttled athletes between the athletic complex and the main campus, everyone would fall silent. I don't know if it was from fear or respect or what, but I never heard of another student having that kind of an effect on his peers. To hear these stories you'd think Kevin was seven feet tall and weighed three hundred pounds. In fact, he was 5-foot-10 and weighed about 185. We listed him in the program at 200, but he never weighed that much. But strong? Oh, man! He bench-pressed more than twice his weight. He was an absolute dynamo. People ask me what kind of football player he could have been if he had been two inches taller and thirty pounds heavier. I tell them I don't know, because we wouldn't have gotten him at Yale. He would have wound up at Notre Dame or Nebraska. In fact, if he had been a little bigger, he would have played in the NFL, I have no doubt of that. As it was he had a tryout as a linebacker with the Cleveland Browns, and they were impressed, but ultimately he was just too short.

Somehow, though, size didn't matter to Kevin. What he lacked in size, he made up for in speed, strength, and ferocity. If there were a way to measure competitive intensity, he would be the all-time leader in the Ivy League and maybe the whole country. He simply refused to lose. As a nose guard, he played the game in the trenches with the biggest players on the field, but he wouldn't give any of them an inch. And you know what? He not only survived, he pre-vailed. In fact, he dominated. He was the heart and soul of two straight championship teams in 1979 and '80 and won the Asa S. Bushnell Award after his senior season as the most valuable player in the league, the only defensive lineman ever to win the honor.

Kevin Czinger may have been a great player, and he may have been loyal, intelligent, intense, and a whole lot of other wonderful things, but he was a handful, too. I never knew what to expect next. I'll never forget the phone call I got one Friday night from a panicked nurse at the Yale infirmary. Earlier in the week, Kevin had suffered a hip pointer, which is a bruise on the pelvis that is so painful and limits movement so much it can keep a player, even a tough one like Kevin, on the sidelines. Ironically, he didn't get hurt in a game; he slipped during practice and crashed into the blocking sled. He didn't do anything halfway, not even in practice. If he had just been going through the motions, he might not have gotten hurt. But that wasn't

Kevin. To be safe, the doctors decided to keep him overnight in the infirmary. They wanted to limit his movement as much as possible and monitor his medication. At first, Kevin took the advice, but as the evening wore on, he started to worry that if he stayed in the infirmary on Friday night, the doctors wouldn't let him play on Saturday afternoon. Suddenly, he decided he wanted out and he wanted out right then. But the nurses wouldn't release him.

Despite his reputation, Kevin was quiet and studious most of the time, almost shy, really. But when something like this set him off, look out. He was determined to do something dramatic to convince the nurses that he was healthy enough to get out of the infirmary. Late that evening, a nurse called me at home. She was terrified. Kevin was going from room to room, picking up beds and bouncing them on the floor. The trouble was that there were people in some of those beds. He was so strong that he was just lifting the beds, even the occupied ones, and letting them drop. I told the nurse to put him on the phone. He said, "Coach I have to get out of here or they're not going to let me play." I said, "Kevin, I want you to stay there overnight, and if you don't calm down, I'm going to come down and stay with you." I told him that the doctors had already cleared him to play. Well, that's all he needed to hear, and he finally settled down.

Kevin was so quick and had such great anticipation that he excelled at middle guard despite his size, or lack of it. He would get right up in the center's face and thoroughly intimidate the guy after only a few plays. He'd watch the center's hands on the ball, and as soon as he saw them tense, he was off like a shot. He might fake a move to the right side, put a swim move on his opponent, and blow by him on the left. He did things you can't coach. In fact, Czinger did things you shouldn't coach. He used his natural instincts as an athlete to execute moves that simply wouldn't work for the average player. Dave Kelley, his position coach, would get frustrated trying to teach him the proper fundamentals of line play. Finally, I told Coach Kelley to just let Kevin play his game. Forcing him to use basic techniques just limited his imagination. Kevin knew better than we did what he could and couldn't do.

Kenny Hill, who became a fine NFL defensive back with the Oakland/Los Angeles Raiders and New York Giants, was Czinger's teammate at Yale. He tells the story about Kevin's dream of intercepting a pitchout in the opposition's backfield and running it back for a touchdown. I can't tell you how many times he almost did. His unexpected presence in the backfield caused a number of handoffs to be mishandled or pitchouts to be fumbled.

He gave every team fits, but he seemed to inflict particular damage on Brown, beginning with his very first start as a sophomore in 1978. He got a couple of quarterback sacks and forced several fumbles in a game we won 21–0. The next year, he blocked two punts that led to our only touchdowns in a 13–12 victory. That game stands as an example of his toughness. He was just recovering from a bout of mononucleosis and was about ten pounds under his playing weight. Imagine someone playing football in the trenches at the Ivy League level at 175 pounds. Not only that, but the Brown offensive line double-teamed him throughout the game. They remembered how much time he had spent in their backfield the previous year. Kevin may have been frustrated at the double-teaming, but he still found a way to win the game for us by breaking loose to block those two punts. He always found a way to beat you.

We considered moving Kevin to linebacker before his senior season. Actually, he was the one to suggest the change. He was tired of being smothered by two and sometimes three blockers, and he longed for the freedom of movement of a linebacker. We worked him out behind the line of scrimmage for much of the training camp, and, believe me, he would have been a standout linebacker, but ultimately we decided that he was just too valuable at nose guard.

He wanted so badly to move to linebacker that I dreaded having to tell him he couldn't, so I played a little trick on him during our preseason scrimmage against Montclair State. He was prepared to play at either position, and for a while he was in at linebacker. As the scrimmage wore on, he took a breather and was standing next to me on the sidelines when Montclair ran a trap play up the middle for a short gain. The backup middle guard made a reasonably good tackle, but I started yelling at him as if he had let the kid run over him for a touchdown. I ripped off my hat and stomped around, then grabbed Kevin by the jersey and told him to get in there at middle guard. He raced onto the field as though he were rescuing a damsel in distress. I don't think it dawned on him that I had put on an act for his benefit until he took his three-point stance. Then he looked over at me as if to say, "You snookered me, you son of a gun." He was disappointed, but he played middle guard the rest of the season without a peep. He knew it was the best thing for the team, and that was as important to him as it was to me.

So Kevin was at his familiar position when we opened the season against Brown in 1980. Early in the game, I noticed some commotion going on in the area around the center, but I couldn't tell exactly what was happening. I asked Jeff Rohrer, who later played seven seasons with the Dallas Cowboys, what was going on. He said, "Their center called Kevin a little shit." Well, that was not a smart thing for the Brown player to say. The next thing I saw was the center's head snap back like someone hit him in the chinstrap with a baseball bat. Kevin had come up under his chin with a clenched fist and put him on his butt in the backfield. The Brown kid—and he was a big kid, too—played the rest of the game terrified of what Kevin might do next. It actually disrupted the center snap. We won the game 45–17, thanks largely to John Rogan's passing and Curt Grieve's receiving, but I guarantee you that their coach, John Anderson, was glad to be finished with Kevin Czinger.

What people don't realize is that Kevin Czinger was one of the two or three brightest kids I had at Yale, which is saying something, considering that I had five Rhodes scholars and God knows how many high school valedictorians. His College Board scores were almost perfect, and he breezed through Yale with a double major in pre-med and history. When it came time to take the test for medical school, he changed his mind and took the law boards instead. He breezed through them and was accepted at all five schools he applied to. He chose, naturally enough, to attend Yale Law School.

His professors would tell me that he was a real challenge. In the first place, he was brighter than most of them, and he had such a thirst for knowledge that they couldn't keep him satisfied. That kind of intelligence doesn't always carry over to the football field, but in Kevin's case it did. He was always thinking, always observing what was happening and figuring out what he could do to get an advantage.

As a graduate student, he agreed to help us out as a volunteer coach, working with the freshman coach, Joe Benanto. I figured if he could impart just some of his tenacity to the new kids it would be a good thing. One afternoon—I'll never forget this—I looked over to the freshman practice field, and there's Kevin running across the field pulling one of our linemen by the face mask. The kid didn't dare complain. He just ran wherever Kevin pulled him. Obviously, Kevin's reputation had preceded him. You don't want to do anything to set this guy off. As I watched what was happening, I didn't know whether to laugh or cry. I wanted Kevin to motivate the kids, but I didn't want him to scare the hell out of them doing it. After practice I asked Kevin what he was doing. He said, "Aw, Coach, the kid wasn't running fast enough, that's all." I told him there were other ways to get a kid to run faster.

The fourth game of Kevin Czinger's senior season was against Boston College on a rainy night in Chestnut Hill, Massachusetts. We had won fourteen of our last fifteen games, including a 17–16 victory over Air Force the week before, but the oddsmakers had us as fourteen-point underdogs. And they were probably right, given the Eagles' superior manpower and schedule. I remember joking with the press that if our kids had found out how big the BC players were, they never would have gotten on the bus. Still, we gave them a good game, trailing just 14–3 in the third quarter before losing 27–9. A few days after the game I got a phone call from an assistant coach at Florida State, who said to me in his deep southern drawl, "Coach, who is that No. 40 you got?" Florida State was playing BC the next week, and this coach had seen the film of our game. He couldn't get over how effective Czinger had been against the biggest linemen we had faced in years. Some of them were five or six inches taller and maybe sixty pounds heavier than Kevin, but it was all they could do to handle him. They doubled up on him and held him all night. It was the most frustrated I had ever seen him.

I told the coach his name was Kevin Czinger, and he said, "How big is he, anyway?" I told him we listed him at 200, but he was more like 185. He said, "My goodness, what do you feed that little gnat? Those big redwoods up there at BC never did block him, did they?" I said, "No, but they held him a lot." I said that if Kevin were a little bigger, FSU could use him down there. He said, "Coach, we could use him here right now! My lord, he's a tenacious young man."

Tenacious, yes, and a lot of other qualities, too, like loyal and intelligent and honest. I could always count on Kevin to tell the unvarnished truth. So could his teammates, who respected him enormously. They knew he was a step beyond as a player, but I think it was the other intangible qualities that impressed them most. One of the wonderful rewards of football is being part of a family that works and sacrifices together for a common purpose. Kevin, an investment broker in New York City now, understood that as clearly as anyone I ever coached. Having him on the team magnified that familial experience for me and all of his mates.

I dug out an old newspaper clipping that pretty well explains Kevin's philosophy about college football. These were his words when a reporter asked him about his reputation as a wild man on the field: "Yeah, I'm a fanatic on the field. Football is a waste of time if you're not fanatical on the field, and time is the most valuable commodity a human being has. You can't be anything but fanatical and do justice to your own life. Football takes four or five hours a day, and when you put that much time and energy into something, you don't expect to lose. I am simply not mentally prepared to lose."

No more need be said.

CHAPTER EIGHT

Fred the Dog, Etc.

Not all my recollections fit neatly into a particular chapter. There are humorous tales to tell and random thoughts to express that have no logical place in the sequence of these pages. So I have strung together a few observations and anecdotes in this catch-all chapter in the hope that these bits and pieces help tell the story of Yale football in my time. My only regret in writing this book is that I can't mention each person who touched my life or acknowledge each event that held meaning for my family and me, but there simply isn't room. Every one of my assistant coaches enriched my life. Every one of my captains increased my confidence that the future of America was in good hands. And every one of my teams left me with an overwhelming sense of gratitude for the opportunity to share their college football experience. I am particularly grateful to my administrative assistants, Grace Lewis Jacunski and her successor Maude Schmidt. They were loyal, dedicated, and tireless workers who went well beyond mere clerical duties to become integral parts of the football program.

What better place to start than with the story of Fred the Dog?

Fred belonged to Dave Holahan, a free-spirited defensive back on the 1969 and '70 teams with Dick Jauron, captain and Rhodes scholar Tom Neville, future NFL player Donny Martin, and the future mayor of Baltimore, Kurt Schmoke, among others. Holahan was an undersized but talented player who distinguished himself as much by marching to his own beat as he did by intercepting passes, though he did a little of both. Dave was the kind of free spirit who didn't think twice about bringing his dog to practice. He escorted the dog through the walkway under Derby Avenue and tied him to a bench beside the field with a leash. If I had been smart, I would have put a prompt end to this foolishness after Fred's first appearance, but the players seemed to get a kick out of the dog, and I figured anything that kept them loose couldn't be all bad. Besides, Fred just sat there quietly watching practice. So I figured, hey, what's the harm?

I was wrong. During a full-contact drill one afternoon, the action spilled over the sideline, and one of the players landed on Fred and broke his paw. The players were heartbroken. So was I. We gathered around poor Fred, and after a moment I realized the players were looking to me to handle the situation. I guess they thought I was some sort of veterinarian. I told one of our managers to take the dog to the animal hospital and get him fixed up, and I would take care of the bill. Well, Fred and the manager were back before the practice was over and received a spirited ovation. The dog had a splint on his paw, but other than that he was as good as new.

From that day on, Fred was the unofficial team mascot. Don't tell Handsome Dan, the official Yale Bulldog, but he was the No. 2 canine in the hearts of the players that year. After the season, we had our usual team banquet in the elegant President's Room in Woolsey Hall. As always, the dinner was a dressy affair, harkening back to the more formal days of the early 1900s. The players wore their best suits, and the tables were set with fine China and crystal stemware, and the stately presence of President Kingman Brewster added to the ambience. My place was set next to the president's, and as I leaned forward to take my seat, I glanced to my left and caught a glimpse of, yes, Fred the Dog, wearing a bib and tie and sitting in a chair like the rest of us.

I didn't know what to do. I didn't know whether Kingman had seen the dog and was waiting for me to say something, or whether he was in on the joke, or whether for once in his life he had encountered a social situation that he didn't know how to handle. But I was keenly aware that the players were watching me to see what I would do. So I took the coward's path. I didn't do anything. I flat-out pretended that I didn't notice this dog sitting a few seats away from me with his paws on the table, wolfing down a steak dinner with the rest of us. Every time Kingman leaned forward in his chair, I did the same, hoping to block his view. To this day, no one has ever said a word about the incident. Not President Brewster. Not any of the players. And certainly not me, until now.

Dozens of my former players became famous, or at least famously successful, outside of football. They include men like Rhodes scholar Kurt Schmoke, the mayor of Baltimore, and Tone Grant, CEO of Refco, one of the nation's largest commodities trading firms. I shouldn't start listing them because I'll leave out more names than I include. The roster of doctors, lawyers, scientists, educators, influential businessmen, and powerful entertainment executives goes on and on. Calvin Hill was famous three times over as an All-Pro back with the Cowboys, Redskins, and Browns, as vice president of the Baltimore Orioles and consultant with the Cowboys, and as the father of NBA superstar Grant Hill.

Thanks to the pervasive presence of television, however, no former players have become household names quite like Jack Ford and Stone Phillips. Both Jack and Stone were first-string players on championship teams, and both had record-setting running backs as teammates. Jack was a hard-hitting monster back on the 1969 team that went 7−2 and shared the championship with Dartmouth, and he was on Dick Jauron's teams in 1970 and '71. Stone was the quarterback when we compiled a record of 7−2 in 1975 and shared the championship with Brown in 1976 with an 8−1 mark. He was in the backfield for John Pagliaro's sophomore and junior seasons.

Jack wasn't very big, about 5-foot-11 and 185 pounds, but he had really quick reactions and surprised us by cracking the lineup as a sophomore after missing most of his freshman season with injuries. He had a 77-yard interception return for a touchdown as a soph and was a solid performer throughout his career. He was a spirited young man, and he nearly got us all killed down at Princeton in his senior year. We had just eaten our Friday evening meal in one of the Princeton dining halls and were walking back to our rooms when Jack stopped in the middle of the campus to lead the team in the Yale Fight Song. I couldn't believe it. Those people hated us down there, and here he was right in the middle of the campus leading a dozen of our players in a Yale song. I walked up to him and said, "You'd better win tomorrow." We did, but only by a 10–6 score.

I knew Jack went to law school after graduation, but I had no idea that he had gotten into television until I saw him doing legal commentary on the O. J. Simpson trial for NBC. Now he seems to be on various NBC news shows at all times of the night and day. He's the weekend co-host of NBC's *Today Show* and does news and commentary on a variety of other shows.

Stone was a very good college quarterback, who played nearly every down for us as a junior and was the starter in his senior year, too, although he shared time with Bob Rizzo. He passed for exactly 1,500 yards in those two seasons, as we won fifteen games and lost only three. I didn't know he had gotten into television until Christmas week in 1976, when I was in Atlanta just after I had been elected president of the American Football Coaches Association. I got a message in my hotel room that a Mr. Phillips from the local TV station wanted to interview me. When I got down to the lobby, there was Stone with his camera crew. It wasn't long before he became a national correspondent for NBC, and you could just see him growing into the job. Later, of course, he became co-anchor of NBC's *Dateline*.

Stone wasn't the only former Yale player to appear on *Dateline*. Bob McKeown, the center on our 1969 and '70 teams, was a regular NBC correspondent who gained national attention as the first civilian newsman to cross the Kuwaiti border during the Persian Gulf war. He is a native of Ottawa, Ontario, and was working for a Canadian station at the time. I got phone calls from several newspapers that were doing stories on him, asking whether I was surprised that he would go into such a dangerous area without a gun. I said that as our center he had taken so many blows to the head that nothing he did would surprise me. I hope they realized I was kidding.

My wife, Jean, would get so excited at our games that she had a hard time getting anyone to sit next to her. My daughters will tell you how she would roll up her game program and swing it like a club. Whenever Yale scored, or whenever we got called for a questionable penalty, she would get so pumped up she would whack the person next to her on the shoulder without realizing what she was doing. It makes me laugh to think about it because, though of course I was never with her in the stands, I can just see her doing it.

It was great to have her so involved with the team and the kids, though I must admit that I seldom made eye contact with her during games. I would get so wrapped up in the action on the field that I'd forget she was there. But it was wonderful to know that she shared my love for the players and my passion for the competition. Of course, she had a stake in the outcome: she had to live with me for the next week, and I don't suppose I was a very pleasant housemate after a loss. There was an added benefit to having her in the stands. I don't think she did it on purpose, but she had a way of letting me know what the people around her were saying. She would say things like, "Why didn't you throw more passes on first down?" Or "Why didn't you change quarterbacks when the offense stalled?" I knew that she was getting that from the fans sitting near her, who had no idea she was my wife.

I was always sensitive to criticism, or maybe I should say attentive to it. I didn't always take it seriously, and I certainly didn't always heed it, but I didn't mind it, either. Sometimes the criticism was ridiculous and uninformed. Other times, people had legitimate questions and sound advice. Either way, I believed that fans and particularly alumni had a right to express their opinions. If nothing else, it showed they cared about Yale football. The two most common areas of criticism were play calling and substitutions. Any play that didn't work or any defensive alignment that failed to hold the opposition was fair game for criticism. In a way I almost welcomed criticism because I knew that second-guessing the coach is an inalienable right of all fans. I wouldn't enjoy my Sunday afternoons watching NFL games if I couldn't grouse about the play calling and the use of personnel. But I always believed our coaches knew more about the abilities of our players as they related to the opposition than the most knowledgeable fan in the stands. God knows we made mistakes, but I think the record shows we were right more than we were wrong. Whether it was Seb LaSpina on offense, or Buddy Amendola, Dave Kelley, or Don Brown on defense, our coaches did well to consider the subtleties of various situations and the variables of personal abilities that were not always obvious to the casual fan. By and large, over thirty-two years, they did a terrific job. I wouldn't have lasted all that time as the head coach if they hadn't.

The other common area of criticism was substitution. People would ask why I took Brian Dowling out of the game so early, or Stone Phillips, or Dick Jauron. There were several reasons. One was to keep harmony on the team. People might not realize how important it is to keep your players motivated and feeling like a part of the team. Yale players are not paid athletes, after all; they're students. I was the one who had to look these young men in the eyes during practice when they were working as hard, if not harder, than the starters. Getting as many players into the game as possible is what the team concept is all about. Second, I never wanted to destroy another team, even if we had the capability, because that team might help us win a championship down the line by beating someone else. I tried never to take away another team's confidence or hurt them physically. And third, it made sense to give the younger players an opportunity to play. Game experience was invaluable for a player when he became a starter the next year.

Kickers were always a little different, to put it kindly. But I loved them. The kicking game was the one phase that I coached personally. We always had a specific assistant coach for linebackers or defensive linemen and so on, but I was the position coach for the kickers and as such was directly responsible for all aspects of kickoffs, punts, field goals, and extra points. I did it partly to show how much importance I placed on that part of the game, and partly because no one else had the patience to deal with these young men who tended to be, well, colorful. My assistants would say to me, "Coach, you don't pay me enough to work with the kickers."

One of the great characters was Tony Greblick, our kicker in 1982. I guess I should have known better than to recruit a barefoot kicker from Binghamton, New York. Hell, the ground doesn't thaw up there until August, and this kid kicked with no shoes on. During his freshman year, he was playing up at Harvard on a brutally cold day, and to keep warm he zipped himself into one of the ball bags. The problem was that the zipper handles were on the outside of the bag, so when Coach Harry Jacunski called for him to kick an extra point, he couldn't get out. Finally, someone saw the bag moving and let him out, but by then it was too late. They had to go for a two-point conversion.

Then there was Jim Nottingham, our punter in the early 1970s. He could really boot the ball, but he had trouble catching the snap from center. The week before the Cornell game he was dropping every snap during practice. I kidded him about having stone hands, but he was the best punter we had. That Saturday at Cornell, when the first punting situation arrived, I half closed my eyes, not knowing what to expect. Well, he got off a shot that would have hit low-flying aircraft. And he did it again in the next punting situation. And he did it again and again. I thought, geez, maybe I should just leave him alone.

A week later, we were playing Princeton, and by now I was feeling comfortable with him. We had a 13–0 lead in the first quarter but stalled and had to punt from our own 8-yard line. Once again, I was a little worried about whether Jim was going to be able to handle the snap as he stood in our end zone. What I didn't know was that he had made a bet with his roommate that he was going to take off with the ball sometime during the game, and this was the time he picked to do it. When I looked at the game film the next day, I could see him look up in the stands before the snap and nod his head. He handled the snap all right and began to run it out of there. Here was a kid with a brace on his knee who wasn't in the best of shape, and he was running the ball out of our own end zone with no blocking. Somehow, he not only made the first down, he ran all the way to the Princeton 19-yard line. Of course, he thought he had done something great. He came running over to the sidelines and jumped up in my arms. I wanted to punch his lights out for taking such a chance. Then again, he had gotten us out of a hole. After the game, a reporter asked me if I had called the play. I looked at him and said, "Do I look like an idiot?"

Two years earlier, Nottingham had run with the ball in a punting situation against Penn. That time, though, he got tangled up with an official, who was zig-zagging desperately to get out of his way, and didn't make the first down. It was almost a disaster. Penn scored two quick touchdowns and we barely escaped with a 32–22 victory after having led 25–7 in the third quarter. Coincidentally, the official was a Princeton grad who had made some of the calls against us two years previously in The Tie at Harvard. He told me he couldn't get out of Nottingham's way. I believe that's true. On the film I could see that every time he turned one way, Nottingham followed him as though he were a blocker. Jim insisted the run wasn't premeditated. He said the snap was high, which it was, and he didn't think he could get the kick off without having it blocked.

I mentioned Brian Clarke earlier as one of the first players to challenge me by wearing a beard and long hair during the Vietnam war years. Well, he was quite a character, as well as a really fine place kicker, who held the Yale record for most field goals in a season and in a career when he graduated in 1974. He was also a tough competitor who was an all-conference fullback and linebacker at Shaker Heights High outside Cleveland. I'll never forget the Friday practice before his first game as a sophomore. We always went through a full kicking drill on the day before games. I called Brian out for the drill and he looked me in the eye and said, "Coach, I don't kick on Fridays." I said something sarcastic like, "Well, do you kick on Saturdays? That's when we play our games, you know." I was dumbfounded, but he just turned and walked away. I don't know whether it was a superstition or if he wanted to save his leg or what, but he was serious about it. Frankly, I didn't know what to do. He was obviously the best kicker we had. The next day, he kicked a couple of extra points and a field goal, and the week after that, he hit two field goals, one from forty-three yards. Now, I'm not a dumb coach, so I decided we wouldn't kick on Fridays as long as Brian was there.

In time, Brian became a good friend. He got to know our youngest daughter, Karen, a little, and he told her stories about how he was going to go to Hollywood after he graduated. And sure enough, that's what he did. The first time we saw him on TV he was acting in a Tuborg Gold beer commercial. He was dressed like Tarzan and swinging on a rope. Then he was in a Chrysler commercial dressed in a tuxedo and opening a door for a young lady. After that, he got regular acting roles on *General Hospital* and *Eight Is Enough*.

Dan Begel was my first place kicker. His field goal at Brown provided the only points in my first victory, a 3−0 win in 1965 after the embarrassing inaugural loss to Connecticut. My most vivid memory of Dan, though, is of an incident during training camp before the school year opened. After lunch in the Ray Tompkins House, I noticed that he would slip downstairs by himself. I was worried because drugs were just coming on the scene, and I wasn't sure what he was doing. So I sneaked downstairs, and there he was playing the cello. I came to find out that he was an outstanding cellist, but he was a little embarrassed and didn't want the other players to find out. I don't have the musical background I wish I had, but I could tell this kid could really play. He was a very bright kid from Whitefish Bay, Wisconsin, and I was really proud of him. He's a psychiatrist now and has remained a good friend through the years.

Although Danny had no real cause to be concerned about what his teammates would think of his cello playing, the story brings up an interesting point about the way kickers are treated on football teams. They take a lot of teasing, both the good ones and the not so good ones. They hear things like, "Gee, I hope you didn't get your uniform dirty." As a coach, I was concerned about this because, all joking aside, kickers did tend to have a different mentality and they could easily lose their confidence. Once they proved themselves in game situations, you could tease them, but until then, you had to be careful because you could destroy a kid's psyche. I always told the kickers to run with the other players and to join in all the workouts to show that you're a part of the team. I didn't want them on the sidelines looking in the mirror while the players were busting their humps on the field. Luckily, I never had any real problems. I didn't have to explain to Yale students that the kicker could mean the difference between a win and a loss. They were plenty smart enough to figure that out for themselves.

Sometimes I wonder whether I took my coaching staff for granted. Or if I let them know how important they were to my family and me over the years. God knows we spent enough time together. In the heat of the season, or during the most intense recruiting periods, the coaching staff was like a second family. There were periods during each year when the coaches saw more of each other than we saw of our wives. A lot more. You've no doubt heard the expression "We interrupt this marriage to bring you the football season." Well, for us, it was a case of interrupting our real marriages for our football marriages.

We worked long hours during the season, and that means seven days a week. It was not unusual for us to be in the office late at night going over film or revising game plans. The work week began on Sunday morning, when I went to the Yale infirmary to visit any players who had been injured. Jean would bake brownies and I would deliver them. On Sunday afternoon we had the first team meeting of the week, after which the staff would send out for pizza. We'd shoot the breeze for a while, talking about the previous day's game and whatnot, then get serious about making plans for the next Saturday.

Recruiting season could be just as hectic, especially for the coaches who had responsibility for the Midwest and Far West. Because of the time difference, they were up late nearly every night making phone calls. I gave the staff a few weeks off before the players reported for two-a-day practices in August, and I tried to take some time off, too. I tried to stay close to the office, however, in case some recruits and their families wanted to visit the campus. Often a family would spend time on its vacation to tour campuses, and I wanted to be there to escort them around or show them a highlight film.

One day each year, right before the team reported for two-a-days, the whole staff got together just to have fun. We would either go out fishing on a charter boat or play some golf or sometimes just gather at our house for a cookout. Those were fun days. I remember how Buddy Amendola would get seasick every time we went out in the boat. As soon as he got aboard, he'd be lying down groaning. He'd swear he was never going out again, but the next year he'd be raring to go. And I remember putting a couple of big rocks in the bottom of Dave Kelley's golf bag. The big guy carried that bag around for a couple of years before he discovered them. Then Bill Narduzzi dropped them into Seb LaSpina's bag, and Seb lugged them around for the next few years. Still, when I look back, it wasn't those off days that made working with my staff so special. It was the day-to-day contact with a succession of wonderful men. Collectively, they were as knowledgeable and caring a bunch of coaches as you'll find. They made the drudgery of long hours enjoyable and the pain of losing almost bearable.

On Christmas Eve 1990 I was on the sidelines at Yokohama Stadium in Tokyo. On Christmas Day, I was home with my family in Connect-icut. In fact, I walked in my front door in Orange, a suburb of New Haven, just as the clock struck midnight on Christmas morning. I didn't need Santa's sleigh to accomplish this seeming miracle, just a fast jetliner and a fourteen-hour time difference.

I was in Japan with my offensive and defensive coordinators, Seb LaSpina and Don Brown, to coach a team of Ivy League All-Stars in the Epson / Ivy Bowl. The game was played before an enthusiastic mostly Japanese crowd of thirty thousand at noon Tokyo time—10 P.M. the night before on the East Coast of the United States. Needless to say, I had a major case of jet lag when I got home, but I also had six days of terrific memories. What an experience! The people over there couldn't have been nicer or more respectful. And they couldn't have picked our brains any more than they did. They were intensely interested in anything we could teach them about the game that had been invented at Yale more than one hundred years before. If we had practiced from six in the morning until midnight, they would have been happy. The game was a big deal in the press, too. Early in the week, we attended a press conference in a television studio where there must have been one hundred reporters and photographers.

The Japanese treated the Epson Bowl like a serious competition, but frankly they didn't have the size or skill to beat us. Don, Seb, and I had six days to put together a team of forty players from all eight Ivy League colleges. We had Kevin Callahan, John Furjanic, Chris Gaughan, Terry Johnson, Darin Kehler, Chris Warner, and the Michalik twins, Chris and Rob, from Yale. Chris Gaughan, our captain and linebacker, was majoring in Japanese, and I told him to stick close to me and let me know if anyone was swearing at me. He said, "Coach, don't expect too much. Japanese is a tough language." We had no problems, though. Everyone was as helpful as could be, and it was amazing how many people spoke English. It was embarrassing, really. Here we were with a group of the smartest college kids in America, and only one of them could speak any Japanese, but the majority of the Japanese could speak English.

Actually, Chris Gaughan proved to be as helpful on the field as he was as a translator. The Japanese had a quarterback who must have been 6-foot-5, and they put him in a deep shotgun formation, as deep as a punter would normally stand. The first time they had the ball, he hit four consecutive passes, and they moved right down to our 1-foot line. For a moment, I thought we might be in some trouble. There was just no way we could get to the guy that deep in the backfield, and he was hitting his targets at will. On the fifth play of the series, Chris blitzed through the line and nearly cut the quarterback in half. Really gave him a pop. From that point on, the game was over. The guy was so tentative he wasn't effective at all. They weren't used to getting hit like that. They had quick, skilled athletes in the backfield, but when they got into our secondary, our tough defensive backs really whaled on them. After that, you could see them back off. We won 47–10, and when they scored near the end of the game, our guys were so happy for them that they cheered.

The Japanese tried a little intimidation before the game. They lined up at the 50-yard line and started to chant something. Of course, we didn't know what the hell they were chanting, but I thought, oh boy, this is going to be a tough game. Their players weren't all small either. They had some sumo wrestlers' sons out there. But as always, our kids were smarter than I was. I don't think they even noticed the chanting. If they did, they were entirely unimpressed.

A couple of summers later, we had a Japanese college team at Yale for a week of practice before a game at Harvard Stadium. We had the Wasedo team, and Harvard was host to Keio. The two schools were Japan's answer to Yale and Harvard. I spent as much time with them as I could and took some satisfaction when Wasedo beat Keio the next year for the first time. I figured our Japanese guests would want to practice in the morning, then take some short trips to places like Yankee Stadium in the afternoon and evening. No way. They had their minds on football and nothing else. They asked me every question they could think to ask. If I went to the restroom, they followed me in. Jean and I had the whole team out to the house for a cookout and a swim in the pool. Over there, the head coach was sort of on a pedestal, and they were surprised that I would have them out to my house. They loved it and we enjoyed having them. They must have bowed to Jean a thousand times.

I told people to expect the Japanese teams to get better and better with time. I said they would copy everything we do, then do it better, just like they did with the automobile. I kidded my son-in-law, David, who was a vice president at Sikorsky Aircraft, that pretty soon they would be selling helicopters to us instead of the other way around.

I made sure everybody got to play in the Epson Bowl. I had them substituting for each other every other series, almost like the honor system. Near the end of the game, a big lineman from Cornell asked to go in on the kickoff team because his coach never let him. I said "Sure." Well, Christ! He ran down the field like a man possessed and put a hit on a kid that nearly killed him. I think if the Japanese player had dodged him, the Cornell kid would have put a dent in the goal post. I told him, "On the next kickoff, I want you to stand over here with me." He didn't care. He'd had a chance to do something he had always wanted to do.

Sometimes the Ivy League was a little too zealous in guarding its ethics. It was so intent, for example, on protecting the academic side of the student-athlete equation that for many years it prevented football players from taking part in some very healthy and rewarding postseason experiences. In 1981 Rich Diana had to give up his senior year of eligibility in baseball in order to participate in two postseason all-star games. He was given permission to play in either the Blue-Gray Game or the Japan Bowl, but not both. That made no sense whatsoever, as far as I could see. A case can be made for the conference's ban on full teams playing in bowl games, which was still in place when I retired, because that means an extra five or six weeks of football. No doubt that would be a drain on a young man's academic life, particularly during final exams. But a single individual going to an all-star game requires only a week or so, and I saw no reason to prohibit that.

At one time, coaches were forbidden to participate in any postseason games, period. In 1970 I went to President Brewster to ask for an exception so that I could coach in the East-West Shrine Game in San Francisco. Donny Martin and Tom Neville had been invited to play, and I had been asked to be one of John Pont's assistants. I told President Brewster that it was a wonderful opportunity for all of us. He agreed and got the other presidents to grant me an exception. The next year, I was invited to be the head coach and asked Kingman for another exception. He agreed that the rule was wrong, but there wasn't time to change it, and I was not allowed to go. Fortunately, I was asked to coach the team again the following year, and by then the Ivy ban had been lifted.

That East-West Shrine Game in 1972 was one of the highlights of my career. Dick Jauron was on the team, and Jean and the girls came with us because it was during the Christmas break from school. They got to know Dick in a way that was impossible during the regular season. In fact, Dick took my rental car and drove my family around while I met with my assistant coaches to devise a game plan. Those assistants were Bob Blackman, my longtime friend and adversary at Dartmouth and Cornell, and Bo Schembechler, my old teammate from Miami. Bob ran the defense, Bo ran the offense, and I drank coffee. Jean was finally able to relax and enjoy the game without becoming a nervous wreck—it was an all-star game with little riding on the outcome. It was a special time for me, too. I discovered that Dick had a sense of humor I hadn't recognized before. My family was with me in 1981, too, when I coached Rich Diana, Curt Grieve, and Pat Conran in the Blue-Gray Game in Mobile, Alabama. I enjoyed a kind of bonding with my players at those three all-star games that I couldn't achieve during the regular campaign.

The all-star games also allowed me to coach a team of extraordinary athletes that I could only dream of at Yale. Don't misunderstand me—the Yale players I brought with me handled themselves very well at that level. Jauron and Diana had especially good games. But I never had more than two or three athletes of that caliber in any one season, and here I was with twenty-two of them. The big difference at that level was speed. Whew! Some of them could really fly. It wasn't so much that they were bigger and hit harder that impressed me, it was their speed at every position.

After those games, it was only human for me to dream about coaching in a big-time program. It got my competitive juices going. I admit that it would have been fun to see how I would fare in the big time. But coaching, when you reduce it to the basics, is dealing one on one with individuals, and I felt that I got as much satisfaction in my career as anyone, regardless of the level, because of the caliber of young men I was blessed to have. I mean that with all my heart. Yale's student-athletes were the cream of the crop of student-athletes. They were quality young men in all respects. I would not want to deal with the problems other coaches had. I never had a player who didn't want to go to class, for example. I was more likely to have a player who couldn't come to practice because he had fallen behind on an assignment or had to make up an exam he had missed because of our travel. Given a choice, I'll take the problems of Yale players ten times over.

It was always tough for me to find a balance between my passionate desire to win and the need to teach young men that they couldn't always win, and that when they didn't, they must be gracious and learn something from defeat. That was hard for me because I absolutely hated to lose. At anything. I couldn't stand to lose at Ping-Pong or golf or racquetball or even a game of cards with my family. Winning was like a narcotic. It gave me a rush. Defeat was pure agony. It made me sick to my stomach. Literally.

As far back as I can remember, I did everything I could to make myself a better athlete. In high school, I admired an older kid named Mel Burke, who was a great left-handed pitcher. He used to walk around school with his head tilted slightly to the left. I don't know whether I thought that was cool or whether I thought it would make me a better pitcher, but pretty soon I found myself copying him. It took me a while to realize how stupid I was being. Christ, I was right-handed! That was a good lesson for me to learn. You can't be someone you're not. You have to be yourself. You have to use what talent you have to the best of your ability and not try to imitate someone else.

It bothers me that many people today are trying to restrict competition. Some educators, think it's wrong to rate students by letter grades. In the lower grades, teachers don't give a mark of C, they write a note that little Johnny is improving but needs to work harder. They don't hand out an F, they write a note that the student is "falling behind grade level." I'm told that this is because school officials don't want students to lose self-esteem. In other words, if they don't compete, they can't lose. I think that's wrong. Even the pass-fail courses they offer at Yale are questionable, to my way of thinking. When a youngster gets out of school, whether he's a high school dropout or a Yale graduate, he is going to compete every day for the rest of his life. He's not going to get an A, a B, or a C from his boss, but he's going to be graded in subtle, inevitable ways. Life is a competition, and not teaching young people how to deal with it is wrong.

There is a danger, of course, that you can put pressure on kids too early in life. That's why I haven't always supported Little League baseball or Pop Warner football leagues. If every coach played every kid an equal amount of time and stressed enjoyment and development as much as winning, I'd be for it. A lot of coaches are doing that, but not all of them. Maybe I'm old-fashioned, but there is something to be said for a kid's knocking on a friend's door for a pickup game, as opposed to parents organizing everything and driving the kids all over the place. I don't think that kind of competition is good when the kids are still very young.

So it's a balancing act. It's a mistake to push kids too early, but it's just as big a mistake not to let them know that competition is out there and they are going to have to deal with it. I always wanted my players to take it to heart when they lost. I didn't want them smiling and laughing on the bus coming home from a loss. But I didn't want them to think about jumping off a bridge either. That was the other extreme. I know, because that's always how I felt.

Sabby Frinzi, God love him, was one of the real characters of Yale football. He had no official tie with the team or the university, but it seems as though every time I turned around, he was there with his camera. Sabby was a freelance photographer who made his living on Yale athletics. The sports information directors hired him to take pictures for brochures, program covers, and publicity shots for all Yale sports, but that was only half the story. He would make friends with the athletes, so when it came time for them to graduate or get married, they would hire him as the photographer. Many of the pictures in this book are courtesy of the Frinzi Studio.

Sabby added a wonderful flavor to the Yale football experience, with one exception. Sometime in the 1970s he visited his daughter, who was a student at UConn, living in a high-rise dormitory overlooking the football field. Sabby used her window as the vantage point to get an elevated shot of the stadium to use in our program.

The problem was that Coach John Toner was running a practice at the time. When someone told him the Yale photographer was hanging out a window taking pictures, he went crazy. He called me at home and accused me of spying on his practice. He was really angry. I assured him that in the first place I would never do something like that, and in the second place I had no idea what the hell he was talking about. When we finally figured out what had happened, we both had a good laugh.

Through the years I was honored at a number of dinners, and I appreciated them all, though there were times when it seemed that I was getting more attention than I deserved. Being named Man of the Year by the Walter Camp Football Foundation was special. So was my induction into the Miami University Hall of Fame and, of course, my retirement dinner after the Princeton game. Perhaps the greatest honor I received, though, was the black-tie dinner at New York's Waldorf-Astoria in January 1990 to commemorate my twenty-fifth anniversary as head coach. More than one thousand of my former players attended it, including all the members of the 1989 team and a number of important Yale people who played before my time. President George Bush was invited but couldn't make it, sending his son George W. Bush instead. He also sent a telegram explaining that he had another engagement that night. He sure did. He was giving the state of the union address to Congress.

Just about everyone in attendance was a Yale graduate, except for Harvard coach Joe Restic. He had some nice things to say about me in his speech, and he presented me with a Harvard sweat suit. Years later, at a dinner for him in Boston, I presented him with a sterling silver replica of Yale Bowl.

Tom Schmidt walked into my office just before noon one day in August 1966. I had no idea who he was or what he wanted. He was a scrawny kid who looked like he hadn't had a meal in a week. It was the first day of preseason camp before my second season, and we were busy getting the players settled in the Ray Tompkins House, where they would live for the next few weeks until school opened. This kid looked at me and said, "Coach, I'd like to try out for the team."

Well, I don't think I laughed, but I probably felt like it. There was just no way he was ever going to play football for us. He had been up all night driving back to school and hadn't had anything to eat. Our cook fixed him a meal, and I told him to go upstairs and get some rest. Meanwhile, I had my secretary check to see whether he was really a Yale student or just some guy who walked in off the street. It turned out that he was a junior from Ohio who had played some high school football as a defensive lineman at Cincinnati Country Day. Harry Jacunski, the freshman coach, used to say that they didn't play football at schools like that, they danced with each other. But he was a legitimate student, and he seemed like a nice kid, so I gave him a shot. That's what the Ivy League is all about, after all.

I don't think he cared if he made the team or not. He just wanted to practice with the guys and have some fun. We put some pads on him and before long he was working with one of the defensive units as a middle guard. He was the most unorthodox football player you ever saw, but when I paired our starting offense against his defensive squad in a controlled scrimmage, we couldn't block the sucker. He bent thirty different ways and we couldn't put a good hit on him. He did things—like leaping over people, for example—you can't coach. Things, in fact, you wouldn't want to coach. But I figured, hey, if we can't block him, and we were pretty darn good, how was anybody else going to block him? The only question was whether I should try and coach him or just point him toward the opposition and say, "Sic 'em!"

Sure enough, Tom Schmidt worked his way into the starting lineup in both his junior and senior years and played on our 1967 championship team with Calvin Hill, Brian Dowling, and Company. Furthermore, he was a two-time All-Ivy League selection. So much for the importance of recruiting.

It's probably not a good idea to mention specific alumni who helped Yale football through the years, because I'll surely fail to mention a number of deserving people. I want to say publicly and emphatically, that as a group, the alumni were invaluable. Many were former players and members of the Football "Y" Association. They were always there to help raise money for travel expenses, find summer jobs for the players, or support the program with their attendance at alumni functions around the nation.

Ted Blair, who was known as "Mr. Yale," was wonderful to the team. He was our host at a team cookout after two-a-day practices every year at the nearby Madison Beach Club. After he died, Dr. Lenny Fassano carried on the tradition. In the days when alumni were allowed to approach high school candidates, Bob Anderson did more to recruit in the Chicago area than anyone before or since. Bob Spears and Jim Mourkis did the same in Pittsburgh, and Jack Ember-sits worked hard in the New Haven area. Harris Ashton helped endow the coaches' travel fund in the name of Charlie O'Hearn, the former university vice president. Joel Smilow endowed the football head coaching position and was the major contributor to the reno-vation of the former Lapham Field House, now the Smilow Field House. Marty Dwyer, Bill Stack, and Bob Hall did wonderful things for the program. So did many of my players—Fred Leone, Pat Ruwe, Bob Sokolowski, Gary Fencik, Calvin Hill, Dick Jauron, Jon Reese, Rich Diana, and John Pagliaro, to name just a few. Even Chris Dudley, who played for many years in the National Basketball Association, helped us out. If my memory serves, I think the other members of the "Y" Association in my first year were Win Lovejoy, Walt Lever-ing, Chuck Willoughby, Jerry Roscoe, Birch Williams, Jim DeAn-gelis, and Hal Whiteman.

The alumnus who might have done more for us on a day-to-day basis than anyone, however, was Don Scharf, who lived in the area and was a fixture at games, practices, and various functions. He was terrific in placing the players in summer jobs and helping them find employment after graduation. I can't say enough about what he did to help us. I can't say enough about what all the alumni did, purely for the love of their alma mater.

I know, of course, that many alumni were critical of me when

I congratulate Dick Jauron (40) in the end zone after his amazing touchdown run against Columbia, 1972. (Milton M. Smith)

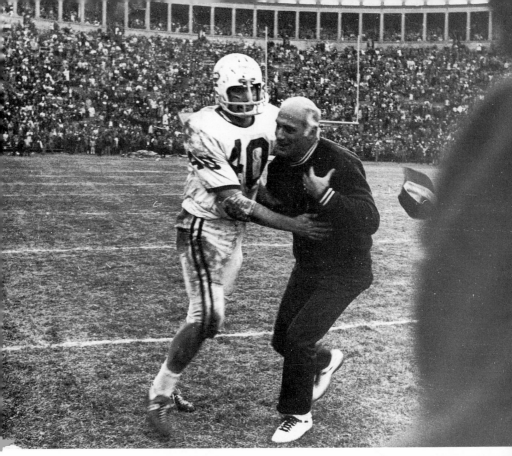

Another Cozza-Jauron touchdown celebration, this one in Harvard Stadium, 1972. We won 28–17.

1936 Heisman Trophy winner Larry Kelley with Dick Jauron and me at the 1972 National Football Foundation and Hall of Fame dinner in New York. (Bill Mark)

Levi Jackson, Yale's football captain in 1946, wi Dick Jauron. (Yale University Sports Archives

The team takes the field at Cornell in the early 1970s. (S. Frinzi)

With the Yale Bulldog. (S. Frinzi, Yale University Sports Archives)

Carried off the field after the Elis defeated Harvard in 1972.
(Yale University Sports Archives)

With Gerald Ford.

Brian Clarke (31) wouldn't kick on Fridays, but he was reliable on Saturdays, as he was here against Princeton in 1973. (S. Frinzi, Yale University Sports Archives)

Gary Fencik hauls in a pass. (S. Frinzi, Yale University Sports Archives)

Former players Jack Ford, left, and Chuck Sizemore
return to Yale Bowl as alumni.
(S. Frinzi, Yale University Sports Archives)

At right, with captain Rudy Green.
(S. Frinzi, Yale University Sports Archives)

Below, Gary Fencik (22) blocks for Rudy Green (43),
1974. (Yale University Sports Archives)

In my office with members of the Class of 1975; from left, Tom Doyle, Rudy Green, Greg Dubinetz, and Elvin Charity. (S. Frinzi, Yale University Sports Archives)

Many years after my career as a minor league player in the Indians and White Sox organizations, I take a cut in the Yale Alumni game, circa 1975. (S. Frinzi)

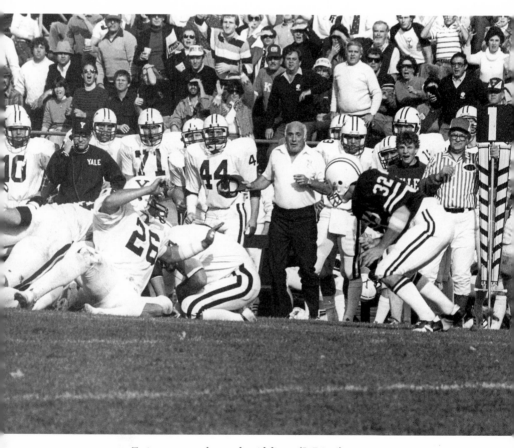

Trying to stay calm on the sidelines. (S. Frinzi)

Former Yale players Calvin Hill and
Dick Jauron at the NFL Pro Bowl, 1975.
(S. Frinzi, Yale University Sports Archives)

John Pagliaro (40) carries the ball in the 1976 win over Harvard.
(S. Frinzi, Yale University Sports Archives)

Pagliaro tries to run over the Columbia defense, above.
(S. Frinzi, Yale University Sports Archives)

Stone Phillips (16) rolls out against Dartmouth, 1976.
(S. Frinzi, Yale University Sports Archives)

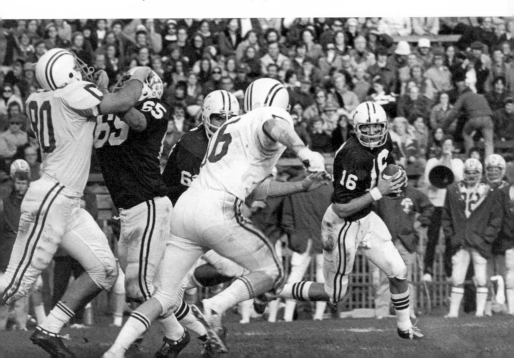

With Pat Ruwe, Yale's 106th
football captain and later the team doctor.
(S. Frinzi, Yale University Sports Archives)

Talking with Pat Ruwe while the team stretches. (Lorenzo Evans, Yale University Sports Archives)

High blood pressure at practice. (The Hartford Courant)

Kevin Czinger (40) stands up a Brown runner, 1980.
(S. Frinzi, Yale University Sports Archives)

Kevin Czinger, Yale's tough
middle guard, 1981.
(Yale University Sports Archives)

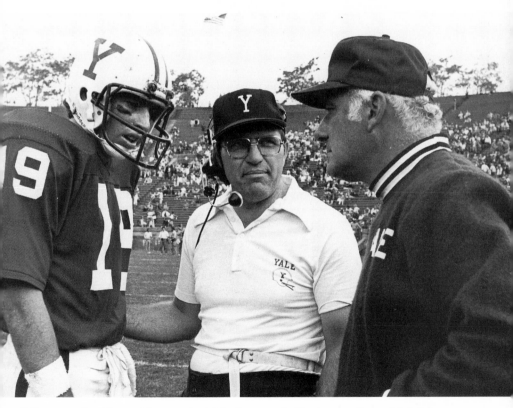

Talking over the offense with quarterback John Rogan and offensive coordinator Seb LaSpina.
(Yale University Sports Archives)

Getting a ride off the field after the 14–0 championship win over Harvard in 1980.

we had some tough seasons in the late 1980s and '90s. There were some, I'm sure, who wished that I had retired before I did and who voiced that opinion to the president or athletic director. Some criticism is inevitable, I guess, especially when you're not winning. And maybe there was more of it than I realized, because, of course, I didn't hear it directly. What griping there was went on behind my back, and I would pick it up secondhand. But I can say in all honesty that I had the enthusiastic support of the vast majority of alumni throughout my stay, and I am very grateful for that.

At times, enthusiastic alumni could cause problems. In all my years at Yale, we received only one sanction from the NCAA, and that was because of a well-meaning alumnus in a midwestern city who broke a minor rule without realizing it. He sponsored a gathering of alumni and high school seniors who were interested in attending Yale. There was nothing wrong with that, because there were prospective students in attendance who were not athletes. The problem was that he sent out a notice that called it a Yale football meeting, instead of just an alumni meeting, and that broke the strict letter of the law of what the NCAA allowed alumni to do. I immediately notified Associate Athletic Director Colleen Lim, who is our compliance officer, and she informed the NCAA. Because it was such a minor infraction, and because we reported it voluntarily, our only penalty was a one-year reduction of paid visits by recruits from seventy to sixty-five and some temporary travel restrictions on the assistant coach responsible for recruiting in that area. It's not easy to stay within the rules. In fact, you have to work hard at it.

I should also mention the Faculty Advisory Committee on Athletics and the Football "Y" Association. Over the years, there were literally hundreds of people who served on one of those two groups and rendered invaluable service to Yale athletics. The Faculty Committee is particularly noteworthy because some people have the false impression that the professors at Yale are all eggheads who resent the football program for all the attention and publicity it receives. There might have been some who felt that way, but the majority of them were enthusiastic about helping us in any way they could. The committee members were there basically to serve the athletic director as liaisons with the rest of the university, but they were always willing to talk to our recruits about academics or the residential college system. It seems as though every time we had a recruit on campus for the weekend, some dean or college master was available to meet with him. Don Kagan, who served a year as interim AD, was a big help. So were John Blum, Gaddis Smith, Stan Wheeler, Paul Frey, Skip Stout, Hugh Flick, Kelly Brownell, and many others.

There were many wonderful advantages to coaching at Yale and living in New Haven. I mentioned how much I enjoyed conversing with the players about anything from politics to history to the theater and how honored I felt to have been associated with men like Kingman Brewster and A. Bartlett Giamatti. I also had great respect for the other presidents, Benno Schmidt and Rick Levin, and especially the interim presidents Hannah Gray and Howard Lamar, although there never seemed to be enough time to get to know any of them very well. It also was marvelous to have so many academic and entertainment opportunities to choose from, though I wish now that Jean and I had taken more advantage of them. We saw some great shows at the Shubert Theater in New Haven, like Mame and Hello Dolly. We particularly like fine music and enjoyed many live performances at Yale's Woolsey Hall. And speaking of music, our three daughters gave us a wonderful fortieth anniversary gift. They treated us to a concert by the Three Tenors at the Meadowlands in New Jersey. They even arranged for a limo to pick us up at the door.

My one-year term as president of the American Football Coaches Association was both an honor and an eye-opener. I was proud to represent the entire nation in a profession that is very meaningful to me, but I was surprised at some of the things I discovered at other universities around the country. I wasn't so naive that I didn't know about unethical practices taking place in the big-time programs, but this was the first time I had come in contact with them firsthand. It was the first time I had faced the reality of coaches keeping $100 bills in their desk drawers to pass out to recruits, or assistant coaches tampering with student transcripts. I remember Darrell Royal, the Texas coach, getting really upset when a team that had beaten him presented the game ball to an assistant who had just been charged with adjusting a player's grades. That's why I was pleased to follow up on a proposal that had been made before my term to put coaches on probation along with a school for rules infractions. Until then, a coach could do something to put his university on probation, then move to another school without any personal consequences.

I don't want to leave the impression that abuses like these were widespread. They weren't. I believe 99 percent of the coaches, even in the major schools, had the interest of their players at heart. They did nothing unethical themselves and tried to rein in the abuses committed by alumni and others in the name of their schools. There were some outlaws, though. For the first time, I was exposed to coaches who were under enormous pressure to win or risk losing their jobs. Their universities needed money, big-time bowl-appearance money, to sustain their programs, and a coach who didn't win didn't keep his job. Some of those coaches felt as though they had to bend the rules to compete.

If nothing else, that year as head of the AFCA made me realize that Yale was a pretty darn good place to coach. The administrators and the alumni still wanted to beat Harvard and Princeton, but not at the expense of using or abusing young men in the process. And not at the expense of telling a young man that he couldn't be an engineer because science majors had afternoon labs, when he was supposed to be on the practice field. That year also made me realize the joy of being around students of superior intellect. Among the rewards of coaching at Yale were the conversations I had with players about subjects other than football. I can't tell you how much I learned from them over the years. Now and then, a player would make a stupid mistake on the field, and one of my assistants would call him "a big dummy." I'd remind him that all the coaches' board scores combined wouldn't equal the player's.

CHAPTER NINE

Just One Miracle Short

I t has been more than ten years since I watched from the sideline as Kelly Ryan performed his string of miracles, but I still get palpitations. Every time I think of those three games, almost four, when he snatched victory from the jaws of defeat in the last minute of play, I have to breathe deeply to calm myself. That son of a gun nearly drove me crazy, winning games that looked hopeless as the final seconds ticked off. Three times in 1987, Kelly led us to victory in the last minute of play. In a span of five weeks, we beat Connecticut, William and Mary, and Pennsylvania with turnovers and touchdowns as the clock ran out. I used to tell that team, "You guys might think you're having fun, but you're going to give me a heart attack if you keep this up."

Kelly had plenty of help from his teammates, no doubt about that. Mike Stewart threw one of the deciding touchdown passes on a tailback option, Dean Athanasia made a sensational diving catch in the end zone, and Bob Shoop turned a simple quick-out pass into the most memorable single play in my time at Yale. But Kelly Ryan was the young man who made it all happen. Without his leadership and contagious confidence, as well as his extraordinary passing skills, those last-minute victories wouldn't have happened. The season ended on a sour note when we couldn't quite pull off one final miracle against Harvard, but I still think back on Kelly Ryan's senior season as one of the most eventful and exciting in all the years I coached.

In some ways, it reminded me of the Brian Dowling era. Even though Kelly and Brian were very different personalities with an entirely different set of skills, they had many similarities. Both of them were outstanding young men and great team leaders, as well as supremely confident and gifted athletes. They were both elected captain (Bob Rizzo was my only other quarterback/captain), and both of them ended their careers with a disappointing game against Harvard.

The first I knew of Kelly Ryan was when we got a promotional flyer on him from his high school coach in Springfield, Illinois. It was the kind of brochure that college publicity offices sometimes send out to hype a player for All-America or the Heisman Trophy, except that this was about a high school kid. Right away, I was skeptical. But we knew that he was from a good family because his older brother, Mike, was a linebacker on our freshman team at the time. And Dave Kelley, who was one of my best recruiters through the years, if not the best, was really high on the kid. He told me that the high school coach was someone who had always been honest with us, and he was insisting that Kelly was for real.

Well, all I had to do was look at some film of his high school games and I was convinced. Coach Kelley told me that they wanted me to speak at their awards banquet, so I jumped on a plane without a second thought. After I spoke at the banquet, I met with Kelly and his parents in their home, and we hit it off right away. They were really solid people. I think Kelly had already been on our campus to visit his brother, but we brought him in on a paid visit anyway, then held our breath while he made his decision. We weren't the only school in the hunt. He had offers from some scholarship schools, including Indiana, and I think Notre Dame was interested, too.

There is never any guarantee when you take a recruiting trip like that. First of all, you hope that you make a good enough presentation to convince the prospect to come to Yale. Then you wait to see whether you can get him through the admissions process and whether the family is eligible for financial aid. Finally, you hope he turns out to be worth the effort once you get him to New Haven and put him in pads. Well, I wish every trip turned out as well as that one to Illinois in 1984 did. It produced one of the finest young men I've ever had the pleasure of coaching.

Right from the beginning, I knew we had something special in Kelly Ryan. He had as quick a release as I've ever seen in a quarterback. In spite of his obvious potential, however, he didn't become the starting quarterback until his junior year. He was probably ready for the first-string role in his sophomore season, but we had a fine senior quarterback at the time by the name of Mike Curtin. He was another great kid and an awfully good player, too, who went on to medical school and became a doctor in Utah. In fact, Mike set the Yale record for completions in a career, with 207. He didn't hold the mark for long, however. Kelly Ryan blew it away with 348 completions just two seasons later.

I tried to give Kelly some playing time as a sophomore because I knew he was going to be a great player, but it didn't make sense to put a player like Mike Curtin on the bench. Toward the end of the season, when it was obvious that Kelly was ready to step in, I had a talk with him. I sat with him on the bus trip to Princeton and explained that this was Mike's senior season and with all the success he was having, he deserved to have the reins. Kelly said, "Coach, I fully understand." When his junior season finally arrived, there was a palpable sense of excitement surrounding the team. I was certainly excited, and I know the assistant coaches and the players were, too. We all had great expectations for Kelly. Man, could he throw a pass! He could set and release the ball like a shot. I know it's a lot to say, but in many ways he reminded me of Dan Marino, the great Miami Dolphins passer. That's the kind of quick trigger he had. There were times when I would see good coverage on our receivers and I'd think, "Oh no, don't throw the ball," but Kelly would find a way to get it to a teammate. Time and time and time again. He could throw it through a moving window fifteen yards downfield. The receivers would be running with their backs to him and when they turned, the ball was right in their stomach. He just had that knack. And he used all his receivers, too, the way Brian Dowling did. If you got open, wherever you were on the field, you were going to get the ball. And you'd better be ready for it, because it was going to get there quick. He was so strong, such a great leader, and really tough inside. He was just super.

Needless to say, we were psyched when it came time for our Blue-White intrasquad game at the end of the training period before Kelly's junior year. For the coaches, that annual scrimmage was an opportunity to get a line on some of the players under game conditions, especially the first-year kids. For the players, it was a chance to have some fun as well as make an impression. After three weeks of hitting blocking sleds—and occasionally each other, under carefully controlled conditions—they finally got a chance to let off some steam in a competitive situation, with officials and first-down chains and even a small gathering of hard-core fans in the stands. As it turned out, though, that 1986 Blue-White game was a near disaster. Instead of building confidence for the season, we nearly lost the one player who promised to make it special. Because of a single thought-less act, one of the most talented quarterbacks ever to play at Yale suffered an injury that hobbled him for the rest of his career.

I still shudder when I think of the moment. Here was this wonderful player, wearing a protective red jersey, as quarterbacks always do in intrasquad scrimmages, to remind the defensive players to be careful, and he gets cut down by one of his own teammates. He had just thrown the ball and was standing there defenseless when one of our middle guards, I won't mention his name, plowed right into his knees from the front. It wasn't really a cheap shot. It was only a split-second after he released the pass. But the whole team wanted to kill him. He was nobody's friend after that and eventually dropped off the team. I never said anything to him; I didn't have to, because he felt terrible. And after I calmed down, I felt sorry for him, too, because he had to live with what he had done. I'm sure he didn't mean to hurt Kelly. He just wasn't thinking. One thing the kids know is that you don't ever hurt your quarterback, especially when he's wearing a red jersey and he's the star of the team.

The injury turned out to be a torn posterior ligament, which is the toughest of all the knee ligaments to heal. I had Kevin Lynch, our team doctor, look at him, and other doctors did, too. Kevin told me, "You know, there's a possibility he's going to be okay." Well, it turned out that he did recover fast enough to play after missing only a few games, but he never regained full strength or stability in that knee, not that season or his senior season either. Kelly had never been fleet of foot, but he had some of the same instincts on his feet that Brian Dowling had. He had a sense of how to move and how to make the most of what running ability he had. Now he had to wear a brace and he had trouble running at all. We did the only thing we could. We put him back in a shotgun formation, where the quarterback stands about five yards behind the line of scrimmage to catch the snap from center. That saved the stress he would have put on his knee backing up from center.

The third game of the season was against Army in the Bowl, and to be honest, they were a much better team. We didn't really have a strong enough defense to hold them in check, and we were going to have to play them with a one-legged quarterback who still didn't have any significant game experience. Well, we didn't win the game—in fact, we lost 41–24—but Kelly Ryan was sensational. He set a Yale single-game record for passing, 426 yards, which still stood when I retired a decade later. He just cut them to ribbons. The Army coach, Jim Young, told me after the game that he considered himself lucky to get out of the Bowl with a win.

In spite of the injury and the brace, Kelly had a fine junior season, even though we struggled to a 3–7 record as a team. He struggled a little, too, but he did things that other quarterbacks would love to do with two good legs. Here's a statistic that proves the point. Because of his inability to run, he had minus 126 yards rushing for the year, but he still netted more yards of total offense than any Yale quarterback before him except Brian Dowling. He passed for 1,739 yards, for a net offense of 1,613. Dowling's best numbers were 313 yards rushing and 1,554 passing for 1,867 total yards in 1968.

It wasn't until Kelly's senior year that he really showed his stuff. He was still hampered by the injury and still wore the knee brace, but, wow, he and the receivers, Bob Shoop, Tom Szuba, Dean Athanasia, tailback Mike Stewart, and fullback Troy Jenkins turned in one of the most heart-stopping seasons of my time at Yale. In fact, Kelly's total-offense record that season was 2,120 yards, a mark that still stood more than a decade later. And yet he rushed for only ten yards.

Passing statistics don't tell the whole Kelly Ryan story. Another mark of his greatness was his coolness under fire and the way he pulled out last-minute victories seemingly at will. Even with the crucial roles that Shoop and Stewart played in two of the victories, all three of those clutch wins had Kelly's signature all over them. He had full command of that team, which is essential when close games are on the line. And he had a confidence that spilled over to the rest of the team. Years later, when Bob Shoop became an assistant coach on our staff, he often talked about Kelly's strength of character and leadership. He said Kelly was like a commander in the huddle, someone who could raise the level of play of the people around him. Praise like that, coming from a teammate, is a powerful testimonial.

There was another dimension to Kelly Ryan that I admired as much as his football talent. He was an outstanding captain and a caring young man. There were a lot of examples of this in the way he went about his life on the field and on campus, but one story of his response to a teammate's tragedy will always stand out in my mind. It happened during the off season, when Coach Kelley and I were in Chicago, meeting with a group of alumni in a downtown restaurant. The father of one of our running backs, Kevin Brice, collapsed with a heart attack right there in the room. By coincidence, Bob Rizzo, our captain in 1977 who had become a respected heart specialist, was there. Dr. Rizzo went to work right away. Unfortunately, he couldn't save Mr. Brice, who died later that night in the hospital.

To make matters worse, Kevin, who was back at Yale, didn't have the ready cash for the flight to Chicago for his father's funeral. There was nothing I or any of my coaches could do because of the stupid NCAA regulations that prevent us from lending money to players for any reason at all, even to attend a family funeral. Well, when Kelly heard about the situation, he put Kevin's ticket on his credit card. Not only that, he bought a ticket for himself and flew out to the funeral to give Kevin the emotional support he needed. That's the type of young man he was.

We opened the 1987 season with a 17–7 loss against Brown on a rainy day and muddy field in the Bowl. It was a disappointing start because it was a game we might well have won, except for six turnovers. We came right back the next week, however, with the first of Kelly's miracle victories, beating Connecticut 30–27 in the final seconds before a crowd of thirty-four thousand. Kelly hit Tom Szuba, who was a real "go-to" receiver from suburban Pittsburgh, with an 11-yard touchdown pass with just eighteen seconds to play. It was Kelly's fourth TD pass of the game.

The next week it was off to sunny Hawaii. The Rainbows were a Division I-A team that played in the Western Athletic Conference, with the likes of Brigham Young University. They played Wisconsin, Air Force, and Arkansas the same year they played us. A lot of people said that we had no business scheduling a team like that. Frankly, we had little chance of winning and a big chance of getting roughed up physically. But I have always felt that kids enjoy a stiff challenge, and unless there is a risk of serious injury or embarrassment, they should get the chance to play against really good opponents at least once in a while.

It's funny, but the thing I remember most about being in Hawaii is the way the television and newspaper reporters reacted when they saw that our kids had brought their textbooks with them. They just couldn't believe the players would be doing any real studying on a trip like this. What they didn't see was a planeload of dead-tired athletes flying back across the Pacific Ocean on Saturday night after a bruising defeat—with their overhead lights on, studying.

Actually, we gave Hawaii a good game for most of three quarters. We were only six points behind with eight minutes left in the third period, but their superior size, speed, and depth just wore us down. It was 62–10 at the end. I knew we were in trouble early in the game, when we pitched the ball to our tailback, Mike Stewart, on an end sweep, and he was run down from behind by a freshman linebacker who must have weighted 240 pounds. Stewart was a good 4.6 or faster in the 40-yard dash, but this big linebacker was even faster. I thought, oh boy, this could be a long day. In an odd way, though, that loss to Hawaii showed just how special that team was in Kelly Ryan's senior year. A loss like that could have broken our spirit,

especially with the brutal travel time and the six-hour time difference. We weren't in bed at all from Saturday morning until we got
back Sunday night. The only sleep we got was on the plane. I got up
Monday morning feeling as though I had been drugged. I was really
whipped. I thought, there's no way these guys are going to come
back. But you know what? They did. They won the next six games,
and if we hadn't fumbled in the last minute against Harvard, it might
have been seven in a row, with an Ivy League championship in the
bargain.

The week after Hawaii, we were back in the Bowl to play William
and Mary. Somehow the players had found the energy to have a good
week of practice, so I was feeling better about the prospects for the
remainder of the season. Still, until we got back into a game situation, I really didn't know what to expect after the physical beating in
Aloha Stadium. Well, it was as if the Hawaii game had never happened. Not only did this team win, but it won in thrilling fashion,
with the second last-minute miracle in three weeks. This time, Kelly
Ryan was the costar. He shared top billing with the tailback Stewart,
who had been a two-time all-state quarterback at Central High
School in Manchester, New Hampshire. Stewart not only ran for 188
of our 338 yards that afternoon before twenty thousand fans, he also
threw the winning touchdown pass from three yards out with just
twenty-eight seconds remaining. We were down by a single point
when he took a pitchout from Kelly and threw to a diving Dean
Athanasia in the end zone.

The Yale faithful had only two weeks to wait for Kelly Ryan's "cardiac
kids" to perform their next act. And this one was the most amazing
of the season, a real Houdini escape from near-certain defeat. We
had beaten Columbia the week after William and Mary, and now we
were playing host to a Pennsylvania team that was better than its 2–3
record showed. The Quakers had lost two Ivy League games by a
total of six points and had played a tough game against Navy before
losing by ten points.

By now, the news media and the students were beginning to take notice of Kelly Ryan's heroics. We were only 3–2 as a team, but the word was spreading around the league and in the New Haven community that we were an exciting team with a talented quarterback who had a knack for the dramatic. That team created a following that frankly had been on a slow decline over the previous ten years or so.

Actually, if the Quakers hadn't mounted a late comeback of their own, we wouldn't have needed a last-minute miracle. We were up 21–7 in the fourth quarter, but they scored two touchdowns and ran for a two-point conversion to take a one-point lead. I remember someone joking after the game that being behind with time running out meant we had them right where we wanted them. That's the aura these kids had. And true to the script, we drove into Penn territory with just under two minutes to play. You could just feel the tension building. There were twenty-three thousand in the stadium, and I think every one of them thought we were going to pull it out. That's where our good fortune stopped. We failed to convert on a fourth-down play, and I remember thinking, well I guess our luck has finally run out.

Talk about a hopeless situation, we were behind by a point, they had the ball at midfield with a half-minute left, and we had no timeouts left. They tell me that one of the Philadelphia writers left the press box when we ran out of downs to go back to the field house and start his story. Who could blame him? The stands were beginning to empty, and I was thinking about what I was going to tell the reporters in the postgame press conference. It was all over except for the final whistle. For us to have any chance of winning, they would have to fumble. That was pretty unlikely, because their quarterback just had to wrap his hands around the ball and fall into the line. Even if they fumbled, we would have to recover and find a way to score from fifty yards away, with almost no time left and no way to stop the clock except to run out of bounds.

So what happened? Their quarterback fumbled the snap from center, and our sophomore lineman Mike Browne recovered. After we got the ball back, it was one of those rare occasions in sports when you think there's just no way a team is going to get out of a hopeless situation, and at the same time you half expect it will. When Kelly Ryan was in there, it was a lot like Brian Dowling. You never thought you were going to lose. These kids had pulled out last-minute wins twice before, and everyone in the stadium was watching with a mixture of disbelief and expectation to see whether they could do it again.

We had the ball near midfield, and the obvious play was a quick-out pass pattern to pick up a few yards and get out of bounds. Coach Seb LaSpina called "77 Pass" to Bob Shoop, and it worked perfectly. Shoop caught Kelly's pass to the left side of the field and stepped out of bounds right in front of our bench, stopping the clock. In fact, the play worked so smoothly that Coach LaSpina grabbed Shoop by the arm and told him to tell Kelly to run the same play. Once again, it worked perfectly. Shoop caught the pass and ran out of bounds at the 32-yard line, where Coach LaSpina was waiting to give him the next play.

If we could gain another ten yards and get out of bounds, our kicker, Dave Derby, would have a reasonable chance of making a winning field goal. We figured, hey, they hadn't stopped the quick-out pass on the last two plays, why not call it again? So for the third straight time, Coach LaSpina sent Shoop into the huddle with a play for Kelly. This time he called "77 and up." It was the same play, except that Shoop was to turn up field and run along the sideline as far as he could go before stepping out of bounds. Coach LaSpina had another message for Shoop to take to the huddle. He wanted Mike Stewart to run a post pattern out of the backfield to clear his defender out of the area.

What happened next was certainly among the wildest and most memorable single plays in my time at Yale. In a situation like that, a coach becomes more like a spectator than a part of the action. Once the play is called and the team comes to the line of scrimmage, it's too late to do anything but watch. To have any chance of winning, we had to complete the pass, gain sufficient yardage to be within field goal range, and get out of bounds. So, like everyone else in the stadium, I held my breath. At least I knew I was working with Yale students, who were smart enough to understand the situation and execute the plan to the best of their ability.

Well, I didn't count on Bob Shoop taking matters into his own hands. He caught a third straight pass from Kelly. No problem there. And he turned up field to get what extra yardage he could. No problem there either. But when he was about to get tackled, instead of stepping over the sideline and putting the game in the hands of our kicker, he turned in toward the middle of the field and headed for the end zone. I can't imagine what my expression must have been as I watched this act of derring-do. Bob was going to be either the hero or the goat. Either he was going to make it to the end zone and win the game, or he was going to get tackled and time was going to run out. Either way, I was going to wring his neck.

Apparently, he saw enough daylight in front of him to make a split-second decision to go for broke. Not only did he leave the relative safety of the sideline, but he angled in almost to the hashmarks before he raced into the end zone. Somehow he made it, proving once again what a great coach I was. It was one of the most thrilling football moments I ever experienced. Bill Gonillo, the play-by-play broadcaster for the local radio station, WELI, was yelling into the microphone that it was one of the greatest moments in the history of Yale sports. I guess he took some kidding from the sportswriters in the pressbox who thought he was getting carried away. But you know what? He might have been right. A lot of our coaches got a copy of Gonillo's tape and kept it as a memento.

Shoop was mobbed after the touchdown, and it seemed forever before he made his way to the bench. I honestly didn't know whether to hug him or strangle him. I just asked why in the world he hadn't stepped out of bounds. He said something like, "Coach, what are you worried about? We had six seconds left." If he had been tackled, that might have been how long he had to live once I got my hands on him. I'm kidding, of course. I had real affection for just about every one of the two thousand or so players I coached, and

Kelly Ryan, Bob Shoop, and the others on that team were among my favorites. In fact, two years later, I hired Shoop as a graduate assistant coach, and five years after that, I brought him in as my defensive coordinator. He never let me forget that catch, either. Any time I got after him because I wasn't happy with the way his defense was playing, he'd say, "Hey, Coach, remember that Penn game in '87 when I . . ."

I've heard Shoop tell people that if he hadn't scored that touchdown, I might not have given him a job and his whole career might have been different. That's not true, but it makes a good story.

After the Pennsylvania game, we were 4–2 and developing into the kind of team that didn't have to rely on last-minute heroics to win games. Several sophomores had matured into solid starting players. Jon Reese, who would be captain two years later and one of the most inspirational athletes I ever coached, was on his way to leading the team in solo tackles at linebacker. And three sophomores—Brian Hennen, who moved to linebacker the next year, Steve Essick, and Rich Huff—played significant roles in the defensive backfield with senior Mike Sullivan. In fact, a fourth sophomore, Chris Rutan, saw more and more action in the secondary as the season went on. He had eleven tackles and an interception against Cornell, the same game in which Huff, who needed a second helping of potatoes to get to 170 pounds, was named Ivy League Sophomore of the Week with eight tackles and two interceptions. There were important juniors in the mix, too, like Don Lund, the next year's captain, who worked with Reese and senior Tony Cappelino at linebacker.

Whether the miracle finish against Penn gave us the momentum we needed I don't know, but we knocked off the next three Ivy League foes in good order. We beat Cornell, Dartmouth, and Princeton in successive weeks, then hunkered down for Kelly Ryan's final game against Harvard in the Bowl. Kelly didn't provide any last-minute thrills in those games, but he had one of the best statistical days any Yale quarterback ever had in our 34–19 win over Princeton. He completed 21 of 30 passes for 329 yards and three touchdowns without an interception. That's more than fifteen yards per completion and nearly eleven yards per attempt. The Princeton quarterback that day was Jason Garrett, who went on to be Troy Aikman's backup with the Dallas Cowboys.

It was unseasonally warm the day before the Harvard game in 1987. In fact, we practiced in shorts. I mention this because just twenty-four hours later we were faced with weather conditions so cold and windy that I marveled that the kids could play football at all. And yet both teams played very well. I was amazed that anybody was hardy enough, or maybe foolhardy enough, to come to the Bowl to watch, yet there were 66,548 fans huddled under blankets, eager to watch the two archrivals play for the undisputed Ivy League championship. That's pretty close to capacity.

It was the most uncomfortable I have ever been on the sidelines. The conditions were the most physically demanding and competitively challenging I ever experienced in a half-century as a player or coach. The temperature was in the low teens, and there was a steady wind that gusted up to forty miles per hour. Usually, I'm so involved in the game I hardly notice the weather, except to adjust the game plan for rain or wind or a particularly sloppy field. But that afternoon against Harvard, my face actually hurt from the cold and wind. How the receivers were able to catch the football is beyond me. And remember, the passing game was our main weapon. The newspapers dubbed it the Freeze Bowl. People still call it that today.

Not only was it a surprisingly well-played game, but it was an exciting one, too, right down to the final minute. We had a chance for a fourth Kelly Ryan miracle finish, but this time things didn't go our way. We were behind 14–10 late in the game when we mounted what was certain to be the last drive of Kelly Ryan's career. The setting was perfect for a storybook ending to a storybook season. Here we were with about two minutes left on the clock and moving toward a touchdown that would have given us the Ivy championship. I think every coach and player on our team was dead certain Kelly was going to get us into the end zone.

For a few moments, things looked hopeful, as if we were following a scripted destiny. We converted on successive third-down situations and moved the ball into Harvard territory. Bob Shoop caught a pass of about eight yards from Kelly on the first third-down conversion, then Mike Stewart made a sensational one-handed catch on the next one. Maybe the scenario was a little too perfect. The winning touchdown that seemed almost inevitable fell out of reach when our fullback, Troy Jenkins, fumbled and they recovered. I try not to make excuses when kids make mistakes, but it was hard to blame Troy for that turnover. He was still healing from a pinched nerve in his shoulder, the tackler put his helmet right on the ball, and the subzero wind chill had turned his hands to ice. It was a huge disappointment, as any loss is, especially against Harvard with the title on the line. But it was a well-played game, and to be honest we had gotten our share of breaks during the season. Still, I guarantee you that if we hadn't fumbled, we would have won the game. Kelly Ryan would have found a way to get us into the end zone—again.

Bob Shoop reminds me that we found a way to laugh a little the next week at Troy's expense. He took the train to New York for a couple of job interviews with investment banking firms. In the first one, the bankers who were interviewing him told him that they had been in New Haven over the weekend for the Yale-Harvard game, and if some son of a gun hadn't fumbled the ball, Yale would have won. Apparently they didn't realize they were talking to the son of a gun who had fumbled. At his next interview the prospective employer said, "Troy, I want you to know I don't hold you responsible for our loss to Harvard. Not entirely anyway." Finally, when he got back to New Haven that night, he got into a cab. The driver looked in the rearview mirror and said, "The guy put his helmet right on the ball didn't he, Troy?"

What a season! What a wonderful group of young men! And what a terrific leader in Kelly Ryan! If only he hadn't suffered that dumb knee injury in the Blue-White scrimmage as a junior, who knows how good he might have been? It's astounding what he accomplished playing most of his career with a bad knee and a leg brace. His bad luck didn't end with the loss to Harvard, either. After the season, he got an infection in his elbow that was so serious he could have died from it. He had gotten nicked during the season, but he didn't think anything of it and didn't bring it to the attention of our medical people. The elbow began to swell and eventually he was bedridden with blood poisoning. I visited him every day in the infirmary and I'll tell you, I was scared. He was a very sick young man.

In time he recovered, graduated, married a local girl, and went back to the Chicago area to work in the banking field. But he never got a shot at pro football, even though I think he was a legitimate prospect. Actually, he signed a free-agent contract with the Dallas Cowboys, but he failed the physical before he reported to training camp and was released. The doctors detected a weak pulse and residual blood clots in his throwing arm and decided not to take any chances with him. It still saddens me to think how the ill fortune of two injuries diminished the playing career of such an extraordinary athlete. Still, he made the most of the situation, and he never complained.

CHAPTER TEN

Broken Jaw and All

I t was just after dark when I left the field house on a rainy Halloween night, one of those spooky October twilights that stir childhood memories of ghosts and goblins. I can't say that I felt any particular apprehension as I drove past the cemetery on Derby Avenue on my way home to supper. Maybe I should have. Our Tuesday practice had gone well. We were in high spirits after the previous Saturday's 23–22 squeaker over Penn. In fact, that 1989 team was loaded with high-spirited players, very much reflecting the inspirational leadership of the captain, Jon Reese.

The victory over Penn before nineteen thousand fans in the Bowl had been significant. Both teams had entered the game unbeaten in the Ivy League, and Penn had a tailback named Bryan Keys who was the leading Division I-AA rusher in the nation. He was averaging 171 yards per game and 5.4 yards per run. The game lived up to expectations. It was a well-played contest that could have gone either way right down to the final ten seconds, when our kicker, Ed Perks, drilled a 28-yard field goal to win it. And I mean drilled it. He hit one of those low line drives that couldn't have cleared the crossbar by more than a few inches. The papers quoted me the next day as saying the ball might have dented the crossbar if it had hit it. Actually, the ugly kick was the result of a low snap from center, which threw off the timing. Our holder, Adam Lenain, did a marvelous job of scooping the ball off the turf and setting it up for the kick. Incidentally, Perks, who was a sophomore then, went on to set Yale records for most field goals in a season and career, including a 52-yarder against Cornell the next year.

So it's no wonder that there was an added level of enthusiasm at practice that Halloween afternoon, despite the gloomy weather. We were 6–1 on the season and 4–0 in the league, with Cornell at home, Princeton away, and Harvard at home still on the schedule. Our success was something of a surprise, because we had been picked to finish fifth in the league. It was due in large part to Darin Kehler, the undersized, overachieving quarterback who had been coaxed off the fall baseball team the year before when injuries left us threadbare at that position. The Kehler story is a great one, which I'll get to later.

I hadn't been home more than a few minutes that Halloween night when the phone rang. It was the Hospital of Saint Raphael. There had been an accident. A car with five Yale football players in it skidded through a rain-slick intersection and slammed into another car that had run a blinking red light. Both cars were total wrecks, and two of the players were in the hospital. I told Jean to forget about dinner, and I promptly drove back to New Haven. By the time I got to the hospital, I was sick with worry. Ed Woodsum, the athletic director, arrived at about the same time. Jon Reese, who had been driving, got the worst of the crash. He was thrown forward, collapsing the steering column with his chest and smashing his mouth against the dashboard. He looked terrible. The lower part of his face was a mess of cuts and bruises, and I could see that his whole mouth had been pushed in. He must have been in serious pain, though he would be the last to admit it.

I felt so sorry for him. What a shame that this fine young man should end his football career like this, just three weeks from his third and final appearance in The Game. He was the epitome of the all-American kid, with rugged good looks and an almost military bearing, six feet tall and 220 pounds. His love of competition and the joy he took from life just bubbled out of him and infected every player on that team. The kids just loved him, and so did I. It was hard to look at him lying there in a hospital bed. He was to have surgery later that evening to fix his teeth, set his broken cheekbone, and wire his jaw in place. It could have been worse, I suppose. The people who saw the car said that it was a miracle nobody was killed. The only other player with a significant injury was senior defensive back Bob Bennett. He suffered a concussion and was kept in the hospital overnight.

I gave Jon a hug, careful not to jostle his face or shoulder, which had sustained some ligament damage as well. I said, "Thank God you're alive. Now just relax, you're going to be well taken care of."

And what does he say? He apologizes. Imagine that. Instead of feeling sorry for himself, which he had every right to do, he felt bad for me and the team. He wasn't thinking about his broken jaw or the fact that his football career had skidded to a halt on a rainy Halloween night on the way home from practice. He was thinking about what this might do to our chances for the Ivy League title.

In many ways Jon Reese was the classic Yale student-athlete. He came to Yale, instead of going to Syracuse, where his father had been MVP of the lacrosse team, because he wanted to play two varsity sports. He was as good an attackman in lacrosse as he was a linebacker in football. Maybe better. He thrived on the family atmosphere of a team sport and didn't want to limit his college sports experience to just lacrosse, as he would have been forced to do if he had accepted the full scholarship to Syracuse. Athletes at Yale are not only allowed to play more than one sport, they are encouraged to. That is in contrast to most Division I universities, where scholarship athletes in the revenue sports are prohibited by the coach from playing a second sport.

Things are different now that Yale football has twelve days of spring practice, but in 1989 Jon was able to move from one sport to the other with no problem. It meant that he was able to integrate the valuable learning experiences of athletics with his academic life throughout the school year, just as amateur sports in general and the Ivy League code in particular intend. Still, the choice of a college was a tough one for Jon because of his father's close ties to Syracuse. The Reese family on Long Island, New York, was a loving family, bonded by its participation in sports. Jon's father, Walter, was the football and lacrosse coach at Copaigue High School, while Jon and his brother Jason played both sports at rival West Babylon High. I'm told that Jon's mother, in order to keep peace in the family, was forced to ban all talk of sports in the weeks before the two high schools played each other.

Ultimately, Jon chose Yale, where his brother was already on the lacrosse team. I think that Walter Reese, the loyal Syracuse alum, was secretly pleased to have both his sons at Yale. He certainly was proud four years later, when Jon set the NCAA record for most lacrosse goals in a season, at fifty-four. Yale went to the national semifinals that year, 1990, under coach Mike Waldvogel. Jon's mom and dad were in the stands when he set the scoring record. In fact, the game was held up until Marian Reese, tears of emotion running down her cheeks, came out of the stands to accept the ball as a memento.

Needless to say, my mood had changed dramatically as I drove home for the second time that dark, rainy night. As concerned as I was for Jon's health, I had to put him out of my mind and think about replacing him for Saturday's game in the Bowl against Cornell. The idea that he might recover fast enough to play football four days after that scary accident never entered my mind. It seemed out of the question that he would return at all. Well, I should have known better. I should have known that he was lying there in the hospital determined that nothing would keep him out of Saturday's lineup.

As the week progressed, I was amazed to learn that there was indeed a possibility that Jon could see some action against Cornell. He had been fitted with a plastic mouthpiece to protect his loosened teeth, and his jaw was wired in place to prevent further damage. What's more, his helmet was fitted with a dark shield that made him look for all the world like Darth Vader from the *Star Wars* movies. Still, we weren't counting on him for any real help. He had moved from Saint Raphael's to the Yale Health Center, but he wasn't able to practice, and he was growing weaker by the day on a restricted diet of liquids and baby food. Just the same, as game day approached, I got the feeling that he might at least be able to make an appearance on the sidelines, and that alone would give us a tremendous emotional lift.

Jon left the infirmary on Thursday afternoon long enough to show up at practice. Slurring his words through a clenched jaw, he gave a terrific talk to the team, reminding them of the importance of the Ivy League title. Then on Friday afternoon, he showed up in sweats and led the team through calisthenics. The reaction from the players was enough to send shivers down your spine. I know I had goosebumps. Even then I had doubts that he could actually get into the game the next day, but I think the players believed that he could. Darin Kehler was quoted in the papers that Jon would show up in his hospital gown if he thought he could help the team.

Jon was still confined to the medical center on Friday night, and when he woke up Saturday morning, he wasn't sure that he would be strong enough to play. All he knew was that he was determined to suit up and run through the tunnel into the Bowl with his teammates. Dr. Robert Parker, who had done the surgery, cleared him to play as long as he wore the special mouthpiece and facemask. I didn't know what to think. I wasn't sure how effective he could be in his condition, and I was worried about how well he would be able to breathe through the mouthpiece once he exerted himself. Most of all, I didn't want to risk further injury. Football is just a game, and he had the rest of his life to live. The thought of his taking a knee to the helmet was almost too dreadful to think about.

So we played it one step at a time. He suited up and took a few gentle hits during pregame warmups just to get a feel of contact, but that left him all the more apprehensive. We started sophomore Kevin Skol in his place at middle linebacker. Jon went in for a few plays to test his strength, but he was obviously tentative. You could see he was hesitant to stick his head into a tackle the way he normally would. But he was actually in the game, something I simply wouldn't have believed four days earlier. Then, suddenly, I think it was in the second quarter, the moment of truth arrived. Skol got injured and had to leave the game. Nobody had to ask Jon whether he was ready for full-time action. He was already running onto the field, strapping that Darth Vader contraption on his head as he ran. He took a few good licks in his first series, and when he came out, he said he was afraid to take his mouthpiece out for fear his teeth would come out with it. Later in the game, unbelievably, one of the trainers found him smashing his helmet on the bench, trying to get the protective facemask to come off. Apparently it was steaming up from his body heat on a cold day.

Jon played the entire second half, and though he wasn't at his best, he did make nine tackles, which was a major contribution to our 34–19 win. Darin Kehler had a great game, rushing for 89 yards and passing for 158, including two touchdowns. But it was a defensive victory as much as anything. Rich Huff, the youthful looking defensive back who was a dead ringer for the actor Richard Thomas of John Boy Walton fame, intercepted two passes. The first one was a diving catch in the end zone that proved to be a turning point in the game. The second, his seventh of the season, tied him for the Yale single-season record with the 1937 Heisman Trophy winner Clint Frank. Rich had a baby face and a nice smile, but in the heat of a game he'd tear your head off to make a tackle.

There is no way to measure the importance of Jon Reese's courageous play that afternoon against Cornell. I'm sure he made a larger impact emotionally than he did physically, but his performance should silence forever those cynics who say Ivy League athletes aren't tough. Like Kevin Czinger ten years before him, Jon was a model of courage and tenacity. As a reward, he got to spend the next week in the heady atmosphere of preparing for a championship game. On the afternoon we beat Cornell, Princeton had pummeled Penn 30–8, the same team we had struggled to beat by a single point two weeks earlier. Believe me, that got my attention. And it set up a huge game at Princeton's Palmer Stadium the next Saturday. The Elis and the Tigers were both 5–0 in the conference, and the winner would clinch at least a share of the Ivy League title.

We hadn't won the championship outright since 1980 and hadn't shared it since 1981, when we tied with Dartmouth. Those seasons came at the end of a very good stretch of 107 wins, 28 losses, and 3 ties, and only one losing season in fifteen years. It was good to have the championship excitement back again. Weeks like that magnify the joy of college football a hundred times over. The players and the coaching staff were very much aware of the increased excitement on campus and around New Haven.

It was a special season for me personally because it was my twenty-fifth anniversary as head coach. I'm sure it was also special for assistant coaches Seb LaSpina and Rich Pont. Seb was an All-Mid-American Conference nose guard at Miami of Ohio when I was an assistant on John Pont's staff, and he had been on my staff at Yale from the beginning. When I retired in 1996, we had been together for thirty-two years. Rich, Jon's younger brother, was on my staff form 1968 to '94. Coach LaSpina had reason to be particularly proud that week as we prepared our surprisingly good team for the title game. He was the one who had urged me to switch to a modified wishbone offense at the beginning of the season to take advantage of Darin Kehler's running ability. The gamble had worked beautifully. With fullback Chris Kouri and tailback Kevin Callahan behind him, Darin was on his way to setting an Ivy League rushing record for quarterbacks, and we were looking at the possibility of Yale's first unbeaten and untied Ivy League season since 1967. We were un-beaten in 1968, too, but we had that blasted tie with Harvard.

Princeton also had a record-setting back in Judd Garrett, the third of the Garrett brothers to be outstanding players for the Tigers. First there was John, an All-Ivy split end, then Jason, the quarterback who became Troy Aikman's backup with the Dallas Cowboys. Now Judd was on the threshold of a whole slew of Princeton rushing records. All three Garretts had transferred from Columbia when their father, Jim Garrett, left as the Lions' head coach.

Our kids needed no extra incentive that week to get juiced up for a championship game at Princeton, but they got it anyway from their captain, Jon Reese. He was as exuberant that week as could be. The local papers quoted him as saying this game exemplified what college football was all about. I was pretty excited myself. People say I don't always show my emotions, and I suppose there is some truth to that. But I feel them inside. Believe me, I do. When I walked into Palmer Stadium that crisp autumn afternoon and saw thirty-seven thousand fans streaming in from their tailgate parties, I was wired, and grateful to be a part of Ivy League football.

The game lived up to its hype in every respect. It was an epic struggle that neither team deserved to lose. It was filled with outstanding individual efforts and pivotal plays, but at the end of the day, we prevailed because of one of the best defensive games any Yale team played in my thirty-two years. Judd Garrett got his yardage— 149 yards on 33 carries—but we held the Tigers to a single touchdown, which they scored on the first series of the game. After that, we played steady defense and took advantage of a half-dozen huge plays that turned the game around.

We were still down 7–0 in the third quarter when running back Maurice Saah turned in the most significant offensive play of the afternoon. He took a pitchout from Darin on a standard option play and was immediately boxed in by Princeton defenders. It looked as if he was going to be tackled for a loss, but somehow he spun away from at least two tacklers, bounced off a couple of others, and ran thirty yards for the score. (Just another example of great coaching.)

Rich Huff accounted for at least three pivotal defensive plays. His first key play came in the third period, with the game still tied 7–7. We forced Princeton to punt from deep in its own territory when our two big tackles, Scott Wollam and Glover Lawrence, stuffed Garrett at the line of scrimmage on a crucial third-and-short situation. We put ten men on the line of scrimmage in an all-out attempt to block the punt. Huff, who was wide to the outside, timed his rush perfectly, found an open lane inside his blocker, and got a hand on the punt. The ball bounced out of bounds at the 17, and we scored two plays later.

Not once, not twice, but three times the Tigers threatened to tie the game (or win it with a two-point conversion) in the fourth quarter, and all three times we came up with big plays to hang on. On the first occasion, they went for it on fourth and one at our 14, but we forced Garrett to fumble, and Tom O'Brien recovered. Later, they had second and seven at our 33, but Huff sacked Princeton quarterback Joel Sharp on a safety blitz, forcing a fumble that Chris Rutan recovered for us. That sack was an example of Huff's speed. Sharp was rolling to the opposite side of the field when Huff caught him from behind. Finally, with just twelve seconds left, Jim Parsons intercepted a desperation pass from Sharp at the 2-yard line, clinching the victory and a share of the Ivy League title.

Sadly, that triumph turned out to be the last really high point of my thirty-two years. We had many wonderful young men come through the program in the years that followed, a few winning seasons, and some very satisfying individual victories, but 1989 was my last championship. After beating Princeton we were ranked thirteenth in the country in the NCAA Division I-AA poll. I remember the mob scene after the game, when a group of fans carried Jon Reese off the field.

If you ask me to define a dangerous situation, I'd say it is a Yale football team with an unbeaten Ivy League record going into The Game against a Harvard team with no chance at the title. That's the way it was that last week of the 1989 season, as Jon Reese and the other seniors prepared for the last game of their football careers. Emotion was running as high as I ever felt it, but in many ways, the Harvards had us right where they wanted us. They were 4–2 in the conference, 4–5 overall, and not in contention for the championship. But they had an opportunity for a successful season by spoiling our bid for an unbeaten record. That made them loose and aggressive, and it made us tight and defensive.

Harvard week was always a bittersweet time for me. The Game was the highlight of any year, especially a good year like we were having. But it was also time to say goodbye to the seniors who had been my second family for four years. I felt a heightened importance to everything we did. The recent history of The Game was not on the side of the more successful team. So often the underdog, whether it was Yale or Harvard, would win The Game and tarnish the better record of the other. I thought about The Tie in 1968 that blemished the Dowling-Hill era. I remembered 1974, when we came in 6–0 in the league but lost 21—16 to tie Harvard for the title. I remembered 1975, when we were headed for a 7—7 tie and a three-way share of the title with Harvard and Dartmouth, only to lose 10—7 in the final minute. I remembered 1979, when we were 8—0 on the season but lost 22—7. And of course I remembered The Game two seasons earlier, when both teams were 5—1 and we came up just short in Kelly Ryan's final contest. Our senior tackle Glover Lawrence could tell you about another disappointing loss to Harvard. His father, Ab Lawrence, was the captain in John Pont's final game in 1964, when Yale lost 18—14, only its second loss of the season. The trick was to use this history as motivation without making the players defensive and tentative. It does no good to play scared. A team that dwells on how awful it would be to lose often fulfills that destiny.

I counted on Jon Reese that week as much as I ever depended on a captain to motivate the team. He commanded enormous respect from the players, not only because of the work ethic and enthusiasm he had displayed consistently for three years but because of his courage after the accident. He was still feeling pain in his face, but he played at full strength. It helped, too, that Reese and the other seniors had known both victory and defeat against Harvard. They had bounced back from the Kelly Ryan loss to beat Harvard 26—17 the next year. That was an example of how a win in The Game made a struggling year feel like a glorious one. We were 2—6—1 on the season and 2—3—1 in the league going in, but beating Harvard washed away a lot of the disappointment.

Nearly sixty thousand people jammed Yale Bowl to witness the last chapter of what had been a storybook season. Unfortunately, the script had an unhappy ending for us. We lost 37—20 and had to settle for a share of the Ivy League title with Princeton. Harvard had saved its best performance of the season for The Game. Its multiflex offense had sputtered on and off during the season, due partly to injuries, but it worked with dazzling efficiency that afternoon. Our defense, which had controlled Princeton the previous week, simply couldn't contain the reverses and crossing pass patterns that Coach

Joe Restic's forces threw at us. Harvard used plays it hadn't run all year. We were known for our aggressive defense, and they used it against us. They made us overcommit to the point where we were tackling the wrong people. Glover Lawrence made a beautiful tackle in the backfield only to find out that the kid had handed off on an end-around play.

I walked through the locker room after the game among a bunch of brokenhearted kids. Many of them were just sitting in front of their lockers with their heads hanging down. Except for Jon Reese. He was going from one teammate to the next, hugging them and thanking them for being such an important part of his life. What an amazing gesture. In this moment of heartbreak, Jon had the presence of mind to find something positive. He understood that this would be the last opportunity for the team to be together in the moments after battle, and it would be a waste not to find some joy despite the pain. Not only that, he understood the need to share it. It was an exhibition of maturity and character that made me as proud as anything a player could do on the field. When he saw me, he walked over and we stood there looking at each other for an awkward moment. I was trying to find the right thing to say, but it wouldn't come. It was dreadfully still except for the murmur of conversation and the locker room sounds of cleats dropping on the floor or water in the showers. After a moment, as if on cue, we both said the same thing. "I wanted so much to win this one for you."

CHAPTER ELEVEN

Unlikely Hero

Most good athletes run with their toes pointed slightly inward. Darin Kehler ran like a duck, with his feet pointed out. Most good quarterbacks are taller than six feet, with enough body weight to sustain the punishment of on-rushing linemen. Darin Kehler stood just under 5-foot-10 and weighed about 165 pounds. Most good quarterbacks work on their throwing skills year-round and go to sleep at night with visions of pass receivers picking their way through zone coverage. Darin Kehler gave up football after a freshman season spent primarily as a defensive back to concentrate on baseball. In September of his soph-omore year at Yale he wasn't dreaming of completing third-down passes, he was dreaming of turning ground balls into double plays as an infielder on the fall baseball team. Given these facts, you can imagine how desperate our situation was on September 26, 1988, when I called this wisp of a second baseman—pitcher in his residential college and asked him to help us out at quarterback.

It was 8:30 on a Monday morning, two days after Connecticut had punished us 41–0. I remember staring at the phone in a moment of hesitation, listening to the traffic outside my second-floor window in the Ray Tompkins House. I had never openly solicited a student to come out for the team, but there was a first time for everything. I wondered how my longtime friend Bo Schembechler would feel if he ever ran so low on quarterbacks at the University of Michigan that he had to draft one from the fall baseball team. Bo had teased me publicly about how easy it was to coach in the Ivy League, but if he had been with me in my office that morning, he might have had second thoughts.

Finally, I dialed the phone and made my pitch to Darin. My call wasn't a total surprise to him, because Joe Benanto, the head baseball coach and freshman football coach, had already sounded him out on the idea. Still, it must have seemed odd for him to pick up the phone and hear my voice. I had been aware of him as a freshman player, but I doubt that we had ever had a personal conversation of any significance. I made sure he understood our situation, that our No. 1 quarterback was out for the season with a torn knee ligament and our two backups, senior Mark Brubaker and sophomore John Furjanic, were hobbled by injury. I told him I could empathize with his desire to concentrate on baseball, because I had had my sights on professional baseball when I was a sophomore at Miami of Ohio. But I let him know that we had a need, and I asked him to help us out. He was terrific. He just said, "Coach, if you think I can help, I'll be glad to."

His only concern was how the players would feel about his joining the team two weeks into the season. He had missed the brutal two-a-day practice sessions during preseason. So I put the question to the team as a whole, and they left no doubt that he would be welcome. Darin Kehler did more than just "help us out." Over the next three seasons, that little son of a gun left his mark on the history of Yale football and became the central figure in the last of my ten Ivy League championship teams.

Bob Verduzco was the heir apparent to Kelly Ryan at quarterback as we began the 1988 season. He wasn't as big as Kelly and didn't have as strong an arm, but he had the all-around talent to become one of the best in the Ivy League. He had been an all-state quarterback at Soquel High School in Santa Cruz, California, where he was team captain and most valuable player. He also started at point guard on the basketball team for four years and played baseball for two years. Furthermore, he was class salutatorian and senior class president. A typical Yale recruit, you might say.

After a sophomore season as Ryan's understudy, Bob stepped into the starting role as a junior. He was under center when we opened the season against Brown on a sunny day in Providence, Rhode Island. For the first time in two years, I had a quarterback with two healthy legs. It was a good feeling that lasted for slightly less than one half of one game. On the last play of the second period, Verduzco was caught flat-footed just as he delivered a pass and was cut down by a Brown tackler who drove his helmet into the side of his knee. Bob's cleats got caught up in the grass, and the impact bent the joint to the inside, tearing the ligaments. It was less a cheap shot than an awkward moment when Bob became a stationary target and paid the price.

What happened in the second half was truly amazing. There is simply no way to explain how that young man managed to play the rest of the game despite obvious pain. But he did. We didn't realize the extent of the injury or we never would have let him play. He was so eager not to lose the starting berth that he convinced the trainers that he was okay. They taped him up, and he struggled through the rest of the game, which ended in a 24–24 tie. In the locker room after the game, Bob leaned on a pair of crutches and told reporters that he might have to miss a couple of practices but assured them that the injury was just a bruise and that he would be in the lineup the next Saturday. Sadly, it was two years before he was healthy enough to play football again.

The injury was far worse than anyone imagined at the time. The doctors told me later that there was absolutely no support left in his knee because the ligaments were torn completely away from the bone. They were dumbfounded that he had been able to stand up, let alone play football in the second half at Brown. There was nothing but tape holding that knee together. Bob Verduzco didn't give up easily. After surgery, he spent two years of intense and painful rehabilitation. He was back in preseason training camp two years later. He never got back into the starting lineup, however, because by then his replacement, Darin Kehler, was firmly entrenched, and Nick Crawford, another mobile quarterback, was a solid backup.

Joe Benanto gets the credit for suggesting the call to Kehler. As head baseball coach and freshman football coach, he knew what kind of athlete Darin was. It took me a little longer to be convinced. Kehler's high school credentials in Valley View, Pennsylvania, as a scholar and and athlete, were not unlike Verduzco's. He was an honorable-mention all-state quarterback for two seasons and made the all-county team at quarterback and defensive back both years. His team was 13–0 in his junior year. He also wrestled and played baseball, making the all-country team as a second baseman and pitcher in his last two years. Furthermore, he was junior class president and graduated No. 1 in his class. Yet another typical Yale recruit.

Five days after the emergency call-up, Darin was in uniform for our game at the Naval Academy. He watched from the sideline as Navy trounced us 41–7 with its well-oiled wishbone offense. If I had known then that we would retool our offense to the wishbone the following year to take advantage of Darin's running skills, I would have had him pay particular attention to the Midshipmen's offense that afternoon. The situation was almost the same the following Saturday, when a high-powered Army team invaded Yale Bowl as a thirty-point favorite. It was the last game in a murderous three-week stretch against Connecticut, Navy, and Army, and it was the second consecutive week we faced a wishbone offense. We fared a little better, but we still lost 33–18. Linebackers Jon Reese and Don Lund sparked a strong defensive effort, and tailback Buddy Zachery ran eighty-two yards from scrimmage for a touchdown. Without that fourth-quarter run and a fumble recovery on the ensuing kick-off that led to a touchdown, the score would have been worse. Still, there were some things to be encouraged about. Or, to state the case another way, I didn't get the feeling the kids were entirely demoralized by three straight physical beatings. The resilience of Yale athletes never ceased to amaze me.

The best thing to happen that afternoon was that Columbia beat Princeton 16–13 to end its forty-four-game losing streak, the longest in the nation. That took the pressure off us for our game with Columbia the next Saturday in Yale Bowl. I tried never to look beyond our next opponent, but I must admit that I had begun to worry about Columbia even before the Army game. The potential embarrassment of being the first team to lose to the Lions in five years was hard to ignore. I didn't want that fear hanging over our heads all week, certainly not when we were 0–3–1 on the season,

physically hurting from three tough games, and without a quarterback healthy enough to run the option. I was also happy for Columbia coach Larry McElreavy. He was an assistant on my staff for a few
years and the head coach at the University of New Haven before
moving to Columbia.

Instead of a potential embarrassment, the game against Columbia was a turning point in our season and a coming-out of sorts for
Darin Kehler. We were tied 10–10 midway through the third period
when I figured it was time to see whether Kehler could open up our
offense with his mobility. He had taken a few snaps the week before
against Army, but this was his first extended experience and his first
taste of action with the game still on the line. Poor Mark Brubaker
simply couldn't run well enough on his injured leg to make the
option work, and we sorely needed to get Kevin Callahan, Kevin
Brice, and Buddy Zachery to the outside to open up our running
game and spread the defense. Kehler was exactly what we needed.
He completed only one pass in four attempts, but he added a dimension to our ground game that led to two late touchdowns and a
24–10 victory. Zachery had touchdown runs of thirty-four and
thirty-two yards and amassed 138 yards in 18 carries. It was the first
indication that Darin might become more than an emergency call-
up to provide depth at quarterback. It was obvious he had the
potential to be a first-string player.

Both Brubaker and Kehler played the next week at Penn, but,
to be honest, neither of them sparked much of an offense. It's too
bad, because our defense gave us a chance to spring a significant
upset against the undefeated Ivy League leaders. Oddly, despite our
troubles, we entered the game unbeaten in the conference. The
season-opening tie with Brown and the win over Columbia had
been our only league games. Penn was 5–0 overall and 3–0 in the
Ivies. Penn was determined to avenge its last-minute defeat of the
previous year, when Bob Shoop had caught Kelly Ryan's pass and
scampered into the end zone in the final seconds. The Quakers
barely hung on, however, for a 10–3 squeaker before a homecoming crowd of twenty-eight thousand at Franklin Field in Phila-

delphia. We had the ball deep in their territory in the final minute but couldn't score.

The Darin Kehler era began in earnest at Dartmouth on October 29, 1988. That was the first time we started him and the first time he showed himself to be an impact player. Buddy Zachery was the star of our 22–13 victory, rushing for 174 yards on 26 carries, but it was the threat of a running quarterback that made the yardage possible.

At the end of the third period we mounted a drive that previewed Kehler as a dominant quarterback in the Ivy League. We were in a vulnerable situation. Dartmouth had come back from a 12–3 deficit to take a 13–12 lead, and I could tell that we were flat. Maybe the offense didn't yet believe in the new quarterback. Maybe he didn't yet believe in himself. I'm not sure I believed in him yet myself. Whatever the case, we had lost our first-half momentum and were in danger of reverting to a pattern of short offensive possessions followed by long, debilitating series for the defense. Starting from our own 11-yard line, Darin engineered an offensive drive that changed the complexion of the game and the team. The march took nineteen plays, consumed nine minutes and twenty-six seconds, covered eighty-two yards, and concluded with a 24-yard field goal by Scott Walton. We didn't score a touchdown, but the three points put us in the lead to stay. More important, the sustained drive gave our offense confidence and our defense a needed rest. On our next play from scrimmage, Zachery ran fifty-seven yards for an insurance touchdown and a 22–13 final margin of victory.

The emotional boost we got from Darin Kehler and Buddy Zachery didn't last long. We got hammered by Cornell 26–0 the next Saturday. I don't know which was tougher on us, the Cornell defense or the gale force winds that whipped through Cornell's hilltop campus in Ithaca, New York. At any rate, we barely managed a hundred yards of offense. The wind was so strong that we called only three pass plays all game. Darin completed all three of them, but our offense was unbalanced and ineffectual.

I don't imagine that I was very pleasant to be around the next day. I was exhausted after the five-hour bus ride from Cornell, which began in a rainstorm and ended around midnight. I woke up Sunday morning tired, worried, and disappointed. When I got the usual day-after-the-game phone call from Bob Casey at the New Haven newspaper, I wasn't sure what to tell him or what he was going to ask. I thought that we were doing the best we could as coaches with the talent we had, and I felt some sense of excitement at the dimension Darin Kehler had provided, but I wasn't sure we were ready for the season-ending games with Princeton and Harvard.

Maybe I should have anticipated the question Casey asked me, but I didn't. It came out of the blue, and my answer was probably a little more candid than it would have been if I had been prepared for it. I didn't say anything that wasn't true or anything I'm sorry for, but I surprised myself with some of the things I said. Casey, who was a veteran sportswriter and a real pro, wanted to know whether the next season was going to be my last. It was a legitimate question, I suppose. I was two games from the end of my twenty-fourth season at Yale, and it was natural to wonder whether I had decided to call it quits after my twenty-fifth. But good heavens! Retirement was the farthest thing from my mind. Oh, I knew the day would have to come sometime. I wasn't getting any younger, after all. But, gosh, I was enjoying the job at fifty-eight as much as I ever had, and the thought of giving it up voluntarily was ridiculous. I certainly didn't feel old or burned out. In fact, I burned with more competitive desire than ever. People say that you lose a little of the competitive edge as you grow older. That wasn't true with me. If anything, the victories felt better and the defeats hurt worse as the years went on. Furthermore, retirement was simply not something I would ever contemplate in the middle of a season.

I might have been annoyed at the question if another less-seasoned sportswriter had asked it. Somehow it seemed to carry the suggestion that if I wasn't planning to step aside, perhaps I should be. But I knew Bob was just doing his job. He had to ask the question on the off chance that the answer was yes. Besides, he knew that unexpected questions sometimes result in unguarded comments, and that's just what he got. The column he wrote in the next day's *New Haven Register* was accurate and sensitive. After a fifteen-year stretch with only one losing season, we had struggled through three losing seasons in the last six and were about to have the fourth. We hadn't won the Ivy League title since 1981, and I could feel Yale's dominance within the conference slipping as the Academic Index began to work against us. The Academic Index was a formula that tied the academic standards of the football team to those of the student body as a whole. It was intended to level the playing field within the Ivy League, but instead it forced us to recruit teams with stiffer academic standards than other teams in the conference, because Yale's admission standards were higher.

I don't know whether I was feeling pessimistic and defensive about our long-term prospects or whether I was just down after the loss to Cornell. Whatever the case, Casey's question struck a nerve. I made a few cutting remarks about the Academic Index and the Yale admissions process that were out of character. It was one of the few times I disparaged Yale or the league in public. I can't say that I'm sorry I did. The things I said were true and became obvious to everyone in the years ahead.

Casey wrote that Yale was competing with "one hand tied behind its back" and quoted me as saying, "Yale has to get into the fold with the rest of the league in admissions and everything else. Right now we're not near it. We need a complete turnaround." If only my warnings had been heeded. My candid remarks did us no good against Princeton the next Saturday. The Tigers came into Yale Bowl and beat us 24–7 before nearly twenty-four thousand people. It was their first win in New Haven since 1966, the year before their quarterback, Jason Garrett, was born. Garrett, incidentally, completed 21 of 26 passes for 259 yards, five of them to his brother, Judd, who also ran for 76 yards.

Thank heaven for Harvard. Yale graduates like to joke that the only reason for Harvard's existence is to provide an opportunity for Yale football teams to redeem losing seasons. Come to think of it, maybe some of them aren't joking. Anyway, 1988 was one of those seasons when we were plenty happy to have Harvard as the final game of a disappointing season. The Game is even more important at the end of a losing campaign than at the climax of a winning one. The rivalry is so strong that a victory can make the most frustrating season feel like a successful one. The significance is magnified for the seniors who will remember The Game for the rest of their lives. Our captain, Don Lund, made that point to the players, reminding them that he and the other seniors had never beaten Harvard. He told them that he didn't want to go through life with that stigma attached to his football career.

Coincidentally, Harvard coach Joe Restic had also lost his first-string quarterback in the opening game, when Tom Yohe suffered a stress fracture in his shin. Yohe was back for The Game, but Restic, cagey as always, wasn't saying whether he or the backup, Rod Mac-Leod, would start. The noisy crowd of thirty-six thousand on a cold, gray day in Harvard Stadium was typical for The Game, even though each team had only two wins and there was no Ivy League title at stake. Not even the Big Three crown was in play, because Princeton had beaten us both. The national telecast by ESPN may have added some excitement, but I don't think the players paid that much attention. There was nothing on the line but pride, and that's when character counts most.

Our offensive game plan was as simple as it was obvious. Run the ball. Run it again. Then run it some more. A successful Ivy League coach quickly learns to make the most of the talent he has. That's true in all sports at all levels, but it's particularly true in a conference in which the truly outstanding players are few and far between. You can't always employ the kind of offense you would like if you don't have the players who can make it work. I was not deaf to the criticism over the years that our playbook was too conservative. Alumni sometimes asked me why we ran so many off-tackle plays instead of passing more. It was an understandable criticism, but when a coach makes a cold assessment of his quarterback's throwing ability, his receivers' speed, and the skill of the opposition's defensive secondary, it's sometimes best to run the ball up the gut and accept whatever criticism comes with it. Our best attack that afternoon against Harvard was on the ground. So that's what we did. On the very first series, we ran the ball seventeen consecutive times, all the way into the Harvard end zone. It was the same kind of sustained drive that Darin had given us against Dartmouth. It covered eighty-three yards, lasted for just under nine minutes, and set the tone for the game, which we won 26–17.

I was delighted for all our seniors. In fact, I got every one of them into the game. But I was particularly pleased for Mark Brubaker, who played a critical role in the win. He had been shoved to the background because of his early injury and Darin's surprising emergence, but when we needed him at a crucial time in his final game, he responded brilliantly. We put him in at the end of the second period, when we needed a hurry-up passing attack. We had taken possession on our own 36-yard line, but with only 2:22 left in the half, there wasn't enough time to grind it out on the ground. Mark, working out of the shotgun formation, took us sixty-four yards for the score, hitting Kevin Callahan for the go-ahead touchdown just twenty-nine seconds before the half.

We ended up running the ball sixty-one times, occasionally out of the wishbone formation, and throwing only six passes, just one of them by Darin. It was incomplete. Callahan rushed for ninety-seven yards and Kevin Brice for ninety-eight. It had been an up-and-down season, but it ended on a high note. I shudder to think what a disaster it might have been if Darin Kehler hadn't tossed his baseball mitt on the shelf two games into the season to take up a sport he never expected to play again. Hey, you do what you have to do.

When Darin Kehler reported for two-a-day practices before his junior year, he was ready for football and we were ready for him. Having him in camp from the beginning made a huge difference. We had made a decision during the off-season to retool our offense to the wishbone to take full advantage of Darin's mobility. I wasn't in favor of the change at first, but Seb LaSpina, the offensive coordinator, and Bob Estock, the offensive line coach, talked me into it. Of course I take full credit for it now. We might not have taken the chance if we hadn't had a transfer quarterback from Davidson named Nick Crawford as a backup. He was swift enough to step into the wishbone if anything happened to Darin, which was always a possibility, given his size.

I was concerned about introducing wholesale changes to the offense without the benefit of spring practice. The wishbone meant a whole new pattern of blocking assignments and pass routes. It wasn't just a matter of getting the running backs and the quarterback into sync for the option play. It was more than that, and we had only a few weeks of two-a-days to install it. Darin Kehler proved to be a natural for the wishbone. Our offense jelled quickly and we went 8–2 on the season, sharing the Ivy League championship with Princeton. If not for the loss to Harvard, we would have had the title outright.

We kept the wishbone under wraps during preseason. We didn't even run it in our scrimmage against the University of New Haven. The surprise worked perfectly in our 12–3 opening-game victory against Brown, when Kehler ran for 107 yards, the most for a quarterback since Tom Doyle ran for 160 against Dartmouth seventeen years earlier. Kehler broke Doyle's record the next game by rushing for 186 yards in a 33–17 win over Lehigh. I was pinching myself, thinking, geez, who's going to stop this kid. Well, Connecticut gave me the answer the next week. The Huskies held Kehler to minus yardage and beat us 31–20. Fortunately, that turned out to be his only bad game. He came back with a 92-yard performance against Colgate the next week and had a 103-yard game against Columbia.

The surprise of Kehler's performance that year was his success throwing the ball. He wasn't a great passer, but he was plenty good enough, especially when our wishbone running attack caught the defense off guard. When we saw the secondary creeping up to cover the run, we found ways to get our receivers open. Darin completed

11 of 15 passes for 130 yards against Lehigh. With his 186 rushing, that was 316 yards of total offense, not bad for a second baseman. He rushed for 903 yards on the season, the best single-season total of any Yale quarterback in history, and passed for 870. We rolled into the Harvard game with seven wins against the single loss to UConn, and we were ranked twentieth in the nation in Division I-AA. So much for reputation and momentum. The Cantabs played their multiflex offense to perfection and handed us a 37–20 loss in Jon Reese's final game.

We were picked to win the Ivy League championship in the 1990 preseason polls, Darin Kehler's senior year. That was always a bad sign. You like to sneak up on people the way we had the previous season with the wishbone. We beat Brown 27–21 in the season opener, but because we were the favorite, the narrow win seemed almost like a disappointment. Brown, under new coach Mickey Kwiatkowski, threw fifty-one passes against our inexperienced secondary, and it almost worked. Fortunately, Kehler had an even more effective passing day. He connected on 9 of 18 passes for 205 yards and two touchdowns. The big play was a fourth-and-fourteen conversion late in the third quarter from Brown's 34. Darin dropped back and hit Jim Gouveia up the middle for twenty-six yards.

We won again the next week, but it wasn't pretty. It was a rainy day made all the more dreary by one of the smallest Yale Bowl crowds I can remember. They announced the crowd at 6,458, but it was closer to half that with all the no-shows. By the end of the game, I doubt whether there were one thousand people left in the stadium. I tried not to let it bother me as the crowds disappeared through the years, but it was hard not to notice so few people in a stadium that holds seventy thousand.

We almost lost the game, too, although we were heavily favored. We were losing 17–10 in the fourth quarter when we got a break and recovered a fumble at their 35. Nick Crawford got us into the end zone in just five plays, which put the pressure on me to either kick the extra point for a 17–17 tie or take a chance on a two-point conversion for the lead. I wasn't sure we would get the ball back, so we took what figured to be our last chance for the win. I sent Kehler back in and called a somewhat risky pass play we had used with considerable success ever since the Brian Dowling era. We called it 432R. The tight end, in this case Chris Warner, lined up like a blocker, then broke toward an open space in the middle just beyond the line of scrimmage. Kehler connected with him and we scored the go-ahead points. Still, we almost lost the game when Lafayette tried a 38-yard field goal with seven seconds left. The kick drifted wide to the right, but only by inches.

The first two games had been victories, but they certainly weren't confidence builders. Particularly not with Connecticut next up at the Bowl. Matters got worse during the week when I got word that Darin was injured and unlikely to see action that Saturday. He had taken a shot in the lower back and was in considerable pain. To be safe, we started Nick Crawford, and we even got Bob Verduzco into a little action as well. But frankly, it wouldn't have mattered who we played at quarterback. Yale played one of the worst games in my thirty-two years, and we got trounced 44–7. Crawford was one of the few kids who played well. He ran for 105 yards and completed 10 of 14 passes for 77 yards. After the game, I told the press we had played like a junior high school team. I figured I could get the players' attention if they read my comments in the newspaper. God knows I had already ripped them as harshly as I could to their faces, both at halftime and after the game. I was really disgusted at the lack of effort.

The situation continued to deteriorate in the next two weeks. Darin recovered enough to start against Colgate, but the back injury clearly affected his speed and strength. After a quarter, I could see he wasn't ready to run the wishbone, and I replaced him with Crawford. We lost 30–7. Darin wasn't at full strength the next week at Dartmouth either, although he played the whole game. We lost again 27–17 in a mud bath. Those first five weeks of the 1990 season show how quickly things can change. High hopes can turn sour quickly. After two ugly wins, we had lost three in a row, and once again we were trying to get things done with a quarterback who wasn't playing at full strength. I felt bad for Darin. Here was an All–Ivy League quarterback as a junior looking to add to the Yale records he had set the year before, but after half the season he still hadn't gotten untracked. The good news was we had only one league loss and our next opponent was a winless Columbia team that was getting better under coach Ray Tellier but was still as good an opportunity as we could ask for to help us out of our slump.

And that's what we did. We beat the Lions 31–7, thanks in large part to a goal-line stand in the last minute of the first half. Ahead 7–0, Columbia had first and goal at our 4, with more than a minute to play. They sent the same running back into the line four straight times but monster back John Furjanic, the converted quarterback; defensive back Maurice Saah, a converted running back; and captain Chris Gaughan, the middle linebacker, wouldn't give ground. Without that defensive stand, the game would have been lost, I'm convinced of that. They had outgained us 211 yards to 83 in the half, and a 14–0 deficit at the half would have been tough for a wishbone team to overcome. Instead, we scored off two quick turnovers in the second half and never looked back. In fact, that goal-line stand might have been the turning point for the year.

We kept the momentum the next week at Philadelphia, beating Penn 27–10, and suddenly we found ourselves tied for the league lead at 3–1. After five frustrating weeks, we had enjoyed two exciting ones. What would be next? Well, the down again, up again season turned abruptly down again. We ran into a powerful Cornell team the next week in the Bowl and lost 41–31. It was an explosion of offense on both sides, particularly on their side, and particularly from a back named Scott Oliaro. He ran for 288 yards on 35 carries, breaking a Cornell record held by the actor Ed Marinaro, who had finished second in the Heisman Trophy voting in 1971. The two teams piled up almost 900 yards of total offense in the game, 395 of it from Oliaro.

Darin Kehler's unlikely football career was down to two final games—Princeton and Harvard. Frankly, I didn't know what to expect from him or the team. It had been an unpredictable year of highs and lows, exciting prospects followed by frustrations. Strange as it sounds, we were still in the Ivy League championship picture. If we won our last two games and Dartmouth and Cornell each lost once, we would share the title. Not likely, but possible. With his injury, Darin hadn't put up the numbers that some people thought he would, but the Big Three games were still ahead, and they were like a second season at the end of every Yale schedule.

First up was Princeton in the Bowl, the last home game for Darin and the other seniors. With a share of the title at stake, we had a spirited week of practices. The game was to be telecast nationally by ESPN, and that just added to the excitement. Unfortunately, the weather on game day was awful. We played in a driving rainstorm with wind gusts of thirty miles per hour. As soon as I walked out of the tunnel into the Bowl, I knew it was going to be a mud bath. In fact, I was glad it was the last home game, because the field was sure to be torn up by the cleats. The rain didn't help the crowd either. With all the no-shows, they estimated the crowd at only 5,500, not exactly a good backdrop for a national TV audience.

I was worried that the field conditions would stymie our wishbone running attack. Slippery turf is not ideal for option plays that depend on speed to the corner and sharp cutbacks. Thank heavens for a duck-footed quarterback. Or maybe I should call him web-footed, in the conditions we faced that afternoon. Darin seemed to be running on a different surface than everyone else. He rushed for a modest sixty-five yards himself, but his quick feet and sure hands sprang Kevin Callahan, Jim Gouveia, and Chris Kouri for important gains. Callahan gained 101 yards in his last home game, his first hundred-yard performance ever. In the second half, Princeton's defense seemed to sag. Perhaps the Tigers were demoralized by the wind and rain, or simply worn out by our steady running attack. Whatever the case, we scored twenty-seven points and won the game 34–7.

The Harvard game the following Saturday shouldn't have been as easy as it was. Granted, the Cantabs were having an off year at 2–6 overall and 2–4 in the Ivy League, but we weren't exactly a power-house, and given the emotion of The Game, we could have been on the losing end of things as easily as the winning end. But fortune went our way right from the beginning. Kehler and the offense had their best game of the season behind the strong senior-dominated front line. And the defense kept a chokehold on Harvard's multiflex offense all afternoon. We won 34–19, and it was more decisive than the score indicates. Not only did Darin rush for 92 yards, he completed eight of nine passes for 113 yards. He finished his career seventh on Yale's all-time passing list with 1,816 yards and eighth on the all-time rushing list with 1,643.

I experienced one of those rare occasions late in the game when I could step back from the action and enjoy a brief moment of reverie. We were up 34–10 with just over five minutes left, and we had the ball around midfield. As I watched Darin break the huddle and bring the team to the line of scrimmage, I thought back to that Monday morning two years before when I called him in his room to ask him for help. Talk about unexpected dividends. That phone call produced a share of one championship, and I'm not sure we wouldn't have had another if he hadn't been hobbled for two or three games in midseason. Over two seasons, we had gone 14–4 when he was entirely healthy. It is fair to call those two seasons the Darin Kehler era. He wasn't the impact player that Brian Dowling, Calvin Hill, Dick Jauron, Kelly Ryan, John Pagliaro, and a few others had been in their time. But no one, except maybe Jon Reese the previous year, had as much to say about our success as Darin during 1989 and '90.

With five minutes to play and a twenty-four-point lead, I figured it was time for Darin to call it a career. I watched him run one final play, a routine pitchout for a 1-yard gain, and sent in a substitute quarterback. The mental picture I carry with me of that season is of Darin running to the sidelines with his arms raised in triumph and leaping into my arms. It was an improbable moment, but a damn sweet one.

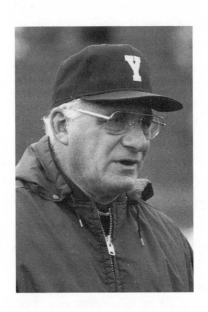

CHAPTER TWELVE

The Last Best Years

There was no more awe-inspiring setting in college football in the twentieth century than a Yale-Harvard game before a capacity crowd in the Bowl. It was more than a football game. It was a celebration of the bright college years at two of the world's greatest institutions of higher learning. And it was a contest between two schools and two sets of alumni whose animosity for one another was born of mutual respect. Neither side will ever admit that The Game contained elements of good humor and play-acting along with genuine feelings of superiority. But athletic rivalries of such intensity grow from balanced competitions between foes of similar ability, values, and preparation. There is no joy in beating a team that you don't fear and respect.

The victories my teams earned against Harvard were all the sweeter because of my admiration and personal fondness for long-time Crimson coach Joe Restic, and John Yovicsin before him. Many people don't know that Joe and his family were very close with my family and me. We spent time together at a summer football camp on Cape Cod, and I tried to recruit his son, Joe Jr., to play at Yale. I teased Joe about making a trade. If he would send Joe Jr. to Yale, I would send my oldest daughter, Kris, to Radcliffe. It didn't work out that way. Joe Jr. became an All-American at Notre Dame, and Kris went to La Salle, then the Yale Nursing School.

They tell me that the tailgate parties in the parking lots before The Game are unlike any others. I never got to do any tailgating myself, of course, so I have no firsthand knowledge. I was always in the Field House trying not to let the players and coaches see how nervous I was in the last minutes before we paraded the hundred yards or so past the tennis courts to the Bowl. But I'm told that the alumni showed up in furs and tweeds, set out tables with crystal wine goblets and fancy silverware, and feasted on anything from beer and hot dogs to champagne and caviar. A Dixieland jazz band wandered up and down the rows of barbecue pits, competing for attention with car stereos playing tapes of the Whiffenpoofs, Yale's traditional men's a cappella singing group.

The crowd for our game with Harvard on November 17, 1979, was the largest for The Game since 1947 and the largest for any game in the Bowl since the Army game in 1954. A record ten thousand tickets were sold in a single day, and by Tuesday the advance sale had reached sixty thousand. To handle the demand, an extra one thousand seats were set up on the field behind the end zones, which swelled the final tally to seventy-two thousand. The sports information office received requests for 150 press credentials. It was great to have that kind of excitement back on campus. As I've said, the week before the Harvard game was always a mixture of excitement and frustration. I sometimes wished that I could take the team off campus to some hideaway where no one could bother us. That would hardly be fair to the players, of course. They deserved the glory and attention, even if it nearly drove me crazy.

But let me back up and put that 1979 Harvard game in context.

Our prospects looked bright when two-a-day practices began in the fall, although I didn't realize at the time just how bright. We had talent, lots of it, and it was evenly mixed among sophomores, juniors, and seniors. We didn't have just two or three outstanding players, as we had come to expect in the Ivy League, we had eight or ten, and they were pretty well divided between offense and defense. I don't like to compare players or teams from different eras, but those players who moved into the rooms on the third floor of the Ray Tompkins House in the weeks before school opened made up the best collection of good players we ever had and launched our most successful three-year stretch from 1979 to 1981.

In spite of the obvious potential, I was a little surprised at our early success. We had graduated some talented players from a 5–2–2 team in 1978, including John Spagnola, the tight end who was drafted in the ninth round by the New England Patriots and ended up playing several seasons with the Philadelphia Eagles. Losing him, along with the other top receiver, Bob Krystyniak, left our passing attack in serious question. Incidentally, there's a classic scholar-athlete story about Spagnola on draft day. Most kids who expected to be selected stayed by the phone or watched the draft on TV, but Spags was fast asleep in his dormitory when the Patriots selected him. He had pulled an all-nighter, studying for a political science final the next day, and he couldn't stay awake. His teammate Rick Angelone knocked on his door with the news, but even then, Spags couldn't afford to celebrate. He just washed his face and went back to his poli sci notes.

The 1979 team had enough talent to make up for the loss of Spags and the other graduates. In fact, we turned out to be even better than people expected. No one predicted that we would become the class of the conference and waltz into the Harvard game undefeated, with undisputed possession of the Ivy League championship already assured. But with an explosive offense and a tremendous defense, that's just what we did.

Our main weapon was tailback Kenny Hill, who was converted to a defensive back when he got to the NFL, à la Dick Jauron and Gary Fencik. He played several seasons for the Raiders and finished his career with the New York Giants and Kansas City Chiefs. He showed up for his senior season a little heavier, at two hundred pounds, but just as fast as he was as a junior when he rushed for 910 yards. We timed him on grass at 4.46 seconds for the 40-yard dash. Believe me, we didn't get many players at Yale with that kind of size and speed. I knew that if we could break him into the secondary, our opponents were going to be picking cinders out of their eyes.

We were lucky to attract him because he had signed a letter of intent for a full scholarship at Louisiana State. Fortunately, the letter wasn't binding in the Ivy League, and at the last minute he changed his mind and came to Yale. His brother Charley was on our team, and I think that had a lot to do with his decision. So did Yale's academic reputation. He was a bright kid who wanted to be a doctor, and he majored in molecular biophysics and biochemistry. It seems as though half my players had that major. One of the qualities I really liked about Kenny was that he always talked about improving himself. You don't always find that in the good ones.

Hill was just one of several good players or good prospects we had in the backfield that year. I remember Dick Jauron visiting our one-day practice the previous spring and saying that he wished he had been surrounded by so many talented backs. Hill's senior year was Rich Diana's sophomore year. It was also the sophomore season for quarterback John Rogan, the junior season for fullback John Nitti, a future captain, and the senior year for tailback Mike Sullivan. As good a quarterback as Rogan turned out to be, he had a hard time getting playing time as a sophomore because of senior Dennis Dunn, a transfer from Montana State, who was a strong enough runner to have played tailback. The same thing happened with future Buffalo Bills quarterback Joe Dufek, who had to wait to become the full-time starter until Rogan graduated. For good measure, we had an excellent place kicker in senior David Schwartz, whose .667 field goal percentage, on sixteen of twenty-four attempts, was still the career mark at Yale when I retired. This was a period of feast, not famine. We were blessed with the best array of offensive talent since Brian Dowling and Calvin Hill in 1968. Still, it was our defense that made the difference. Pat Conran, Fred Leone, Serge Mihaly, and Dennis Tulsiak were sophomores. Kevin Czinger, David Novosel, and Jeff Rohrer were juniors. And captain Tim Tumpane, Arnie Pinkston, and Skip Porter were seniors. That was quite a lineup.

Not surprisingly, defense was the deciding factor in a shaky 13–12 win over Brown in the opener. More specifically, Kevin Czinger was the deciding factor. Although he was still weak from a bout of mononucleosis and he was double-teamed most of the game, he managed to block two punts, which we converted into our only touchdowns. Mike Sullivan, the senior tailback who had eclipsed John Pagliaro's rushing records at Derby High School, scored the winning touchdown. He was tackled before he got into the end zone but managed to stretch the ball over the goal line before his knee touched the ground. I was delighted for Mike. He had missed most of his junior season with a series of injuries, and he surely deserved to have a big play in the Bowl.

Our second win was just as precarious. We beat Connecticut 24–17, thanks in large part to a John Rogan pass that Kenny Hill couldn't quite handle. Fortunately, Dan Stratton caught the deflection and carried it thirty-nine yards for a touchdown. Some of the UConn people dismissed it as a lucky play, but sometimes you make your own luck. In this case, Stratton broke off his pass pattern and ran to the point of the action when he saw Rogan start to throw to Hill. When you put yourself in the right place at the right time, good things happen.

If there was any doubt about our defensive capabilities, it was erased on the third Saturday, when we shut out Colgate 17–0. We intercepted five passes, recovered two fumbles, and held them to minus 14 yards rushing on 31 carries. It was more of the same the next week in a 3–0 win over Dartmouth. Obviously, I wasn't pleased with the offense, but the defense was outstanding. We allowed them only three first downs, 53 yards rushing, and 31 yards passing. They had Jeff Kemp, son of Buffalo Bills great, senator, and and vice presidential candidate Jack Kemp, at quarterback, and future Cincinnati Bengals coach Dave Shula, son of Miami Dolphins coach Don Shula, at split end. Next came a 37–7 win at Columbia. To be honest, the Lions weren't a particularly tough challenge, but I was encouraged that we finally exploded offensively and had one of the best defensive games statistically I ever saw at Yale. For the second straight week, we didn't allow our opposition a first down in the second half. Columbia had minus 11 yards rushing on 28 carries, 45 yards of total offense, and only three first downs for the game to our twenty-eight. Sports Illustrated picked senior linebacker Skip Porter as Defensive Player of the Week.

That catapulted us to the top of the nation's defensive statistics. We led Division I—and remember, all the major schools were in the same division then—in total defense, with 143 yards allowed per game. Texas was second, with 168. And we led the nation in rushing yardage allowed, with 45.5 per game. Nebraska was a distant second, at 67.7. We were under no delusions about the caliber of opposition we faced compared with the teams Texas, Nebraska, and the major powers were playing, but we enjoyed the recognition just the same.

We were feeling pretty good about ourselves the next week when we played Penn in the Bowl, but I knew full well that the opposition and pressure were going to get tougher as we went along. We got past Penn 24–6, thanks to a 100-yard rushing performance from our quarterback, Dennis Dunn. The Quakers were so worried about Kenny Hill's speed to the outside on the option play that Dennis was able to find soft spots by cutting back to the inside. We had one more game to play, at Cornell, before the traditional Big Three games with Princeton and Harvard. We managed to win, 23–20, but it was our third victory by three points or less, and it was the second time we might have lost if not for a deflected pass play. This time the batted pass saved us from certain defeat. We were down 20–17 with fourth and long on our own 33-yard line and just over two minutes to play. Everyone in the stadium knew that we had to pass, and the best option John Rogan could find was a 20-yard throw to Dan Stratton right in front of coach Bob Blackman and the Cornell bench. Their linebacker Paul Dale almost intercepted it, but the ball bounced off his hands. Stratton made a grab for it, but he couldn't handle it either. Finally, Kenny Hill hauled it in to give us a first down and new life. Several plays later, with time running out, Rogan looped a 13-yarder to Bob Rostomily in the end zone for the winning touchdown. Rogan played only the second and fourth quarters but completed 9 of 13 passes for 195 yards and two touchdowns and scored the other on a 1-yard keeper.

We hadn't yet shown ourselves to be a dominant team, but we were riding a ten-game winning streak and a twelve-game unbeaten streak, which had begun with consecutive ties against Columbia and Pennsylvania the previous season. I won't deny that a measure of good luck had helped along the way. Whatever the case, we began preparations for the season-ending games against Princeton and

Harvard with a proven defense, a talented and still-percolating offense, and only one significant injury. Fred Leone had broken his leg against Penn.

Frank Navarro, the Princeton coach, told the New Jersey newspapers that the spirit on his campus the week before the Yale game was the best he had seen it in ten or fifteen years. The kids were pretty well psyched on our campus, too, especially after news got out that some Princeton students had dognapped Bingo, the Yale bulldog. It's no wonder the Princeton kids were stirred up. We had beaten them an incredible twelve straight years, and it looked as though this might be the year for the Tigers to stop the bleeding. They were 4–1 in the Ivy League and could tie us at 5–1 with a win. Furthermore, they had beaten Harvard, and a victory would give them the Big Three title. So passions were running high on both sides when a crowd of twenty-three thousand settled into Palmer Stadium, especially after their mascot, a student dressed up in a Tiger suit, carried Bingo across the field before the game and turned him over to the Yale cheerleaders.

Emotion did Princeton no good, however. We handled them pretty well in a 35–10 triumph that would have been more one-sided if not for a 92-yard interception return for a touchdown in the fourth quarter when the outcome was no longer in doubt. Their offense came close to scoring only once, but we stopped them on fourth and 1 at our 6-yard line. Kenny Hill ran 19 times for 129 yards, including a 64-yard touchdown in the first quarter. The victory gave us the Ivy title outright and increased our unbeaten string to thirteen over two seasons. In other words, we were in deep trouble, emotionally and historically, for John Harvard's visit the next Saturday in the Bowl.

It's easy to see why The Game of 1979 attracted that huge crowd of seventy-two thousand. It didn't seem to matter that Harvard was having an off year, at 2–6 overall and 2–4 in the conference. The Game provided a rare opportunity to see whether Yale could wrap up its first undefeated, untied season since Mike Pyle, the future Chicago Bears center, captained a 9–0 team under Jordan Olivar in 1960. Yale's last perfect season before that had been an 8–0 team in 1923, coached by T. A. D. Jones and captained by Bill Mallory.

Sleep didn't come easy that week. I hadn't been associated with a perfect season since my senior season at Parma High School in 1948, and the prospect of achieving that ultimate satisfaction fueled the normal excitement of Harvard week to an excruciating level. My main emotion, even more than the anticipation of the competition itself, was concern for what my old friend Joe Restic might have in store. Once again, we faced the irrefutable law of Yale football: There is no greater danger than a Harvard football team bent on redeeming an inglorious season with a glorious victory over Yale.

Coach Restic had endured a difficult season, no doubt about that, but the lack of success was due in large part to injuries. He had lost so many quarterbacks that he actually abandoned his signature multiflex offense for a simpler set of plays and alignments. It did not escape our notice, however, that his original starting QB, Burke St. John, was back in the lineup after missing five games with a knee injury. He had started the week before against Penn and thrown three touchdowns in a 41–26 victory.

As the week wore on, I felt like I was the only one at Yale who was worried about Harvard. I'm sure that wasn't the case, but I was an incurable worrier, and I did some of my best worrying in the weeks before we played the Crimson, especially that year, when the scenario seemed perfect for an upset. Naturally, I was relieved when game time finally arrived. I can't say that I was entirely satisfied with our preparation—I never was—but I was reasonably comfortable. We had the two ingredients a team needs most to avoid upsets: a good defense and a powerful running attack. Kenny Hill's rushing yardage as a senior wasn't as impressive as it had been as a junior, but he was such a threat with his size and speed that his presence alone gave us a potent weapon. Every team we played keyed its defense on him, which freed us up to do other things and run other backs. Even with the extra attention he faced,

Kenny averaged four yards per carry and led the team with 669 yards going into that final game.

When we left the field after our early warmups to go back to the halftime room under the stands, I noticed that the Bowl was filling up fast. I guess the fans were more eager than usual to leave their tailgate parties and take a seat for The Game. After our pregame meeting and prayer, we ran back through the players' tunnel into a rollicking stadium. The crowd was on its feet cheering, and so many people were blowing airhorns that I could barely hear the Yale Precision Marching Band playing "Boola, Boola." I took a moment to bask in the atmosphere, then walked to midfield to greet Coach Restic. I don't have the words to describe the emotions I felt in moments like that. There was a vague awareness that this was the culmination of an enormous effort from the coaches, players, trainers, equipment people, and many others. There was a sense that this moment, this wonderful scene, was the result of months of recruiting, two-a-day practices in the summer heat, frosty practices in November twilights, late nights evaluating films, and God knows how many sleepless hours worrying about game plans, injuries, and the crazy bounces footballs take. The reverie was fleeting, just a few seconds perhaps, before I turned my attention to the business at hand. I always liked the expression "put your game face on." In a matter of minutes, I was locked into the game.

It didn't take us long to realize that it wasn't going to be easy. In eight games, no team had mounted a sustained drive against us, but Harvard opened the game by driving seventy-five yards in thirteen plays for a touchdown. I thought, oh boy, we're in trouble. Restic, cagey as always, surprised us with an unbalanced line. He put two tight ends on the same side and ran Jim Callinan, a little-used junior fullback who had been Kevin Czinger's teammate at St. Ignatius High School in Cleveland, to the strong side. It drove us all crazy, but it particularly upset Kevin, who didn't like his former teammate ripping off yardage against our defense, which had led the nation against the run. Late in the game, Callinan did a little hotdogging in front of our bench, and if I hadn't grabbed Kevin by the jersey, he might have gone after him. I told him not to retaliate, just to remember it for next year.

Harvard's early drive rattled us. We committed two offside penalties that cost us possession and led to a Harvard touchdown. Injuries hurt us, too. Kenny Hill got dinged in the head early in the game, and though there was no evidence of a concussion, it affected his play the rest of the game. He fumbled five times, and Harvard recovered two of them. And fullback Mike Sullivan, an essential cog in our running attack all year, ended his career unceremoniously in the second quarter when he popped his shoulder out of the socket. In the locker room after the game, he said that he would just think of the loss as the end of his childhood and move on to the adult phase of his life.

We pulled within 13−7 in the third period when Dennis Dunn scored from four yards out, but we ultimately lost the game 22−7. We had squandered our chance for a perfect season, but as I told the players at the team banquet a week later, none of my teams lived up to its potential as well as that one. They played just one bad game. Unfortunately, it was the last one against Harvard, which meant they would spend their lives explaining how they blew it. Still, that first of three championship seasons was a memorable one. Tim Tumpane was named our Most Valuable Player, John Nitti was elected captain, and Kenny Hill played on national television in the Blue-Gray Game for Coach Restic. He ran 12 times for 52 yards, caught three passes for 31 yards, and scored the winning touchdown.

My main concern going into 1980 was our schedule. It was the toughest nonleague slate we had faced. After the Ivy League opener against Brown, we faced Connecticut, Air Force, and Boston College in successive weeks. We had the makings of a solid football team, even though we had graduated a half-dozen starters on each side of the ball, most notably Tim Tumpane on defense and Kenny Hill on offense. We got a boost when two outstanding players who had dropped out of school for a year rejoined the team. They were Jeff

Rohrer, a 6-foot-2, 215-pound linebacker who went on to a seven-year career with the Dallas Cowboys, and Curt Grieve, a 6-foot-4, 200-pound split end who could leap through the roof. Grieve had spent the year getting his head together, as they say. He worked in a steel mill in Pittsburgh, spent time as a draftsman in Los Angeles, and drifted around the country for a couple of months on a motorcycle. He came back to Yale eager to study and play football and delighted to have quarterbacks like John Rogan and Joe Dufek to throw him passes.

Like so many of our teams, that 1980 group was filled with good players and a slew of interesting and accomplished characters. The people in the sports information office noted that we had forty-eight high school captains, sixty-six members of the National Honor Society, ten valedictorians, five salutatorians, and fourteen high school class presidents on the team. All of which meant nothing when it came to winning football games, but it reminded me that I had one of the most enviable college coaching positions in the country. I read that list as part of my speech at a Multiple Sclerosis Society dinner in my honor, with my old coach Woody Hayes and John Pont sitting beside me at the head table. The accomplishments of our players were no surprise to Pont, of course, because he had coached at Yale, but Woody just shook his head in disbelief. And when I told him that only four of my players had failed to graduate in the fifteen years I had been at Yale, he was stunned.

I was honored that Woody and John came east for the banquet, though I was disappointed that Woody was late arriving in New Haven and missed our practice. It might surprise people to know that he was a scholarly man who told me after touring the campus and spending a few hours in the Sterling Library that he wished he had attended Yale.

Early indications were that the 1980 team would be strong offensively as well as defensively. I was particularly excited about the prospects of Rich Diana at tailback. We had used him at wingback as a sophomore just to get him on the field with Ken Hill, and because he had such great hands. Sure enough, we got off to a fast start with a 45–17 win over Brown that served as an offensive preview for the season. Curt Grieve caught five passes for 99 yards, including two leaping "alley-oop" receptions for touchdowns, one from Rogan and the other from Phil Manley. Brown coach John Anderson called Grieve the best split end he had seen in the Ivy League, including our Gary Fencik and Harvard's Pat McInally. Diana showed his potential, too, rushing for 83 yards in 24 carries.

We beat Connecticut 20–10 the next week before 34,500 in the Bowl, and I think that's when we all started to get pretty excited. UConn had won its first three games, but the Huskies couldn't find a way to stop us from winning our sixth straight over them. Whenever they got close to the goal line, Kevin Czinger would find a way to stop them. He made fourteen unassisted tackles, despite being double-teamed and held most of the time, and triple-teamed and tackled some of the time. Meanwhile, Diana rushed 15 times for 91 yards, scored on a 6-yard run and a 5-yard pass reception, returned a punt for 77 yards, and made a touchdown-saving tackle on a 40-yard punt return. It was an encouraging start to the season, but we couldn't get too excited with Air Force coming to the Bowl and then Yale's first-ever night game the following week at Boston College. Both those teams had the advantages of spring practice, full scholarships, and tougher schedules. They had bigger linemen, faster backs, and a depth of talent that we couldn't approach.

Air Force, which had tied Illinois of the Big Ten 10–10 the previous week, was a heavy favorite. But I must tell you, I had a feeling that if we played our best, we could handle them, even if most of the twenty-three thousand who showed up had a different opinion. I was right. We did play well and beat the Falcons 17–16, thanks to Czinger and Diana, who was emerging as a genuine star. Czinger was in on fifteen tackles and recovered two quarterback fumbles, despite the usual double-teaming. And Diana rushed for 136 yards on 20 carries. He scored the winning touchdown when he one-handed a John Rogan pass and stumbled into the end zone with an Air Force player riding his back.

I was thrilled by the win, but even more touched when my players surprised me with a little presentation ceremony back in the Field House. John Nitti, the captain, gave me a plaque to commemorate my one hundredth victory. I was fortunate to receive a variety of awards through the years, but that plaque meant as much as any of them because it came from my players. They had the forethought to have it made in advance, and I think they really enjoyed giving it to me. Jean got a special thrill that game, too, when one of the Air Force cadets brought their mascot, a live falcon, over to show her.

Boston College brought us back to reality the next week. The Eagles were huge. Czinger was nose-to-nose with offensive linemen who were several inches taller and in some cases forty and fifty pounds heavier. Good players, too. Some alumni thought we never should have scheduled the game because we were in danger of embarrassing ourselves. But the kids were really psyched and we played a very respectable game. We trailed just 17–9 as late as the fourth quarter after John Nitti ran five yards for a touchdown. They scored on a field goal and a 49-yard bomb to beat us 27–9.

Our players were disappointed at the loss, no doubt about that. Especially Czinger, who has as visceral a repugnance to losing as I did, and John Rogan, who had turned down a scholarship at BC, along with Virginia and Syracuse. But the BC game was probably good for us psychologically. I think the kids came away thinking that they had shown they could play football with anybody. And I think they were right. Most of all, we had come through that brutal three-week stretch of nonleague opponents with two wins and our confidence intact.

The final stretch of Ivy League games began with Columbia on Black Athletes at Yale weekend. BAY was an organization of African Americans whose mission was to encourage more black athletes to come to Yale, and to make the environment more comfortable for those who did. I couldn't argue with those goals, and although I thought that some BAY members were overzealous at times, I basically supported them. We had only three blacks on the team that year, so obviously I was in favor of anything BAY could do to help us attract more. Our backup quarterback, Phil Manley, was a founder of and driving force behind BAY and had helped arrange for Levi Jackson to come back to campus as the featured guest for the weekend festivities. It was a wonderful choice. Levi's election as Yale's first black football captain in 1949 was a stunning achievement when you consider the university's wealthy, white, conservative environment at the time. During the week, I announced that Manley would be the starting quarterback against Columbia, and when I did there was some criticism that it was merely a symbolic gesture in honor of the BAY weekend. That wasn't true. Phil deserved the start because of the way he had moved the team the previous week against BC.

We got back on track with a 30–10 win over Columbia, despite a sluggish start. The Lions were ahead 10–0 before we woke up. We held them to minus 6 yards of total offense and no first downs in the second half. On offense, Diana ran 114 yards on 20 carries, and John Rogan, who replaced Manley, threw two TD passes to Curt Grieve. Next came an 8–0 victory over Pennsylvania on a rainy day in Philadelphia. Diana ran 127 yards on 27 carries, and Rogan scored the only touchdown on a 26-yard option play. By now, Diana was attracting national attention. He led Division I in all-purpose running, with 190.5 yards per game. He was our leading punt returner, kickoff returner, and rusher, with 634 yards in 114 carries for a 5.6-yard average. He also was our second leading pass receiver. Obviously, Rich was one of the most versatile backs I ever coached. He wasn't multitalented like Calvin Hill, who could have started at any of the twenty-two positions and been a star, but Rich was the epitome of an all-around back. He was fast, had good hands, and could block. He was built low to the ground, with short, stocky legs, which he turned into an asset with a choppy gait that made him difficult to tackle.

Our 35–7 win over Dartmouth was a mixed bag. Diana kept rolling with 124 yards on the ground, tackle Bob Regan led our best offensive line effort of the season, especially on the pitch-sweep play we called "student body right," and Fred Leone intercepted a Jeff

Kemp pass and returned it thirty-nine yards for a touchdown. But we lost Jeff Rohrer, the future pro linebacker, for the rest of the year with a broken ankle. Only Bob Blackman's Cornell team, which was 2–5 on the season, remained between us and an unblemished Ivy League record going into the Big Three games. Once again, we were in a ripe-for-an-upset situation, but I couldn't convince our players of that fact. I sensed during the week that they were more impressed with themselves than they had a right to be. And sure enough, Cornell made us pay. The Big Red led us 21–0 at the half and beat us 24–6.

I was more than a little ticked off. At the Sunday meeting, I let the players have it. I told them that if they didn't start concentrating on football, we weren't going to get the job done. They seemed to think that the championship was theirs just for showing up. At the Tuesday press luncheon at Mory's, I took the unusual step of telling the reporters that the players might not submit to interviews for the rest of the season because I had asked them to make a total commitment to the team and not let anything distract them. That didn't mean that they should stop studying, of course. It just meant that the casual attitude had to stop. I stressed to the players that if they didn't take their practices and their two remaining games seriously, they would regret it for the rest of their lives. I didn't want them leaving a single practice or game with any regrets that they hadn't done everything in their power as individuals and as a team to win the title. It was a little out of character for me to be that tough with them, but it worked. We had a satisfying 25–13 win over Princeton before thirty-six thousand at the Bowl, which assured us of a share of the championship.

So the second of our three consecutive title seasons came down, as usual, to The Game with Harvard. Instead of being unfocused, as they had been during Cornell week, the players were as emotional as I had seen a team during Harvard week. The final home practice in Thursday's twilight was particularly stirring. It was dark when our workout ended, and a full moon hung in the sky over the West River

Always coaching. (S. Frinzi)

Things didn't always go well. (S. Frinzi)

Gary Fencik returns to Yale as a Kiphuth
Fellow in the early 1980s.

At right, 1987 captain Kelly Ryan. (Yale University
Sports Archives)

I was proud to be awarded the Mory's Cup in 1982 for "conspicuous service to Yale."
I was the first non–Yale alumnus to be given this honor.

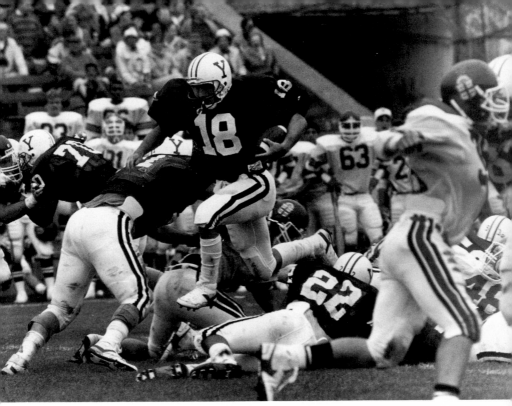

Mike Stewart (18) makes it through a crowd in a 1987 game, above.
(David Ottenstein, Yale University Sports Archives)

Quarterback Kelly Ryan (6) sets to pass.
(David Ottenstein, Yale University Sports Archives)

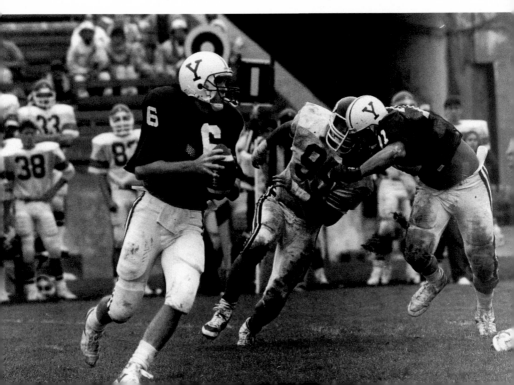

Congratulating Kelly Ryan on the sidelines. (S. Frinzi)

Bob Shoop (17) scores a last-second winning touchdown on a pass from Kelly Ryan to beat Penn, 1987.
(S. Frinzi, Yale University Sports Archives)

Eli linemen John Hansberry (97) and Jim D'Onofrio (95) try to break through
Villanova's sizable front in a 1987 scrimmage.
(Stephen Lefkovits, Yale University Sports Archives)

Players run timed sprints in a 1987 spring practice. (Yale University Sports Archives)

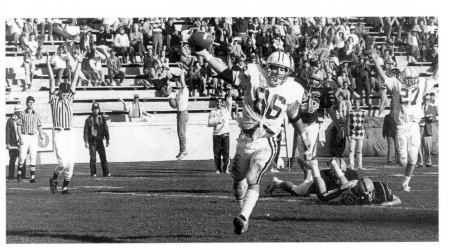

Dean Athanasia (86) scores the winning touchdown against Princeton, 1987.
(S. Frinzi, Yale University Sports Archives)

Fans celebrate with Jon Reese (32) after a victory over Harvard.
(Loren Fisher, Yale University Sports Archives)

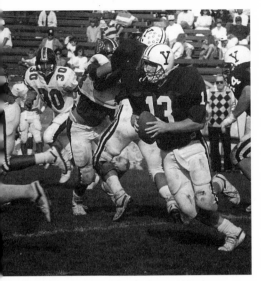

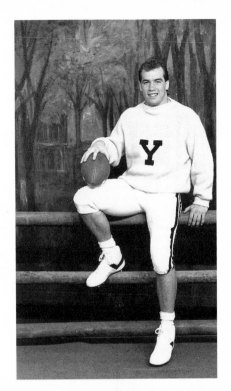

Quarterback Darin Kehler (13) in 1989, above.
(S. Frinzi, Yale University Sports Archives)

At right, 1989 captain Jon Reese.
(Paul J. Penders)

Former Yale football captain Bill Stack greets Jon Reese. Reese played the next day with a broken jaw.
(S. Frinzi, Yale University Sports Archives)

Protected by teammates, Darin Kehler (13) hands off to Chris Kouri.
(David Ottenstein, Yale University Sports Archives)

My twenty-fifth anniversary dinner in New York, 1990. At my left is master of ceremonies Calvin Trillin. (Yale University Sports Archives)

My family, with daughters grown and married, at the twenty-fifth anniversary dinner. From left: Karen and her husband, John Pollard; Jean and me; Kathryn and her husband, Anthony Tutino; and Kristin and her husband, David Powell.

With former players John Pagliaro, Brian Dowling, and Bob Sokolowski at the
twenty-fifth anniversary dinner.

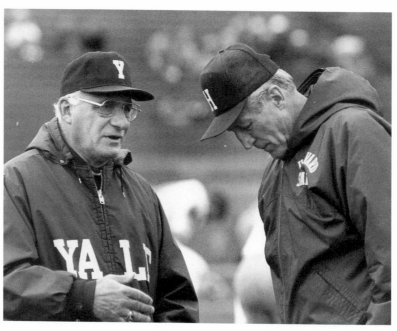

With an old rival—and friend—Harvard coach Joe Restic, 1993.
(David Ottenstein, Yale University Sports Archives)

David Iwan (13) carries the ball while a teammate blocks, 1993.
(S. Frinzi, Yale University Sports Archives)

With my senior players behind me, I announce my retirement
at a press conference, 1996. (Yale University Sports Archives)

Players celebrate on the sidelines after an interception by Rob Masella against Army, 1996.
(S. Frinzi, Yale University Sports Archives)

Former team captains walk to midfield for the coin toss before my last home game, 1996.
(Greg Raymond)

Leaving the field after my last home game, against Princeton.
(Stephen M. Fritzer, Yale University Sports Archives)

At a retirement gala after the Princeton game, my players presented me with a John Deere tractor. (Yale University Sports Archives)

swamp beside the practice field. Mike Pyle and Bob Blanchard, two members of the undefeated 1960 team, watched from the sidelines, and their presence made me aware of the long, rich tradition of our program. Finally, I released the team to John Nitti, who gathered the players at midfield for a few words from the captain before the annual running of the seniors gauntlet. It was an opportunity for me to step back and enjoy the moment as one of the rites of Harvard week unfolded before me. Suddenly, the whole team let out a yell and stampeded over to the adjacent freshman field, disappearing from one set of field lights as they ran, then reappearing in another.

It took me a minute to realize what was happening. It was the final practice for Harry Jacunski, the freshman coach and father figure who had served as an assistant under four different Yale coaches over thirty-three years. Harry had been invaluable to me, especially in the early years as a holdover from the Herman Hickman, Jordan Olivar, and John Pont years. He helped me find my way around Yale and the Ivy League, and his recruiting contacts were absolutely crucial during my first few seasons. He was a large, thick-boned man with a grandfatherly gentleness, an enormous knowledge of the game, and an equally deep affection for the players. He had been one of the fabled Seven Blocks of Granite when he played at Fordham, then played six seasons with the Green Bay Packers before coaching stints at Notre Dame and Harvard. The players surrounded Harry, hooting and hollering and chanting his name, then ran back to the varsity field for the gauntlet. They were so hyped up after the seniors battered their way between the parallel lines of underclassmen that they actually took down one of the goal posts. I had never seen that happen and I never saw it again. True to form, I worried that the kids were too hyped up. There was just no pleasing me, I guess.

When game day finally arrived and we gathered for our team breakfast, I think everyone was relieved. It had been a giddy week, but an anxious one. I usually made a little speech at the hotel before we boarded the bus for the stadium, but I looked at the faces in front of me and I could see in their eyes that they were ready to play. It was only 9:30 in the morning, but they were ready to go right then. On the bus trip to the field, the guys were so tight I wanted to crack a joke or do something to loosen them up, but I couldn't, because I felt the same way. Some of them were crying. Others were hugging. It was the most emotional I had seen any team before a Harvard game. They remembered the year before, no doubt about that.

In a way, it was good to have them so keyed up, but it just made me worry that we were going to be too tight. If we started running in every direction, not using our heads, we were going to be in trouble. Especially against Joe Restic's multiflex. But I needn't have worried. We played one of the best games any of my teams ever played and beat the Crimson 14–0 before a crowd of forty-one thousand, including seven hundred Yalies who had chartered a railroad car for the trip. It was a good Harvard team, too. The Johnnies were 7–2 going into the game, with all their key players healthy, but we really stuffed them. We held the multiflex offense to minus 11 yards rushing and 130 yards total.

Defensively, Harvard keyed on Diana, which freed John Nitti to run for 69 yards and a touchdown. It was a great way for John to end his career. He had played in Rich Diana's shadow, but he was as steady and hardworking a performer as you could want. To top it off, he was named Player of the Game by ABC, which had telecast the game regionally. It was a satisfying game for Kevin Czinger, too, who hadn't forgotten the hotdogging his old teammate Jim Callinan had done in Harvard's win the year before. Early in the game, Kevin tackled him in the backfield with such force that I wasn't sure the kid was going to get up. Everyone in the stadium saw Kevin, in a grand gesture of sportsmanship, grab the kid's arm to help him up. What they didn't notice was that Kevin was standing on Callinan's other hand with his cleats. Once again, Kevin had found a way to get even.

It was a good feeling to look up at the scoreboard with less than a minute to play and know that nothing could go wrong now, as it had so many times before at Harvard. The scoreboard lights were glowing brighter in the dusk, and the wind off the Charles River was

icy cold as it swirled around that concrete horseshoe. But I assure
you I felt no chill. The aftermath of that 1980 win was one of the
half-dozen or so warmest moments of my thirty-two years because
of the wonderful family feeling on that team. John Nitti and Kevin
Czinger and so many others had made it a very special season for me.

Before we could get on with the business of chasing our third
straight championship in 1981, we had to live through a little controversy. Things worked out fine in the end, but for a while we were
in danger of being sanctioned by the NCAA or having some of our
players declared ineligible, all because of a "mystery donor" who
befriended a handful of Yale students. It was a bizarre episode that
my staff and I knew absolutely nothing about until it nearly blew up
in our faces.

As the pieces of the story came together, I found out that a man
named G. Richard Schieffelin had set up what I guess you could call
an unofficial student society, centered in his house just off campus.
He was a wealthy guy who enjoyed helping young people. Once he
got to know a student, he would get the kid to sign a sort of pledge,
and after that, the student was welcome at the house whenever he
wanted, apparently whether Schieffelin was there or not. The kids
would just drop by to relax or study or to make themselves a meal.
He was a middle-aged bachelor, and although his behavior seemed a
little odd, he apparently meant well. One of the stipulations of the
pledge, for example, was that each kid promised to do something to
help someone else once a month and report back to Schieffelin what
he had done.

The problem was that some of the favors Schieffelin did for the
students went over the line of NCAA regulations, and several of the
kids in his society were athletes, including football players. When I
found out what was going on, I got chills and immediately notified
the NCAA, which began an investigation. The man allegedly was
giving loans to some kids, maybe even outright financial gifts. He
was also counseling students about business opportunities and setting up summer employment for others through his business con-

tacts. I asked the guy to meet with me, and to my surprise, he promptly appeared in my office. He seemed like a perfectly good person, and when I explained that what he was doing might be a violation of NCAA rules, he was genuinely surprised. He said he had no intention of hurting anyone, and would immediately stop doing anything that might be out of bounds. Once the story got around, I heard charges that sex and drugs were somehow involved, but my players who were involved assured me there was never any hint of that when they were around. I believe them absolutely. Still, we were in jeopardy with the NCAA. If it had been determined that Schieffelin was an "agent of the university" and gave money or loans to athletes, we could have faced forfeitures, and the players involved could have been declared ineligible. It didn't seem fair that I should be held accountable for the actions of a man I had never met or heard of, but the rules were so strict that any fan could be considered a booster and be subject to NCAA restrictions.

Fortunately, Schieffelin's society included as many nonathletes as it did athletes, and quite a few women as well. Furthermore, Yale was not the only school involved. Schieffelin, who was not a Yale alumnus, had offered his largesse to kids at Harvard, Princeton, and several other schools, too. Eventually, a one hundred–page report on the matter was filed with the Ivy presidents, focusing on twelve athletes from Yale, Harvard, and Princeton who may have accepted loans. I was relieved when Jim Litvack, the executive director of the Council of Ivy Group Presidents, issued a ruling clearing all the schools and players of any wrongdoing.

With "donorgate" behind us, we got serious about the campaign for a third straight championship. On paper, at least, our prospects looked good, and everyone around the league seemed to agree. You'd think by reading the papers that all we had to do to win the title was show up. Rich Diana, who had been second in the nation behind Southern Cal's Marcus Allen in all-purpose yardage (174.9 yards per game), was back for his senior year. So was John Rogan, who would be pushed at quarterback by the eventual NFL player Joe Dufek. And so was the lanky split end Curt Grieve. On defense we had Serge Mihaly and Dennis Tulsiak on the line and Fred Leone and Jeff Rohrer as linebackers. Tulsiak had been named to the All-Ivy team as a junior, even though he was never a starter. As the second man on the depth chart at both tackle spots and middle guard, he got as much playing time as some of the starters.

Diana got us off to a great start in the 28–7 opening win over Brown. Three times I watched him break through the line of scrimmage and speed through the secondary for touchdowns. He scored on runs of 18, 35, and 80 yards and set a Yale single-game rushing record with 196 yards on 27 carries. We didn't realize right away that Rich had set the mark because the record book listed Albie Booth, Yale's fabled "Little Boy Blue," class of 1932, as the standard bearer with 233 yards. But the sports information office determined that Booth's total had erroneously included a 79-yard punt return in that game, dropping his rushing performance to 154. That meant Rich had eclipsed a record Dick Jauron set in 1972, when he ran 194 yards against Connecticut.

Diana's performance was an example of his persistence and confidence. He gained just 15 yards in his first 12 rushes before he tied the game at 7 with an 18-yard run right before the half. The fans were getting restless because we kept calling the same "unimaginative" off-tackle play. At halftime, Rich told the coaches he thought we should stick with the formation because he could feel it beginning to open up. He was right. He ran for more than 150 yards in the second half, and we scored twenty-one unanswered points. When it was over, Rich told the press that the offensive line deserved all the credit.

The Connecticut game was portrayed in the newspapers as something of a grudge match. This was the time when our two programs were going in opposite directions. UConn was upgrading its schedule and scholarship policies, and it was only a matter of time before the Huskies would dominate us. Somehow, we had managed to delay the inevitable. My teams were 13–3 against Connecticut before 1981, including seven straight wins. The papers wrote that Walt Nadzak, the UConn coach, had been so frustrated after we beat them in 1980 that he shattered his wristwatch against the locker room wall. The pregame tension was heightened when I made a public complaint that Nadzak and an assistant had come to the Bowl to personally scout our preseason scrimmage. There was no specific NCAA rule against that, but it was generally considered bad form. We managed to hold off the Huskies one more year, 27–18 before thirty-six thousand in the Bowl, then lost twelve of the next fourteen games to them. It might have been thirteen losses in fifteen years if the 1985 game hadn't been canceled by Hurricane Gloria.

Once again, Rich Diana was crucial to our win. We were behind 18–17 in the fourth quarter and had the ball on our own 20-yard line. Rich threw a tailback pass to Tom Kokoska, who lived in Willimantic, only a few miles from the UConn campus, for twenty-two yards. On the next play, Rich ran twenty-eight yards to the UConn 30. Two plays, fifty yards. We scored the go-ahead touchdown four plays later, two of which were Diana runs of twelve and six yards.

The next week, we played Navy in one of the most memorable games of my thirty-two years. The Midshipmen had damn nearly beaten Big Ten powerhouse Michigan the week before. They trailed by just five points with five minutes to play and had the ball on the Wolverines' 23-yard line, but they couldn't score and Michigan held on for a 21–16 win. I was wary about playing Navy, but I was excited, too. I thought we had the potential to beat them, even though we clearly were the underdogs. We had a solid defense, which is the most important thing when you play a more powerful team. And we had three skill-position players on offense in Rogan, Grieve, and Diana, who could have played for any team at any level. Hell, Diana was in the Miami Dolphins' backfield the next year. Besides, whatever our competition level was, we had won twenty-one of our last twenty-four games. I was particularly excited because the game was to be telecast regionally by ABC, and my old coach, Ara

Parseghian, was coming to New Haven to do the color commentary while Al Michaels did the play-by-play.

The game stirred talk on campus that was typical of the academic paradox we faced. It was a no-win argument for us. If we upset Navy, some academicians among the professors would complain that Yale was putting too much emphasis on athletics. And if we suffered an embarrassing loss, they would say that the game never should have been scheduled. *Sports Illustrated* focused some national attention on the game with a feature story on Diana, referring to the Ivy League as "one of the few organizations left that treats collegiate athletes the way they were originally intended to be treated." The story pointed out that Rich graduated No. 3 in his class of eight hundred at Hamden High and was maintaining a 3.5 academic average as a molecular biochemistry and biophysics major.

It was a memorable day for the thirty-eight thousand who came to the Bowl. The Academy added a military pageantry to the scene when its long blue line of Midshipmen paraded into the Bowl, accompanied by the Navy band. Things went badly for us right from the start. Navy took a quick 12–0 lead, running through us at will. In the TV booth Ara was doing his best to defend us, or maybe he was damning us with faint praise. He said we were a little outmanned on the line of scrimmage and that maybe six of our defensive players were good players, but the others were not equal to the task Navy presented. He kept citing our academic excellence as an excuse for our football weaknesses. That was before we turned things around. It wasn't long before Coach Parseghian was trying to take credit for all the things he had taught me when he coached me in my senior year at Miami of Ohio. I got a kick out of that when I listened to the tape later on. Ara and I have enjoyed a great relationship over the years.

Once we got in gear and shook off a few early jitters, we played a terrific game. John Rogan hit 16 of 30 passes for three touchdowns and no interceptions. Curt Grieve caught two of them, including a 23-yard alley-oop reception in the corner of the end zone with 3:19 to play that turned out to be the winning points. Navy keyed on Diana and held him to just 69 yards in 23 carries, but he gained 172 yards in all-purpose yardage and proved beyond a doubt how tough he was. Phil Tarasovic, the captain of Yale's 1955 team that beat nationally ranked Army, said he was amazed that Diana was still running hard at the end after the punishment he took. Fred Leone recovered three fumbles and was named Defensive Player of the Week by *Sports Illustrated.*

It might have been my most satisfying win ever outside the Ivy League. I got a little extra dose of satisfaction within the family, too. My son-in-law David was a Navy pilot who had played football in his first two years at the Naval Academy. He was aboard an aircraft carrier sailing back from the Mediterranean on the day of the game and called my daughter Kris on the radio-telephone to find out what happened. The conversation went something like this:

"It was a good game . . . We won . . . Over."

"Please repeat . . . Over."

"I said Yale won, 23–19 . . . Over."

After a long pause, David said, "Oh God, it's going to be a long winter with Father."

He was right. I ragged him every chance I got.

We almost lost our momentum the next weekend at Holy Cross, which was 3–1 and had just beaten both Harvard and Dartmouth. But Tony Jones saved us with a 32-yard field goal with thirty-five seconds left for a 29–28 win, our third comeback victory in a row. The Crusaders had taken the lead just moments earlier when we stopped them at the 1, forcing them to settle for a field goal and a single-point margin. Diana was outstanding again, rushing 27 times for 176 yards, including a 67-yard touchdown run when he spun away from at least three defenders.

That led to four straight Ivy League wins—over Columbia 48–17, Penn 24–3, Dartmouth 24–3, and Cornell 23–17. Along the way, John Rogan broke Joe Massey's career passing yardage record, Tony Jones kicked a record 49-yard field goal, and Curt Grieve sur-

passed Ed Woodsum's career touchdown reception mark at seventeen. And, of course, Rich Diana just kept rolling along, including a
38-carry performance against Cornell that netted 178 yards. Needless to say, we were a pretty confident football team as we piled into
the buses on a Friday morning for the trip to Princeton. We were 8–
0, the Tigers were 3–4–1, and we had beaten them fourteen straight
years. I must confess that the anticipation of finally achieving an
unbeaten, untied season was beginning to stir in my gut.

I should have known better. Princeton beat us 35–31 before a
crowd of twenty thousand in Palmer Stadium, ruining my last real
chance for a perfect season. It was a wild game with some remarkable individual statistics racked up by players on both teams. Their
quarterback, Bob Holly, passed for an incredible 501 yards. He
completed 36 of 55 passes, 15 of them to a sophomore named Derek
Graham. Those numbers overshadowed Curt Grieve's six catches for
104 yards, and an extraordinary 46 rushes for 222 yards by Rich
Diana. Both the number of carries and the total yards were Yale
records, and Diana's total for the season jumped to 1,355, also a
school record.

Unfortunately, the game came down to a questionable call by
an official when Pat Conran was charged with pass interference. The
penalty gave Princeton the ball on the 1-yard line with nine seconds
left to play, and their quarterback ran it in on the next play for the
winning points. I won't say that one call cost us the game because we
played the worst defense we had played in years. Not only that, we let
them get back in the game after leading 21–0 at halftime and 31–22
in the fourth quarter. Still, it will always bother me that two of the
best chances any of my teams ever had for a perfect season were
taken away by referees' calls in the dying seconds of road games. The
other instance, of course, was the 29–29 tie with Harvard in 1968.
The questionable call against Conran was made by an official who
came from the other side of the field and threw the flag in front of
another official who was right there on the scene. That's a tough call
to make under any circumstances, but when it gives the trailing team

the ball at the 1-yard line with nine seconds to play, you have to wonder.

Once again, I thanked God for Harvard. It would have been tough to live with the loss at Princeton if we hadn't had a chance for a happy ending to the season in The Game against Harvard the next week. And we didn't waste the opportunity. In fact, we played one of our best games of the season, shutting out the Crimson for the second year in a row. In spite of our loss the week before, the fifth-largest crowd ever recorded in Yale Bowl, 75,145, and the largest in fifty-seven years, showed up to watch our 28–0 win. I hung a large color photograph of that capacity crowd on my office wall right across from my desk. I'm not sure whether it lifted my spirits to look at it over the years or saddened me as our attendance sagged in subsequent seasons, but it was a visible reminder of a very satisfying victory before a rousing crowd.

I was delighted when Fred Leone, the captain, brought me the game ball and said that the team wanted it to go to Jean. She had been suffering with back problems for some time and hadn't been able to attend any of the games that year. She watched the two televised games and listened to the others on the radio. She was thrilled when I brought the ball home to her. She kept it with her all Saturday night, and when I tried to put it with my collection of awards, she said, "No way"—she was keeping it for herself. Lord knows she deserved it, putting up with me all those seasons. And she was truly our most avid fan. That game ball meant as much to me as it did to her.

It had been a great season, thanks to a stalwart defense (except for the Princeton game) and our three offensive stars, Rich Diana, Curt Grieve, and John Rogan. Diana finished the year with a Yale single-season rushing record of 1,442 yards, for an average of 144 per game. His career total of 2,516 was second to Dick Jauron's 2,947 from 1970 to '72. Grieve caught 51 passes for 791 yards and 12 touchdowns, all Yale single-season records. And Rogan's career passing yardage of 2,844 set a school mark.

We had players named to a variety of all-star teams, highlighted by Diana's selection as a first-team All-American by the Football Writers Association of America. He joined a backfield that included three future NFL stars—Heisman Trophy winner Herschel Walker from Georgia, Southern Cal's Marcus Allen, and Jim McMahon from Brigham Young. Diana, Grieve, and cornerback Pat Conran were invited to play in the Blue-Gray Game in Montgomery, Alabama, on Christmas Day, and I went with them as defensive coach. We all came down with food poisoning during the week, but fortunately we recovered for the game. Conran had an interception and a pass breakup, and Grieve caught five passes, including his specialty, the alley-oop, in the corner of the end zone. Diana was also asked to play in the Japan Bowl in Tokyo, though he had to forfeit his baseball eligibility because the Ivy League wouldn't let him play in both postseason games. He was a good baseball player, too, having set the single-season Yale home run record the year before.

In December we were rewarded for our three most productive seasons. From 1979 through 1981 we had gone 25–4, won three consecutive Ivy League championships, beaten Air Force in 1980 and Navy in 1981, knocked off Connecticut three straight years, shut out good Harvard teams in the last two years by a combined score of 42–0, produced a first-team All-American and four NFL players (Diana, Hill, Rohrer, and Dufek), led the nation in defense, drawn two overflow crowds to the Bowl, and averaged thirty-seven thousand fans during the final season. In recognition of our efforts, the NCAA dropped us and the rest of the Ivy League to second-class status as members of Division I-AA, a decision that significantly deflated the program over time.

I remember those seasons and those young men fondly. Still, I can't forget that our 28–0 victory over Harvard in 1981 was the beginning of the end of Yale's stature as a football power in the country. We had managed to hold off the inexorable retreat from national prominence until then—longer than any other Ivy League school, I might add—but the university's slow slide to a lesser level of play had begun. The tide had turned.

CHAPTER THIRTEEN

The So-Called Decline

When I set out to write this book, I knew that there would have to be a chapter on the so-called decline of Yale football. Frankly, if there were a way to avoid the subject altogether, I would. Not because I don't have strong opinions on the subject, but because it is nearly impossible to state the facts honestly and not appear to be making excuses. Furthermore, it is impossible to talk about the top quality players we were unable to bring to Yale without demeaning the ones we did recruit as though they were second choices. That's unfair and untrue. Most of our players would have been welcome in a Yale uniform under any circumstances. The problem was that we couldn't get enough of them. And we couldn't land the half-dozen or so truly outstanding kids we needed each year to really make a difference.

And finally, this is a distasteful subject because the very discussion of a decline in Yale football acknowledges it as a fact. Certainly our national reputation, as well as the level of play in the Ivy League as a whole, has declined since the early 1980s, but there are other ways to judge a college football program. When judged by the really important criteria of college athletics, Yale's record on and off the field never wavered. Not only did we adhere to the highest standards of academic excellence and amateur athletic purity, but we won more than our share of football games.

The last thing I want to do is whine about the problems my coaches and I faced as a series of events weakened the quality of football at Yale and made it harder and harder to win, even within the Ivy League. How well Carm Cozza fared against the flood of corrosive change is not the issue. What is important is to explore the causes of Yale football's so-called decline and the options the university has to reverse the tide. I believe that it is possible to restore much of the glory of Yale football and perhaps double the attendance in the Bowl without compromising the bedrock philosophy of student-athlete integrity. Thankfully, some positive changes are taking place now at the initiative of Athletic Director Tom Beckett, but even more could and should be done.

I accept my share of responsibility for the declining attendance at the Bowl, for Yale's diminished level of play compared with major universities across the country, and for the relative lack of success during the last of my three decades at the helm. But make no mistake, no single person, whether coach, athletic director, or president of the university, was the cause of all the change, or had the power to stop it. Many of the overt actions and subtle trends that adversely affected Yale football on my watch took root outside the department of athletics. Some of our problems could best be described as peripheral damage from the escalating war for TV dollars being fought by the major athletic powers across the country. Other difficulties were the result of Yale's zealous—I think overzealous—guardianship of the lofty ideals of academic standards and equal treatment of all candidates, whether they were linebackers, pianists, or rocket scientists. I know one thing: if the admissions office had worked as hard at admitting the qualified applicants whom we had identified as football players as it did at stamping out any hint of favoritism for our recruits, I would not be writing this chapter.

In my last half-dozen years as coach, a few of my assistants actually believed that there was an overt attempt by the admissions office to sabotage the football program. I refuse to believe that. The men and women whose job it was to sift through thousands of applications from the best and brightest of the nation's high school seniors, ultimately rejecting a large majority of them, had a difficult task. And an important one. After all, the quality of the incoming freshman class is the standard by which the university will be judged in future years. I don't think the admissions people hurt our program intentionally, but there is no doubt that we lost scores of talented players over the years because the admissions office did not act promptly on their applications. It was a matter of timing more than ultimate rejections. There were countless instances when other schools, including Ivy League schools operating under the same regulations, admitted a candidate and spelled out his financial aid package before Yale's admissions office finished its initial processing. There were a few times, believe it or not, when applications were misplaced. You can imagine how my assistants felt when they had to call the family of a recruit for a duplicate copy.

Our admissions people didn't seem to understand how competitive the recruiting process is. When your academic standards are as high as Yale's, there is a very, very limited pool of players to draw from. There simply were not a lot of players big enough, fast enough, and talented enough to really make a difference, who also had 1400 College Board scores and were in the top 2 or 3 percent of their high school classes. And there were even fewer of those kids whose parents were willing to spend from $5,000 to $30,000 a year, depending on their financial need, when they could get full scholarships (board and room, tuition, books, everything) at other schools.

When we identified those kids, we knew that they were being courted by many other schools, including our Ivy League foes. The Yale admissions office never understood the need to act quickly and decisively to have any chance of attracting them, even those who were inclined our way in the first place. Time and again a fully qualified recruit got a prompt acceptance from Princeton or Harvard, including a full explanation of his financial package, while Yale kept him waiting until April 1, the date it announced acceptances for the entire student body. By then, it was too late.

It is important to note that we never tried to sneak a kid into Yale who didn't belong. I never once sought the admission of a young man I didn't think could do Yale work. Not once. All we asked for were quick and fair decisions on a few dozen qualified student-athletes every year. But that was never Yale's priority. The admissions office never understood that when it gave "no special consideration" to an outstanding player whom we had worked hard to identify and attract, that young man often ended up at Yale on a Saturday afternoon in the fall wearing the Tiger stripes of Princeton or the Crimson of Harvard. My staff and I worked nights and week-ends for months to find young men who could handle micro-biophysics and pass defense with equal skill and enthusiasm. We evaluated film, checked academic records, worked the phones, and traveled around the country to isolate a few young men who could excel in the classroom and on the gridiron in the Ivy League. And when we lost those young men to other universities because the admissions office failed to act until it was too late, it was demoraliz-ing. More than that, it directly cost us victories.

See what I mean? I'm just stating facts, but it sounds like a recitation of excuses. So before I go on, let me offer a blanket apol-ogy for the tone of this chapter. I hope my comments will be taken not as a personal defense but as a guide to understanding what happened, or didn't happen, that diminished, at least by some crite-ria, the most storied football tradition in the country.

A lot happened during my thirty-two years to alter the stature of football at Yale. No single decision triggered all the changes. I can think of more than a half-dozen factors that worked against the status quo, and it was the combined weight of all of them that made a difference. Among them were:

- the change from NCAA Division I-A to Division I-AA;
- the advent of coeducation at Yale, which halved the male enrollment;
- the widely misunderstood but damaging "deemphasis speech" by President A. Bartlett Giamatti;
- the skyrocketing cost of an education at a school with no athletic scholarships;
- the escalation of TV money, which encouraged recruiting excesses and abuses at major football programs outside the Ivy League;
- the proliferation of sports on TV, which moved millions of fans across the country from stadium seats to living room armchairs;

- the disastrous Academic Index, which made us less competitive even within our own league;
- and the aforementioned problems with an unresponsive admissions office.

All those factors were harmful to some degree. Some were inevitable, while others could have been avoided. Taken together, they changed the face of football at Yale.

It probably is not fair to characterize coeducation at Yale as a bad thing for football. The decision to accept women as undergraduates beginning in 1969 was entirely proper and a natural reflection of the times. Still, nothing changed the face of the university more visibly than the appearance of women in the classrooms and dining halls of what had long been regarded as an exclusive institution for sons of the privileged elite. Predictably, there was an outcry from some old Blues who cringed at the transformation of their alma mater from a bastion of well-connected males to an institution hellbent on inclusion and diversity. Many of them remained opposed to coeducation until one of their granddaughters decided to go to Yale. That changed their minds in a heartbeat.

It really didn't matter who approved of coeducation at Yale and who didn't. The change, which was made during Kingman Brewster's tenure as president, was inevitable. The United States government, through Title IX, required all institutions that accepted federal funds to provide equal opportunities and facilities for men and women. That meant that there had to be as many seats on the field hockey bus as there were on the lacrosse bus. Coeducation was a welcome change at Yale. I truly believe that. And there is no doubt that the presence of women on campus served as an enticement for recruits. But in many subtle, unintended ways, it dealt a blow to our football program.

After a few transition years, the male enrollment was cut in half. Despite its worldwide reputation, Yale has never had a large underclass population. The number of men dropped from about

5,000 to 2,500 in the early 1970s. That meant that the percentage of football players in the male enrollment had to double from roughly 2 percent to 4 percent to maintain the same numbers. Furthermore, there was an increased demand to admit female athletes to meet Title IX requirements. Suddenly, the quota system for athletes wasn't quite so simple. In the span of several years, we went from seventeen varsity sports to thirty-four, which meant that Yale was flooded with twice the number of "athletic distinctions" among the applicants presented to the admissions office by various coaches. I can only imagine how that changed the attitude of the admissions personnel toward sports. It didn't grease the skids for football players, I'm sure of that.

Yale was not alone, of course, in feeling the impact of Title IX. But at a time when a series of events was eroding the old ways of bringing in football players and filling Yale Bowl, a reduced male enrollment and the increased demand for athletic admissions to fill the women's rosters made the admission of our recruits that much tougher. Furthermore, I'm sure that the major football schools, whose budgets depend on New Year's Day bowl appearances, didn't strike a gender balance by reducing opportunities for male athletes. They simply added opportunities for female athletes. That was not a viable option at Yale.

One measure of hard times for Yale football in the last quarter of the century was the declining attendance at Yale Bowl. There was a time when a crowd of forty thousand was typical for a home game against the likes of Dartmouth or Cornell, and a capacity crowd of seventy thousand for a Princeton or Harvard game at the end of the season was not unheard of. No more. Attendance at the Bowl when I retired was roughly half what it was when I joined John Pont's staff at Yale in 1963. There are several reasons for the decline, but none is more significant than the proliferation of major college football on television just as Ivy League games were dropped from network telecasts.

I say that for two reasons. First, the misguided assumption

arose that if Yale football isn't shown on national TV, it must be an inferior product. It's no different from marketing a commercial product. If a consumer doesn't see a brand of coffee advertised on television, he won't buy it. And if he doesn't see Ivy League football on the tube, he won't go see it. The situation was exacerbated when the major conferences formed the College Football Alliance (CFA) and put a stranglehold on national network telecasts. The CFA effectively excluded nonmember universities, including Yale, from all TV coverage except regional and cable-access telecasts. The last Ivy League contract for national telecasts was with ESPN, but it wasn't renewed after the 1980 season.

The second damaging effect of TV, as the number of telecasts exploded from one or two a week to dozens, was that it just became too darn easy to see the games. A fan could watch nearly nonstop college and professional football from Thursday night through Monday night. Not only did the quantity of telecasts increase but so did the quality. The technological advances of close-ups and replays made the armchair sports experience enormously enjoyable. With expert commentary, a dozen camera angles, and constant updates on other games, college football on television became an enticing alternative to sitting in a cold stadium fifty or a hundred yards from the action.

Much has been written about the way television changed the sports world in the final decades of the century. It was a revolution that didn't just affect Yale football. It took fans out of the stands and away from the sidelines at high school basketball games and Little League baseball games across the country. That's progress, but it's a shame, too. Parents and townspeople getting out to cheer the local team was a wonderful slice of Americana. I miss it, and not just because of the way it affected the crowds in Yale Bowl.

No one at Yale or in the Ivy League can be blamed for our ending up in the second tier of college football teams in the early 1980s. It was not at our urging that the NCAA split the Division I programs into Division I-A and Division I-AA. We were not the ones to devise the series of qualifying criteria, which included stadium size, average attendance, number of scholarship players, and percentage of I-A opponents. And it was not our choice to be placed in the lower Division I-AA classification.

It might have been possible for Yale to qualify for Division I-A, but not without major changes and probably not without leaving the Ivy League. My feelings were mixed at the time. I hated to see us drop down in status, but I knew the NCAA split signaled an escalation of major-college football that would swiftly outstrip our resources unless we undertook fundamental changes in the way we administered the program. It was clear that the Big Ten, the Southeast Conference, and the other high-profile conferences were joining a competition for TV viewers and entertainment dollars that would be anathema to our mission as an institution of learning. Looking back, I realize that we underestimated the importance of the split, not that we had any real choice. The decision was made for us, really, but it stamped us with the stigma of second-level competition, which affected our fan base and our ability to recruit outstanding players who harbored dreams of playing football on national television, perhaps on New Year's Day.

When the CFA came along a few years later to negotiate exclusive TV contracts, our fate was sealed. The big-time schools clearly wanted a clean break from the student-athlete atmosphere of the Ivy League. They wanted to play by their own rules. If they wanted to increase the number of full-ride scholarship players to one hundred, they didn't want Cornell or William and Mary or Youngstown State voting against them. How could Yale, which gave no athletic scholarships, none at all, compete with that? So we contented ourselves with the thought that perhaps it would be better to be competitive among our own kind than to be a doormat for powerful teams with resources we couldn't hope to match. And didn't want to match.

I am not bitter toward those schools that split away. Even when I was president of the American Football Coaches Association, I never presumed to tell another coach, athletic director, or university president what was in the best interest of his institution. Just as I would not have been happy if one of them had told me what Yale should or shouldn't do. Still, Yale has a right to be proud of the extraordinarily high character, academic standing, and graduation rates among its athletes, and if we were left behind when other schools sacrificed their standards and invited excesses in the name of athletic excellence, so be it. Some college teams went to bowl games and brought in millions of dollars for their schools with players who were hardly scholars. They used (an appropriate word) athletes who were not allowed to choose demanding majors that might cut into practice time but were steered instead to courses with comfortable workloads and accommodating professors. The players were led through their schoolwork by paid tutors, and even then most of them were sent into the world when their eligibility was over with no degree and no realistic expectation of getting one.

It was no surprise that alumni and fans criticized Yale for not keeping pace with the rest of the nation in fielding the best possible football teams. Nor was it surprising that the criticism came from people who didn't understand the price of running with the pack of almost professional-level teams. I tried the best I could to explain the hurdles we faced. I did not appreciate the critics who thought Yale should bend the rules in the interest of a better football team. They reasoned that because everyone else was flouting the rules and getting away with it, so should we. First of all, most coaches weren't breaking the rules. Sure, there was abuse, especially where TV revenue and coaches' jobs were dependent on winning. But the idea that abuse by football coaches was rampant and that their admissions people and university administrators were silent partners in the scheme was an overstatement.

In fact, the worst of the abuse was perpetrated by alumni who broke rules without coaches or school officials knowing it. Some coaches might have been guilty of looking the other way when they discovered a graduate slipping spending money to a player under the table. But usually that was the worst of it. I'm not so naive as to think there weren't some outlaw coaches who actively encouraged cheating among their alumni supporters. But I believe they were the exception, not the rule. For that matter, I can't say with certainty that such things didn't happen at Yale. It's possible that sometime during my thirty-two seasons an alumnus took it upon himself to pay for a kid's plane ticket home for Christmas or do favors for a player's family, but if he did, I didn't know about it. I would have gone ballistic, as the kids say, if I had discovered that kind of breach of rules. I would have turned us in immediately to the NCAA, then redoubled my efforts to let the alumni know what they could and could not do. As it was, I sent letters every year to all our alumni supporters summarizing the NCAA compliance manual and letting them know it was our policy to follow the regulations to the letter.

Anyway, what if other coaches were cheating? What would that have to do with Yale? What if there was some falsifying of grades at outlaw universities? What if some coaches were openly encouraging alumni to funnel money or jobs to athletes? That would be no reason to change Yale policy. Or Ivy League policy. Any coach with half a brain understands one basic truth about college football—you can't fool the kids. You can fool your president sometimes, or maybe the admissions office. You might sneak something by the parents or faculty or alumni or even an NCAA investigator, but you can't fool the kids. If you're not playing by the rules, the players will know it. If the star linebacker has a free meal ticket at a local pizzeria, his teammates will hear about it. If the quarterback is steered to a friendly professor who understands the need for a passing grade, it will be an open secret in the locker room. If we had bent the rules, or allowed them to be bent for us, I would have made my players a party to the indiscretion. I would have tarnished their pride at being honest student-athletes playing in a program that was above reproach. And I would have taught them that cheating is permissible in our society as long as the goal is worthwhile—like a winning football season.

In a perfect world, all college sports programs would be more like the Ivy League. That's not to say I'm opposed to merit scholarships for athletes. In fact, I think Yale should employ them in a limited way. But colleges should not be used as minor leagues for professional sports. I watched as college teams became almost professional themselves. The pressures on coaches to win and bring in revenue was intense. So was the pressure on young players, many of them only nineteen or twenty years old. They received celebrity treatment, lived in special dormitories, and grew accustomed to having grown men and women fawning over them. What was worse, the best of them left school after their junior years, sometimes after their sophomore years, to enter the pros. That kind of attention and pressure spells trouble for athletes when they must fend for themselves in society later on. That's why I believed in the Ivy League philosophy. As long as two teams are competitive, the level of play should be a secondary concern. Unfortunately, many fans think they demean themselves by watching a lesser team. Particularly if they can't place a bet on the game. That pro mentality is a shame.

Someone, I've forgotten who, gave me a copy of A. Bartlett Giamatti's deemphasis speech the morning he was to deliver it to a gathering of alumni in April of 1980. Right away I knew it meant trouble. I even called Sam Chauncey, the university secretary and Bart's closest adviser, to see whether he could get the president to rethink the message. It was obvious to me that the speech would be interpreted as a declaration that Yale was taking overt, unilateral actions to diminish the quality of its intercollegiate athletics.

In some ways that was true. If his recommendations had been fully implemented, they would have adversely affected our ability to compete inside or outside the Ivy League. Still, I think the speech was widely misunderstood. I don't think people appreciated the circumstances Yale was in or the pressures Giamatti was under. God knows he was a world-class writer and speaker, and yet I think the words he chose left an unintended impression. What he was trying to do was to get everybody in the conference to play by the same rules. For several years, schools within the league had accused each other of bending the rules, if not outright violation of the Ivy code. The speech was Giamatti's way of telling the rest of the conference in no uncertain terms what Yale's policy was going to be, in the hope that they would fall in line. He seemed to be making a declaration that we were going to be purer than the pure, and that any school that believed in amateur athletics as an important adjunct to academics in the educational process had better follow along. He had submitted a proposal outlining his intentions to the league presidents the previous December, but this was his way of drawing attention to it. He knew that his remarks would be picked up by the news media, and he hoped his message would coerce the other presidents to take similar action.

I think he felt a need to restate Yale's athletic philosophy lest the university drift away from it and get caught up in the rapid escalation of big-time sports competition across the country. It was a right and proper thing to do in many respects, but it probably wasn't wise to do it unilaterally. If all eight Ivy League presidents had made simultaneous statements, that would have been one thing, but it was a mistake to stand up and say, We are no longer going to recruit on the road, and we hope you won't either. At best, it was wishful thinking.

The most damaging of the several proposals Giamatti made was to restrict our recruiting to on-campus visits. He said that he did not believe Yale should send coaches on the road to recruit student-athletes because it tended to create a special and separate group of students. Imagine the advantage that would have handed to our opponents. Their coaches would have continued to visit candidates and their families anywhere in the country, while we asked them to travel to New Haven to be sold on Yale. If we had been the only team in the league to adopt such a policy, we would have sunk to the bottom of the standings like a stone. And if the Ivy League had adopted the policy as a whole, all eight teams would have become doormats for every nonleague opponent. A rule like that could make sense only if every Division I-AA school accepted it at once, but there was never a realistic hope of that. Frankly, I think Yale and Giamatti were guilty of arrogance to believe that we could be the catalyst to make it happen. As I mentioned, even when I was president of the AFCA, I never presumed to tell another school or conference what was in their best interests.

I knew that Giamatti's speech would work against us, and it did, even though most of the proposals were never implemented. There is no way to tell what effect it had on the way the admissions officers viewed our recruits. They may have taken it as a license to be tougher on our candidates, but I don't know that. I do know that the speech gave coaches at other schools the opportunity to tell recruits, "Hey, you don't want to go to Yale, they're deemphasizing athletics." Whether that was true or not, they were free to say it, and they did. I know that because some of our kids who were recruited at other schools told us.

Giamatti also said he wanted us to stop thinking about post-season competition as a "natural consequence of victory" and to "reexamine schedules in terms of length and scope." That pertained mostly to sports like baseball, hockey, or basketball, but the message it sent was clear for football, too. All Yale cared about was winning within the Ivy League. That wasn't what the really gifted athletes we were after wanted to hear. Furthermore, Giamatti wanted the athletic department to move toward "multisport coaching assignments." Imagine what would have happened if, for example, Dave Kelley had been forced to give up his spring recruiting duties to be an assistant lacrosse coach.

Well, the speech got a reaction all right, and it was almost universally negative. Some segments of the alumni were outraged. The Ivy presidents liked it. The university's academicians liked it. But nobody involved with Yale athletics liked it. I was so disappointed that I wrote Bart a letter. It was the only critical letter I ever sent to a president, but I felt our relationship was cordial enough that I could do it without implying disrespect. Here are some excerpts from that letter:

Dear Bart:

One might have expected your address to the alumni on Thursday evening if Yale were [a high-powered football machine]. . . . Please be assured that we are a far cry from such an institution, academically or athletically.

I doubt if anyone at Yale would [disagree] that athletes should be well qualified academically. The record I am most proud of is that out of approximately 1,500 who played varsity football at Yale in the past 15 years, only four have not received degrees. Last year the varsity football team had nine valedictorians, four salutatorians, eight high school class presidents, five high school class vice presidents and 47 high school football captains. Every year we have a good number of pre-med and pre-law students on our squad. Please don't underestimate the academic or leadership quality of our athletes. . . .

If you could convince the entire country not to recruit, I would be the first to endorse your proposal. . . .

You have been misinformed in the area of recruiting. Times are not like they were in the late 1950s or early 1960s. Why shouldn't we strive for excellence in athletics as well as academics? Tom Neville and Bill Crowley were both Rhodes scholars in addition to being superb athletes. [Recruiting] competition is much greater for the athletes who can excel in the classroom. . . .

I sense conflicting views in that our Director of Athletics wants us to play the likes of Northwestern, Boston College and the service academies, and our President doesn't want us to recruit. It doesn't take a mastermind to know that football at Yale would be destroyed with our schedule and no blue chip athletes.

We are already at a disadvantage in that we play these teams early in our schedule without freshmen being eligible or the benefit of spring practice. . . .

Also, I was amazed to hear that television receipts are not important to you when we are asked to cut back our program because of lack of funds.

It may interest you to know that my staff is on the road recruiting for a total of only three weeks a year—two weeks after the season and one week in the spring. In addition, each coach is assigned to another sport or a teaching assignment in the gym. Their work doesn't end on Friday as they must assist me during the winter and spring for 10 weekends when our prospects visit the campus. I would assume that many of our professors are away from the university for three weeks doing consulting work and receiving handsome gratuities. There isn't a professor or administrator who spends more time with or has a greater impact on our students than the coaches do. . . .

Bart, I have given a major part of my life to athletics here at Yale and I would not like to see the varsity programs destroyed. I feel you owe it to yourself, to Yale, to all the coaches and others in the athletic department who have been so dedicated to Yale . . . to look more carefully into this department.

Very sincerely, Carm Cozza

I think Bart was surprised at the reaction to his speech. Obviously, he was a proponent of sports as an integral part of Yale's educational process. If he wasn't a believer in the value of sports, why did he leave Yale to become president of the National League and ultimately commissioner of baseball? Rather than a call for deemphasis, I think his speech was meant simply to be a warning about overemphasis. I was sorry about the reaction because I had enormous respect for Giamatti. We had developed a warm personal relationship, though I wasn't as close to him as I had been to King-man Brewster. When I was thinking about accepting the athletic directorship at Princeton, Bart called me from Houston, where he was speaking to a group of alumni, and asked me to wait until he got back so we could talk. His interest in me wasn't the reason I declined Princeton's offer, but it was certainly nice to know that I had that kind of support from the president.

Bart was a huge baseball fan, as everybody knows. I loved to kid him about the Red Sox cap he wore around campus. I worried, as Sam Chauncey did, that he was working so hard that he was going to burn himself out, especially during his long, drawn-out negotiations with the campus service unions. In fact, it was probably stress as much as his voracious cigarette habit that led to his fatal heart attack before his sixtieth birthday. Being commissioner certainly wasn't a walk in the park, especially with the decision to expel Pete Rose from baseball on his plate in his first year. It's sad that this man who loved sports so dearly should be remembered as the president who deemphasized athletics at Yale. He didn't help matters with his speech, that's for sure, but he never meant to cripple the program. I truly believe that.

Many people think that Giamatti's deemphasis speech was the inspiration for the Academic Index in the Ivy League in the early 1980s. It wasn't. The AI came about because of an incident between Penn and Princeton in basketball. That's not to say that Bart didn't have a hand in it. I think he probably did. But his speech didn't initiate it.

The Academic Index was not well understood among Yale fans or alumni, and the insidious way it worked against us within the so-called comfort of our own league was even less clear. Simply put, the AI is a formula that uses College Board scores, class standings, and high school ratings to determine the average academic standing of the incoming freshman class at each school. That average is then applied as a minimum for the revenue sports, including football. It sounds simple enough. It also sounds fair and appropriate. But it had hidden, unintended pitfalls that worked against us, and our constant efforts to point them out fell on deaf ears. Or at least unresponsive ones.

The problem was that the average academic standing of Yale's freshman class was higher than the other Ivy League schools, except for Harvard's and Princeton's, which prevented us from going after hundreds of recruits who didn't qualify for Yale but had no trouble making the grade at Penn or Cornell. Suppose the average academic profile for incoming freshmen at Yale was higher than that at Brown or Dartmouth. That meant that we were casting our nets in a smaller pool of talented football players than they were. The cruel irony was that the Academic Index was meant to ensure parity within the Ivy League. It was supposed to shore up the conference as a safe haven of competitive equality, where everyone was playing by the same rules. Instead, it created an uneven field.

The AI allowed for some slight statistical deviation from the mean, but that didn't help us. Through most of the 1980s, each school was allowed to accept a certain number of recruits from what were called the lower bands, as long as they were balanced by an equal number from the higher bands. Once again, the rule sounded logical, but it was more trouble than it was worth. We spent time and money recruiting super bright "ringers" whom we ordinarily wouldn't have bothered with in order to help us meet our Academic Index. The kids in our lowest band were no dummies, of course. They met standards that were substantially higher than those at most of the nation's universities.

In later years, the rules got even tighter. When the presidents realized the contortions that coaches were going through, they threw out the ringer system (in football only) and restricted us to just two athletes per year (eight over four years) from the lowest band, while the other schools, except for Harvard and Princeton, could take ten. It was meant to level the playing field between the haves and have-nots, but it just tilted the advantage further away from the Big Three. The other schools would wait to see who Yale, Harvard, and Princeton took from that lowest band, then clean up on the rest of them. Once the new rules were in place, the have-nots wanted no part of repealing them. And they held a 5–3 majority.

Amazingly, the AI was in place for more than a year before we found out about it. The admissions office was using it to balance football acceptances, but nobody bothered to tell the coaches what was happening. I don't think the other coaches in the league knew about it either. Finally, when it became obvious that something was going on, I went to see Worth David, the director of admissions. He told me about the index and how his office was using it. I had a grudging respect for Worth. I didn't always agree with his decisions, but I appreciated the fact that he thoroughly studied all our recruits. I used to meet with him on a weekly basis, and I was careful to do my homework on each recruit, because he knew them top to bottom. When the new director came in, he preferred to have one of my assistants deal with a designated person in his office. Things were not as smooth from that point on.

I never understood why Yale embraced the Academic Index when it obviously lessened our competitive position. I worked twice as hard at recruiting in my last fifteen years, with maybe half the success. The number of players in the football program diminished over the years as well. In the 1960s, we brought in between sixty and seventy freshmen every year. In my last years, after freshmen became eligible for varsity play, that number dropped to thirty-five. In my early years, we fielded three teams—freshman, junior varsity, and varsity. In the final years, with natural attrition and injuries, we had barely enough bodies to field a single team.

One other factor, an important one, eroded our ability to attract the best football players during my last ten or fifteen years—the escalating price of a Yale education. By the time I retired, the annual cost of tuition, books, room, and board had risen to about $30,000. The price tag at other colleges increased, too, but there was a big difference in competing for top-level football talent: Yale awarded no athletic scholarships. All financial packages at Yale, for football players and physics prodigies alike, were grants-in-aid that depended entirely on the family's ability to pay. The university's policy was to accept or reject an applicant first, based solely on his or her qualifications, then determine whether the family was eligible for financial aid.

Once again the football office was confronted with a policy that seemed completely fair and appropriate but worked insidiously against our efforts to build the best possible football team. In fact, need-blind admissions worked against the middle class in general. The rich could afford Yale's full cost, the poor got substantial aid, but working-class families got stuck with more than half the cost. They faced the choice of paying perhaps $20,000 (assuming that they qualified for $10,000 in aid) a year for their son to play football at Yale or paying nothing for him to play football at Alabama or Oklahoma. Contrast our situation with some major-college coaches who had a number of acceptances and full-ride scholarships at their disposal without even checking with their admissions offices. When they saw a kid they wanted, who had the NCAA minimum 700 on the College Boards and was likely to graduate with his high school class, they simply accepted him into the freshman class and offered him a scholarship on the spot.

There is an important point to make here. Yale has an opportunity to move into the new millennium with an invigorated football program, without succumbing to the excesses of the big-time conferences. It has a chance to reverse the so-called decline of football without compromising its status as a world-class academic institution. It can make a simple decision that will bring the crowds back to Yale Bowl without besmirching the purity of the Ivy League code. Yale can do this by offering a limited number of full-ride merit scholarships for gifted students in various fields, including athletics. I believe that the time has come to take this bold step.

It has long been thought of as heresy to treat football players differently from any other group of students. Frankly, I think an argument can be made that they should be treated differently because the competitive pressure to attract them is different from the pressure to attract economic or divinity students. I'm not saying that football players are more important. Not at all. I'm just saying that they must be recruited more vigorously, and that includes offering them merit scholarships. But to avoid the appearance of special treatment, why not offer a limited number of merit scholarships to musicians, poets, and math prodigies as well as linebackers? It would be a way of ensuring a continued flow of the best and brightest candidates to Yale. Besides, in the context of what is being done at other respected institutions across the country, it would be a modest move.

I have discussed this idea with several people in recent years, most notably with Calvin Hill and Tone Grant. I believe that they agree that some type of merit scholarships should be given. Calvin tells the story of trying to recruit a talented young musician. Yale was her first choice, but when she was offered only limited financial aid, she and her family chose a full scholarship to the Juilliard School of Music instead. Obviously, there are other departments in which merit scholarships would ensure the quality of the Yale student body, just as they would for the high-profile sports teams.

Let me state clearly what I think merit scholarships would do, and would not do. They would raise the quality of our teams dramatically. Perhaps as few as twenty-five or thirty merit scholarships over four years (compared with eighty-five at CFA schools) would allow us within a few years to compete again with the service academies, as well as occasional Division I-A opponents like Duke, Northwestern, Vanderbilt, Rice, or Stanford. I don't suggest that we could strengthen ourselves to the point of playing a steady diet of Notre Dames and Florida States. Certainly not. But the excitement and respect we would generate by playing one or two high-profile teams each year would have a significant effect on attendance, and I believe that would more than pay for the cost of merit scholarships. An upgraded schedule would do wonders for our recruiting efforts, too. A full-cost merit scholarship, increased attendance at the Bowl, and a chance to play a few major opponents each year, coupled with the opportunity to get an Ivy League education, would make an enormous difference in Yale's ability to attract truly gifted athletes.

What merit scholarships would not do would be to demean Yale's other students, project us as an outlaw or jock school, alter in any way our academic standards, or cost us money. In fact, revenue probably would increase, with larger crowds and hyped-up fan recognition. A moderate change to limited merit scholarships would simply recognize the obvious truth that the kind of football players who can compete at the highest level and fill the Bowl on Saturday afternoons do not simply flock to Yale because of its tradition and academic reputation. They must be enticed.

In the modern context of Yale and Ivy League athletics, it sounds like heresy to suggest merit scholarships for athletes. But why should a small accommodation to competitive factors be viewed as anything other than a wise strategy to ensure success? Isn't that the sort of thing we teach our business students? I'll tell you what heresy is—letting that magnificent football stadium behind the Walter Camp arch waste away three-quarters empty on Saturday afternoons. I tried not to let the declining attendance bother me, but those afternoons when there were fewer than twenty thousand in the Bowl were depressing. It is heresy not to take a few simple steps to offer students, fans, and alumni a football program commensurate with the world-class reputation of the rest of the university. It is heresy and short-sightedness not to recognize that students who play football do indeed deserve a special status when it comes to prompt action on their applications and merit scholarships for a few of the most talented among them. There needs to be a recognition, starting in the president's office, that recruiting the best players from the nation's tiny pool of top-drawer student-athletes is a vastly different game from attracting the best mathematicians or poets or choral singers. Yale football has too great a heritage, and is too important in the lives of hundreds of wonderful young men, to allow it to wallow in the mediocrity of recent years.

There are signs that the situation is improving, due primarily to the enlightened and forceful leadership of Athletic Director Tom

Beckett. I see small advances as my replacement Jack Siedlecki goes about his recruiting, and I'm hopeful that the trend of improvement will continue. But dramatic improvement will come only through significant change, and there is no better time for that to happen than the dawn of a new millennium.

CHAPTER FOURTEEN

No Regrets

The decision to retire was painful. I won't pretend that it wasn't. Just when it felt as if we were about to turn the corner and get back on the winning track, it was time for me to go. I was sixty-five when I decided to step down, sixty-six when I coached my last game, and I had been in the job for more than three decades, so there was nothing for me to complain about. In fact, I was blessed to have had such a long and successful run. Still, it felt like my life was coming to an end.

It bothered me, it still bothers me, that our fortunes went downhill in the 1990s. I felt like a golfer who double-bogeyed the last two holes to end a round of pars and birdies. The last few seasons were my double bogeys, and the longer I spend in retirement, the more they hurt. In some ways I was like an aging athlete trying to hold back the years, always thinking that his legs could carry him to one more touchdown. It was hard to let go because my will to win was as strong for my final game as it was for my first. Maybe even stronger. If I had grown tired of the grind, if I had lost the energy to compete, retirement would have come easily. It would have been a relief as much as anything. But I was stubborn enough to want just one more season . . . or two . . . or three. I felt the way I did in my youth when my mother called me in for dinner just as I was coming to bat in a pickup game across the street. Only this time I was laying down the bat for the last time.

I didn't want to leave the program when we were struggling because I didn't feel I deserved that, nor did my staff. And it was an excellent staff that really cared about the kids. I don't care how many coaching staffs Yale has had, or will have, there will never be one that cared more about the athletes than mine did. I feel strongly about that, and I feel that we were shortchanged at the end by the admissions office.

It wasn't entirely the fault of the admissions people, of course. We suffered injuries to key people, and I'll take the blame for that. But you can't compete with one arm tied behind your back, and I don't think the powers that be ever realized that. I felt that they never really cared. Some in the administration felt that as long as we were treating the kids right and they were having fun, and we beat Harvard and Princeton now and then, that was fine. I think most of the administration people felt that way, and, hell, maybe they were right. Maybe I was wrong. But when you work 365 days a year and you put your heart and soul into it, you want to win. And you want to win for the kids more than for yourself. If you're not a competitor, you shouldn't be in this business. I felt sorry for the team because I knew that we were only one or two good players away from success. Even in the last few years.

It was my decision to call it quits. I want to be clear about that. No one fired me and no one held a gun to my head. But I would have been blind not to see that President Rick Levin and Athletic Director Tom Beckett thought it was time for a change. I can't blame them for that. We were coming off a 3–7 campaign and three losing seasons in four years. No coach in a big-time program could survive that kind of slump no matter whose fault it was or what the circumstances were. So when I met with the director in the president's office shortly after the 1995 season, I knew that I had come to the end of the run. It wasn't anything either of them said, but I had the uneasy feeling that they would welcome the opportunity to bring in a new coach.

Many of my assistants had turned sour on the administration, especially the admissions office. I didn't blame them. I was frustrated, too, although I tried desperately to remain above the bitterness. I could see the tension in Jean and my family. I'm not a very good actor, and when we lost, it tore at my insides. I think Jean wished I had retired after the 1994 season, when we beat both Connecticut and Harvard. But Tom Beckett and I agreed that I should stay on for a couple of years.

It especially hurt to know that the downslide was not entirely my fault or the fault of my staff. I take the major portion of responsibility, of course. I was the head coach. But at the risk of sounding self-pitying, I felt that fate—in the form of key injuries and an admissions office that was not on the same page with the football staff or with the other universities in the league—was a little unkind at the end. The players were a factor in my decision, too. I had recruited them and I wanted them to win. If bringing in new blood could help, that's what I wanted for them.

At the meeting in the president's office in December 1995, I offered to step down immediately if they had someone they wanted to bring in, but it was decided I would stay on for one more year. They were nice enough to let me handle the announcement in my own way, which proved to be no easy matter. I told no one except Jean for several days until Bob Estock, my line coach, asked me specifically what my plans were. I realized then that I owed it to the staff to let them know about my decision as soon as possible so that they could make plans for their own futures. A new coach was almost certain to bring in his own assistants. I let them know at a regular staff meeting just days before Christmas. I don't think it came as a big surprise to any of them, but you could hear a pin drop in the room. We were all disappointed that the end came just as we sensed a new cooperation from the admissions office and an enlightened approach to early admissions by Tom Beckett. It would have been fun to be a part of what I believe will be a gradual upswing in the program.

As tough a time as this was for me personally, I received another blow with the news that my sister Ange had died. She was the youngest of my four sisters and probably the one I was closest to through the years. Her death and my retirement didn't make for the most joyous of Christmas seasons in the Cozza household.

Keeping the decision secret after I told the staff was difficult. I was determined to recruit the best possible freshman team for the new coach to build on, and if word of my retirement got out, that would be tough. It put me in the uncomfortable position of having to skirt the truth when recruits or their families asked me point-blank if I was leaving. I just told them I could guarantee them I would coach for one more year. In spite of the difficulties, I think we did a

fine job of recruiting a team that we knew we would never coach.
Ten of those recruits ended up starting for Coach Siedlecki as sophomores. A lot of our success that year was due to a noticeable improvement in the attitude and organization in the admissions office.

My retirement was even harder to keep under wraps in the last
weeks before two-a-day practices started in the fall. The news media
had gotten wind of it, and there was one story after another claiming
authoritatively that I was stepping down. That was really embarrassing because I had to fudge my answers, and so did my assistants. I
just told reporters that I would make an announcement when the
team came back to school. I sure as hell wasn't going to announce
my retirement before I had a chance to tell the team myself.

On September 7, 1996, just before our preseason scrimmage
with Plymouth State, I gathered the players in the field house and told
them of my plans. Once again, I'm not sure how much of a surprise it
was, but the players were clearly saddened. Most of them just sat there
silently with their heads down. I don't know whether it made me feel
good that they were so obviously disappointed, or whether it made
me feel worse to be leaving them. Then I went downstairs and made
the announcement at a press conference. My seniors came with me
and stood behind me in their game jerseys. Jean and my family were
there, too, and so were a dozen or so of my former players. Talk about
moral support. I could feel their strength behind me.

Coaches are good only when they have talent. Or, as Yogi Berra
might phrase it, half of football is 90 percent recruiting. But identifying the best applicants and persuading them to come to Yale is just
one part of recruiting. The other part is getting them in the door, and
for that we needed the admissions office as a full partner. In the
1990s, after Worth David left, we were competing at a definite
disadvantage. Our admissions people were not doing everything
they could within the rules of the league and the standards of the
university to admit the players we needed to win. I didn't always
agree with the decisions Worth David made through the 1970s and
'80s, but as I said before, I respected his thoroughness, organization,

and knowledge of every candidate. Unfortunately a new regime came in for the last few years of my tenure and it wasn't on the same page with its counterparts around the league.

There was nothing worse than watching a player we had tried to recruit score a touchdown for the opposing team. When I traveled to the Midwest or California to visit with a high school candidate and his family in their home only to lose him to a rival university, it was devastating. When the recruit showed a definite interest in Yale but committed to Princeton in February because our admissions office hadn't yet processed his application or was holding off on his admittance until April, it was even more maddening. I can't tell you how many times that happened in my last half-dozen seasons.

The first game of my final season was a surprising success, but it created unrealistic expectations. We walloped—and I mean walloped—a good Brown team 30–0. It was the first game of a two-quarterback system, with Blake Kendall and Kris Barber, and both of them had excellent debuts. Our lead runner, Jabbar Craigwell, ran for seventy-seven yards, and our defense dominated Brown all afternoon.

So much for the good news. Connecticut whipped us the next week 42–6 in a game that was about as one-sided as our defeat of Brown had been. And matters got worse from there. We lost Craigwell for several weeks with a severely bruised knee, and we got word that week that Nick Adamo, a starter on the 1994 and '95 teams, had been killed in a private plane crash on a business trip. His death hit the team hard. He was an outstanding young man who had overcome great odds. He had given up football temporarily in his freshman year to earn more money for living expenses. Then came a run of five defeats in six games, including a 39–13 loss to Army after we had led 7–6 in the final minute of the first half. Our only win was 23–21 over Bucknell. At one point we were down to our fourth running back.

So my thirty-two years dwindled down to a final Big Three season against Princeton at home and Harvard on the road. The distractions that week before my final game in the Bowl were incredible. Not only did I receive an endless string of letters and phone calls from former players, alumni, and various other well-wishers, but I got requests for interviews from newspapers and TV stations I had never heard of. It was gratifying, but at the time I just wanted to be left alone to prepare the team the best I could for a very important game.

I couldn't have asked for a more supportive final captain than Rob Masella, who went on to medical school after graduation. He was a wonderful defensive back, too, who returned two pass interceptions for touchdowns, one of which gave us that short-lived 7–6 lead over Army. I think he and the staff prepared the team as well as they could have emotionally for that last home game. They understood the significance of the contest and the importance of it to me, but they knew that their emotions could carry them only so far. They would have to play within themselves. I don't remember anything out of the ordinary about our pregame meeting. I said the Lord's Prayer, as I had since the days of Calvin Hill, and I sent my last team into battle with the words the Rhodes scholar Bill Crowley had first used when he was our captain in 1978: "Leave no regrets on the field." It was always hard for me to show my emotion outwardly, even when my stomach was churning with it, but walking into the Bowl for the last time left me weak in the knees. The week's preparations and distractions were over, and here I was facing the irreversible reality of the last home game. Seb LaSpina and I were the last ones to leave the little room under the stands. I put my arm on his shoulder, and we paused for just a moment to look at each other. Neither of us said a word. We didn't need to. It was the 183rd time we walked through that dank tunnel with the sunlight of the Bowl waiting at the other end. Each of us knew what the other was feeling. It was at the same time a beautiful moment and an awful one.

What greeted me when I stepped into the Bowl will touch my heart forever. I looked to my right and there in the end zone were thirty-one of my thirty-two former captains, each dressed in a game jersey. What a wonderful tribute. I was almost in tears as I went down the line and hugged every one of them. The only captain who didn't make it was Bob Greenlee, who was in Asia on business, and he sent his son, Bob 3rd, who had also played for me, to represent him. There were others of my former players there, too, including Calvin Hill, John Pagliaro, Gary Fencik, Dr. Rich Diana, and others. It was special, really special.

The game that followed was not special, however. Just talking about Princeton's 17–13 victory is difficult. The game was a total embarrassment. Not only did we lose, we didn't play particularly well. I know the players tried their best. I know they wanted to win it for me as much as for themselves. But in truth, they played poorly. I blame myself. Perhaps I had put too much pressure on them to win my final game. I certainly hadn't meant to, but I may have sent them signals I didn't know I was sending.

A crowd of twenty-nine thousand saw us take a 13–10 lead in the fourth quarter, then let Princeton drive in for the winning touchdown with just over two minutes to play. I was devastated. I can't tell you how sad I felt as I left the field for the last time. I hadn't felt that bad after a game since the 29–29 tie with Harvard twenty-eight years before. For the first time in thirty-two years, I didn't even stop at the halftime room under the Bowl to say a word to the team. I walked right by and headed for the field house. I apologized to them later and explained that I was so dejected that I didn't trust myself to say anything until I collected myself.

At the postgame press conference, it was all I could do to keep my composure. I even made a comment about that night's retirement dinner. I'll quote from the newspaper accounts the next day because I don't have a clear memory of my words. "I have a party to go to tonight," I said, "and I dread it. I totally dread it." Well, that was the wrong thing to say. For one thing, a lot of people had worked hard to put the banquet together. More than seven hundred of my former players came back for the dinner, which drew about one thousand people to the Yale Commons, and here I was telling them that I dreaded going. I want everyone who heard those words—and many people did because they were broadcast on the evening news shows—that I regret them. I was thrilled at the banquet and am deeply grateful to all who helped to organize it and attend it. I am especially grateful to Fred Leone and Pat Ruwe.

It was a wonderful affair. They sent a limo to my house for my family and me. Jack Ford, the NBC newsman, was the emcee, and many former players spoke. Presidents George Bush, Gerald Ford, and Bill Clinton, all Yale men, sent congratulatory telegrams, and Governor John Rowland proclaimed it Carm Cozza Day in Connecticut. All three of my daughters were invited to speak, and I was so proud of what they said and the way they said it. It's hard to imagine more disparate memories of a single day—the awful low of that last loss in the Bowl and the warm feeling after the inspiring gathering of so many friends and supporters at the dinner.

Fortunately, I didn't have much time to dwell on it. We had a game to play the next Saturday against Harvard, and my staff and I got to work the day after the banquet. The last home game had diffused some of the attention, but it was still a hectic week dealing with well-wishers and the press. It was hard not to think as the days wore on that everything I did was for the last time. The last Tuesday press luncheon at Mory's. The last Wednesday meeting with the offense. The last home practice on Thursday. That final practice was an especially emotional time. The last home practice of the year always is. As the field lights grew brighter in the gathering darkness, I watched my last group of seniors run the gauntlet, and as the last one emerged from the parallel lines of underclassmen, the chant went up for me to take my turn. That's something I had never done, but I plunged in and felt a hundred pair of hands pounding on my back and arms. I have no words to describe that feeling.

The last game at Harvard was no better than the loss to Princeton, though for some reason it wasn't quite as difficult emotionally. For one thing, it was at Harvard, not at Yale. For another, we played a better game, even though we lost 26–21. We scored the last fourteen points and had the ball on Harvard's 48-yard line when time ran out. And yes, my mind did go back to 1968, when Harvard's frantic last few minutes had stunned us. For a moment, it looked like I might exact revenge in my final game. But it wasn't to be.

On August 23, 1997, the Yale football team returned to campus for the start of two-a-day practices. As the players were moving into their rooms at the Ray Tompkins House, filled with high hopes for the competition and camaraderie of the season ahead, I was on the golf course. They were my players. Every one of them. I had recruited them, coached them, listened to their problems, rejoiced with them over victories, and agonized over defeats. I had traveled with them, laughed with them, yelled at them, even cried with them. I had marveled at their poise and intellect and loyalty and dedication. Their youthful exuberance had kept me young. Their resilience in tough times had kept my spirits high. Their modesty in victory and grace in defeat had made me proud. And now, as these wonderful young men trotted onto the practice field to begin another season of Yale football, I was playing in a golf tournament. I was supposed to be having fun, but I was miserable.

I simply could not keep my mind on my game. I looked at the fairway and thought about the gridiron. It just seemed wrong, all wrong, not to be with my players, not to have a whistle around my neck and a clipboard in my hands. I told myself that it was nice not to be sick with worry about personnel, practice plans, the playbook, and those dreaded injuries. It did no good. I wanted to drop my clubs, climb in the car, and drive to practice. For the first time in thirty-four years I was not there where I had felt so needed and so at home. The young sons of Eli, my young men, were in the blossom of their youth, and here I was struggling with the challenge of retirement.

Oh, I survived. But that first year of retirement was excruciating. It was hard to sit in my old office, which I kept in my new capacity as special assistant. I could hear the voices of my players in the hallways, and occasionally one would stop in to say hello. But it was torture to think that in the meeting rooms down the hall the new coach, Jack Siedlecki, and his staff were planning strategy, breaking down film, and meeting with their team. I wanted so desperately to be a part of it. But, of course, I couldn't. Jack and his new staff were wonderful. They sought and respected my counsel and kept me informed of their progress. I appreciated that. And I hope they appreciated that I kept my distance. Bo Schembechler had told me how tough that first year would be. So had Ara Parseghian and Joe Restic. But expecting the worst didn't make it any easier. It gets easier as time goes on, and it will be easier still when my players graduate. But it was hard. Very hard.

There are great joys in retirement, of course, like spending time with Jean and riding the John Deere tractor my players gave me at my retirement dinner. One of the biggest joys was the opportunity to watch my grandson, Christopher, play Pop Warner football. I will always remember the first time I went to watch him play. He was the smallest kid on the team, just fifty-five pounds, and before the game he said to me, "Papa, I think I better eat a hot dog." I said, "Honey, you can't eat right before you play. And besides, you aren't going to gain another fifty-five pounds eating one hot dog."

I gave him a candy bar for energy and took a seat in the stands. Just before the game was to start a young coach came up and asked me to run the first-down markers on the sidelines. Apparently, the officials who were supposed to work the chains hadn't shown up. I said, "Sure, I'd be glad to." A few minutes later, the guy came back and said, "I'm sorry—I guess I should have asked you if you know anything about football?"

I smiled and said, "Yeah, a little bit."

Honor Roll
Cozza's Thirty-Two Seasons

FULL-TIME COACHES

Buddy Amendola
Paul Amodio
Joe Benanto
Don Brown
Larry Ciotti
Bob Estock
Joe Galat
Dick Hopkins
Harry Jacunski
Dave Kelley
Seb LaSpina
Bill Mallory
Don Martin
Larry McElreavy
Bill Narduzzi
Rich Pont
Neil Putnam
Kevin Ronalds
Jim Root
Bill Samko
Bob Shoop

Larry Story
Russ Wickerham
Mack Yoho

PART-TIME COACHES

Fritz Barzilauskas
Bob Batick
Bob Becker
Jim Benanto
Bob Blanchard
John Bozzi
Sam Burrell
Tony Capraro
Ron Carbone
Jeff Carroll
Tris Carta
Bill Crowley
Kevin Czinger
Vito DeVito
Art Fitzgerald
Chris Getman
Rich Huff

Carter Hunt
Bill Irons
Joe Linta
Doug Magazu
Marty Martinson
Bill McAllister
Bob McHenry
Dan Mellish
Ed Migdalski
Chris Nugai
Mark Peters
Tony Piccolo
Arnie Pinkston
Bob Riggio
Bob Rizzo
Joe Roberti
Archie Roberts
John Rogan
Dave Russell
Pat Ruwe
Mark Salisbury
Jim Schiffer
Bill Simon
Ken Tullo
Bob Verduzco
Mike Waldvogel
Tim Weigel

EQUIPMENT STAFF

Bill Humes
Joe Levatino
Ed Maturo
Lou Scigliano
Jeff Torre

SUPPORT PERSONNEL

Grace Lewis Jacunski
Jennifer Ozols
Maude Schmidt
Tom Smith

TRAINERS

Al Battipaglia
Daphne Benas
Bill Dayton
Vicky Graham
Bill Kaminsky
Rich Kaplan
Dan Kasman
Chris Pecora

TEAM DOCTORS

Rich Diana
Mark Galloway
Barry Goldberg
Isao Hirata
Peter Jokl
Norm Kaplan
Jack Kelley
Dan Larson
Kevin Lynch
Pat Ruwe
Bob Zones

RHODES SCHOLARS

Chris Brown, 1989
Bill Crowley, 1978

Tom Neville, 1970
Kurt Schmoke, 1970
Roosevelt Thompson, 1983

NFL PLAYERS

Rich Diana, RB, Miami Dolphins 1982–83
Brian Dowling, QB, New England Patriots 1972–73, Green Bay
    Packers 1977
Greg Dubinetz, G, Washington Redskins 1979
Joe Dufek, QB, Buffalo Bills 1983–85, San Diego Chargers 1985
Gary Fencik, DB, Chicago Bears 1976–87
Calvin Hill, RB, Dallas Cowboys 1969–74, Washington Redskins
    1976–77, Cleveland Browns 1978–81
Chris Hetherington, RB, Indianapolis Colts 1996–98, Carolina
    Panthers 1999
Ken Hill, DB, Oakland/L.A. Raiders 1980–83, New York Giants
    1984–88, Kansas City Chiefs 1989
Dick Jauron, DB, Detroit Lions 1973–77, Cleveland Browns
    1978, Cincinnati Bengals 1979–81
Don Martin, DB, New England Patriots 1973, Kansas City Chiefs
    1975, Tampa Bay Buccaneers 1976
Chuck Mercein, RB, New York Giants 1965–66, Green Bay
    Packers 1967–69, Washington Redskins 1969, New York
    Jets 1970 (Note: John Pont was Mercein's head coach.)
John Nitti, RB, New York Jets 1981–82
Eugene Profit, DB, New England Patriots 1986–88, Washington
    Redskins 1989
Jeff Rohrer, LB, Dallas Cowboys 1982–88
John Spagnola, TE, Philadelphia Eagles 1979–87, Seattle Seahawks
    1988, Green Bay Packers 1989

ALL-IVY SELECTIONS
1965

Dave Laidley, DG

1966

Bob Greenlee, DT
Bill Hilgendorf, LB

Tom Schmidt, DG
Rod Watson, DE

1967

Don Barrows, FB
Dan Begel, K
Brian Dowling, QB
Kyle Gee, T
Glenn Greenberg, DT
Calvin Hill, RB
Rick McCarthy, G
Schmidt, MG

1968

Mike Bouscaren, LB
Dowling, QB
Ed Franklin, DB
Gee, T
Hill, RB
Del Marting, E
Bruce Weinstein, E
Dick Williams, MG

1969

Andy Coe, LB
Jim Gallagher, DE
Tom Neville, DT

1970

Gallagher, DE
Dick Jauron, FB

Matt Jordan, T
Rich Lolotai, MG
Rich Maher, E
Neville, DT

1971

Jauron, RB
Jordan, T

1972

Jauron, RB
Mike Noetzel, DB
Bob Perschel, LB

1973

Elvin Charity, DB
Rick Fehling, DE
Al Moras, T

1974

Brian Ameche, DE
John Cahill, MB
Charity, DB
Greg Dubinetz, G
Bob Fernandez, G
Rich Feryok, DT
Rudy Green, HB
Moras, T
Charlie Palmer, T

1975

Cahill, MB
Gary Fencik, SE
Don Gesicki, HB
Scott Keller, DE
Palmer, T
John Smoot, LB
Mike Southworth, P

1976

Pete Bonacum, DE
Steve Carfora, G
Jim McDonnell, T
Kurt Nondorf, DB
John Pagliaro, HB
Vic Staffieri, G

1977

Carfora, G
Bill Crowley, LB
Paul Denza, DT
McDonnell, T
Pagliaro, RB
Bob Rizzo, QB
Spagnola, TE
Clint Streit, DE

1978

Arnie Pinkston, DB
Bob Skoronski, DT

Spagnola, TE
Streit, DE

1979

Dave Conrad, DT
Jim Dwyer, DE
Ken Hill, RB
Bob Regan, OT
Tim Tumpane, LB

1980

Kevin Czinger, MG
Rich Diana, RB
Fred Leone, DE
Regan, OT
Dennis Tulsiak, DT

1981

Diana, RB
Curt Grieve, WR
Tony Jones, P/K
Leone, DT
Serge Mihaly, DT
Jeff Rohrer, LB

1982

Paul Andrie, RB

1983

Tom Giella, DT

1984

Hank Eaton, P
John Zanieski, MG

1985

Kevin Moriarty, WR
Steve Skwara, OT

1987

Dean Athanasia, TE
Jeff Rudolph, OG
Kelly Ryan, QB
Mike Stewart, TB

1988

Art Kalman, OT
Rudolph, OG

1989

Chris Gaughn, LB
Darin Kehler, QB
Rich Huff, DB
Glover Lawrence, DT
Ed Perks, K
Jon Reese, LB

1990

John Furjanic, DB

1991

Kevin Allen, OT
Nick Crawford, QB
Chris Kouri, RB
Erik Lee, DT
David Russell, OG

1992

Lee, DL
Bart Newman, OL

1993

Jim Langford, TE

1994

Carl Ricci, LB

1996

Jack Hill, C
Rob Masella, DB

**ASA BUSHNELL CUP
(IVY LEAGUE MVP)**

Kevin Czinger 1980
Rich Diana 1981
Dick Jauron 1972
John Pagliaro 1976, '77
Kelly Ryan 1987
Tim Tumpane 1979

COZZA'S RECORDS

Overall: 179–119–5 (.599)
Ivy League: 135–85–5 (.611)
vs. Princeton: 22–10 (.688)

vs. Harvard: 16–15–1 (.516)
vs. non-Ivy: 44–34 (.564)
Yale Bowl: 116–66–1 (.637)
on the road: 63–53–4 (.542)

Year by Year Records

	Overall	Pct.	Ivies	Ivy Finish
1965	3–6	.333	3–4	4th
1966	4–5	.444	3–4	5th
1967	8–1	.889	7–0	Champs
1968	8–0–1	.944	6–0–1	Cochamps
1969	7–2	.778	6–1	Champs
1970	7–2	.778	5–2	2nd
1971	4–5	.444	3–4	5th
1972	7–2	.778	5–2	2nd
1973	6–3	.667	5–2	2nd
1974	8–1	.889	6–1	Cochamps
1975	7–2	.778	5–2	3rd
1976	8–1	.889	6–1	Cochamps
1977	7–2	.778	6–1	Champs
1978	5–2–2	.667	4–1–2	2nd
1979	8–1	.889	6–1	Champs
1980	8–2	.800	6–1	Champs
1981	9–1	.900	6–1	Cochamps
1982	4–6	.400	3–4	4th
1983	1–9	.100	1–6	8th
1984	6–3	.667	5–2	2nd
1985	4–4–1	.500	3–3–1	4th
1986	3–7	.300	2–5	6th
1987	7–3	.700	5–2	2nd
1988	3–6–1	.333	3–3–1	5th

	Overall	Pct.	Ivies	Ivy Finish
1989	8–2	.800	6–1	Cochamps
1990	6–4	.600	5–2	3rd
1991	6–4	.600	4–3	4th
1992	4–6	.400	2–5	T5th
1993	3–7	.300	2–5	6th
1994	5–5	.500	3–4	T3rd
1995	3–7	.300	2–5	T6th
1996	2–8	.200	1–6	8th

Index